LAW AND ETHICS
A Guide for the
Health Professional

LAW AND ETHICS
A Guide for the
Health Professional

Nathan T. Sidley, M.D.,
Editor

Fourth District Court Clinic
Woburn, Massachusetts

Harvard University
Cambridge, Massachusetts

HUMAN SCIENCES PRESS, INC.
72 FIFTH AVENUE
NEW YORK, N.Y. 10011

Copyright © 1985 by Human Sciences Press, Inc.
72 Fifth Avenue, New York, New York 10011

Printed in the United States of America
987654321

Library of Congress Cataloging in Publication Data
Main entry under title:

Law and ethics.
    Bibliography: p.
    Includes index.
    1. Medical laws and legislation—United States—Out-
lines, syllabi, etc.   2. Medical personnel—Malpractice—
United States—Outlines, syllabi, etc.   3. Medical ethics
—United States—Outlines, syllabi, etc.   4. Law—United
States—Outlines, syllabi, etc. I. Sidley, Nathan T.,
1929–
KF3821.Z9L38   1985   344.73'041   83-26565
ISBN 0-89885-155-6   347.3041

Contents

Foreword

The contents of this book discuss, in a general manner, most of the major areas of American law, including both substantive and procedural issues. The book gives an overview of law and of ethics, going from more general considerations of what is the law and how courts work, to some specific issues that affect health professionals. The ordinary issues of daily life, in which people voluntarily assume legal roles, are then discussed. There is also a brief account of special situations involving the mentally ill.

The emphasis here is on practical understanding of the law. Theoretical concepts which are mentioned represent an effort to help the reader conceptualize the practical aspects of legal situations. Especially intended to be useful are the chapters on personal involvement in legal cases and medical and professional ethics.

When the reader has completed this book, he* will have a broad understanding of how the law gets things done, how legal decisions are argued, rationalized, and made, and what the general principles of law are in the major legal fields. He will be able to understand many of the subtleties in reading about legal cases and situations, as in professional publications, and will also be able to understand better how to approach a legal situation in which he may be involved personally.

The outline format is designed to enable ready discrimination among legal points.** In law, most of the concepts are simple ones and, by themselves, seem straightforward and

---

*For simplicity "he" has been used throughout the book rather than "he/she," which is meant.
**Because Chapter 1, Origin and Functions of American Law, is more discursive than the other chapters, it is in straight narrative form.

easy-to-understand. The difficulty is that there are so many concepts, and the same words in different contexts may have different meanings. The key problem in learning about the law is what are the legal terms and which concepts go together. It is crucial to know which concepts are at which hierarchical level, that is, which are main principles and which are subordinate to the more major ones.

The outline form in which the book chapters are written is designed to facilitate that learning task. At the head of each chapter is an outline of the chapter with the page numbers at which each point can be found. The body of the chapter elaborates on the points of the chapter heading. The sub-points are indented so that they can be recognized as sub-points. The transition from a sub-point to a major heading can be readily appreciated so that the relational roles of the different points can be easily comprehended.

Note that the format used is most useful after the first reading of a chapter. Most readers go through the text the first time in an exploratory manner, to get a broad scan as to where the chapter goes. It is only with the second or third reading, when the individual tries to get the field integrated in his mind, that the value of such a concept-equivalencing organization of the text is manifest. Then, it saves much time and effort to recognize, by the shape of the text on the page, where it fits into the broad picture of the particular legal field being covered.

Each chapter is followed by a set of questions that challenge the reader. It is advisable to go through the questions after, rather than before, the reader believes he has "digested" the material. (It also is wise to read the material with the expectation of answering questions. Attention will surely be greater.)

The Glossary is arranged so the reader may easily quiz himself by covering up the definition with a card. It is recommended that this be done to insure mastery of the meanings, because without knowledge of the terms, one can never come to grips with the law. With that knowledge, one is three-fifths of the way along.

In addition to the specific formal points made, at various places in the book, philosophical comments about the issues are interspersed, especially in Chapter 17, Maxims and Quotations. These comments do not reflect "black letter law" but rather, look at the law broadly, to stimulate the reader's thought about law in relation to the overall human condition.

In short, this is a work which is designed for someone who seriously wants to learn about the law and obtain a broad and firm understanding of it.

It is the hope of the editor and the authors that health care professionals who learn from it will be able to improve their practice. It is our impression, for example, that the legal fundamentals of the doctor-patient relationship are not adequately taught in medical schools, and that as a result, physicians risk compromising the most effective patient care. Knowledge of principles of professional negligence should help one guard against malpractice litigation. Knowledge of evidence and the role of the witness should help a health professional to be a more effective witness when, as is likely at various times in his career, he is called on as an expert witness.

The volume is useful as a textbook in professional school courses on legal aspects of that health profession. The materials can be covered in a 20 class hour course, either in a semester, or, more leisurely, over the course of an academic year.

The book is also designed for the serious individual professional who needs more than a smattering, but who does not wish to be overly technical in his learning about the law.

Like any authors, we hope our readers find our efforts to have been rewarding. If so, we, ourselves, will be twice rewarded.

Contributors

Gertrude M. Allen is law librarian at the 4th District Court, Woburn, Mass. She earned a degree in journalism at Boston University and has been especially interested in Massachusetts court history.

Michael J. English is a staff attorney in the Office of the Legal Advisor at St. Elizabeths Hospital, Washington, D.C. He is a graduate of Georgetown University and Georgetown University Law Center and is a member of the Virginia, D.C., and Federal bars. He has been active in class actions involving civil rights and mental health cases, as well as tort, malpractice, and Constitutional cases, and has had significant administrative involvement in hospital management. He has been especially interested in information management and patient privacy matters.

Ann O'Regan Keary is a staff attorney in the Office of the Legal Advisor at St. Elizabeths Hospital, Washington, D.C. She is a graduate of Wellesley College, where she was a Wellesley College Scholar; she received a J.D. with honors at George Washington University's National Law Center, and she is a member of the Massachusetts and the D.C. bars. She was law clerk for Judge Joyce Green of the D.C. Superior Court. She has represented criminal defendants before the D.C. Superior Court and has worked in the Misdemeanor Trial Section of the U.S. Attorney's Office at that court, as part of her law school experience. In her work at St. Elizabeths she has been particularly involved in legal issues relating to the treatment and rights of mentally ill offenders, and has published articles on the insanity defense.

Colleen Kollar-Kotelly is Chief Legal Advisor in the Office of the Legal Advisor, St. Elizabeths Hospital, Washington, D.C. She attended high school at Escuela Campo Alegre, Caracas, Venezuela, and at Georgetown Visitation Preparatory School in Washington, D.C. She graduated from the Catholic University of America and from the Catholic University of America Law School, where she was winner of the First Year Appellate Moot Court Competition. She has been a law clerk for Judge Catherine Kelley of the D.C. Court of Appeals; she also worked in the Appellate Section of the U.S. Department of Justice Criminal Division, where she wrote Government briefs for cases in the U.S. Supreme Court and the U.S. Circuit Courts of Appeals. She is a member of the D.C. bar. She has been involved in every legal aspect of the activities of the St. Elizabeths Hospital, and she has responsibilities for supervising and training other hospital staff attorneys. She has also been active in legal issues relating to women. As chairman of the Mental Health Committee, D.C. Bar Association, she took a major responsibility in developing the D.C. Mental Health Information Act, the D.C. confidentiality statute.

Michael L. Perlin is special counsel to the Commissioner of the Department of the Public Advocate of the State of New Jersey. Until 1983 he was Director of the Division of Mental Health Advocacy in the State of New Jersey's Department of the Public Advocate in Trenton, N.J. He is a magna cum laude graduate of Rutgers University, where he was a Henry Rutgers Scholar and editor-in-chief of the *Rutgers Daily Targum*. He also graduated from the Columbia University School of Law, where he was Harlan Fiske Stone Scholar and managing editor of *Kent Commentaries*. He is a member of the Federal and New Jersey bars. He has served as law clerk to Judge Sidney Goldmann of the Appellate Division of the New Jersey Superior Court and to Judge Ralph Fusco of the Law Division of the New Jersey Superior Court. Before he affiliated with the Division of Mental Health Advocacy, he was in charge of the Mercer County Office of the New Jersey Public Defender's Office, in Trenton.

He has been most interested in, and published most on, issues involving mental health and the law, especially in relation to the civil rights of the mentally handicapped. He also is a Training Consultant at the Hospital of the University of Pennsylvania in Philadelphia.

John P. Petrila is Deputy Counsel for Litigation in the Office of Counsel in the New York State Office of Mental Health, Albany. He is a summa cum laude graduate of St. Joseph's College, Rensselaer, Ind., and the University of Virginia Law School. He has been an Assistant Attorney General in the Attorney General's Office of the State of Missouri and was the first Director of Forensic Services in the Department of Mental Health in Missouri.

He is a member of the Virginia and the Missouri bars. His present activities involve him in all litigation undertaken against the New York Office of Mental Health. He also supervises several staff attorneys.

Ronald A. Pressman is engaged in the private practice of law in Malden, Mass. His specialty is family law and probate matters. He has an active interest in child abuse cases.

He is a graduate of Clark University and Suffolk University Law School. He has served as a Middlesex Public Defender and is a member of the Massachusetts Bar. Mr. Pressman has been Chairman of Clark University's Century Club, and is active in Lions, Masons, and various religious organizations.

John M. Reed is a partner in the Boston law firm of Sherin and Lodgen and is involved in a general civil practice. He is a graduate of Massachusetts Institute of Technology, where he majored in mathematics, and Harvard Law School. He has been on the faculty of the Boston University and of the Suffolk University Law Schools, where he taught courses on legal methods.

He is a member of the Federal and Massachusetts bars, and the American Law Institute.

Thomas E. Shea is Corporate Counsel for the Commonwealth Companies Inc., Lincoln, Neb. He is a graduate of Regis College, Denver, and has a master's degree in Educational Psychology from Boise State University. He received a J.D. de-

gree from the University of Denver College of Law, where he
was honored with the Order of St. Ives and was an associate
editor of the *Denver Law Journal.* He has served as District
Counsel for the U.S. Corps of Engineers, Galveston District,
and is a member of the Federal, Nebraska, and Colorado bars.

His main areas of interest have been Federal laws, including
Government contracts and environmental impact decisions,
and mental health law.

Nathan T. Sidley is Court Clinic Director at the 4th District
Court, Woburn, Mass. He is a summa cum laude graduate of
the University of Minnesota (Phi Beta Kappa), and the University of Minnesota Medical School (AOA). He received specialty training in psychiatry at Yale Medical School and Harvard
Medical School (where he is presently a clinical instructor),
and is a Diplomate in Psychiatry of the American Board of
Psychiatry and Neurology. He has received special training in
law and been on psychiatry and law committees of the American Psychiatric Association and the Massachusetts Psychiatric
Society. He is a Fellow of the American Psychiatric Association.

He was president of the American Academy of Psychiatry
and the Law and was an associate editor of the *Bulletin of the
American Academy of Psychiatry and the Law.* His main interests
and publications have been in relation to mental health and
law as well as professional ethics.

CHAPTER 1

The Origin and Functions of American Law*

John M. Reed

"And let no one weakly conceive that just laws and true
policy have any antipathy; for they are like the spirits
and sinews, that one moves with the other."
—Francis Bacon

The earliest settlers in what is now the United States came
predominantly from the British Isles as colonists who were
subjects of the Crown. Despite local variations in the colo-
nies—such as the somewhat biblical cast of early legal thought
in New England, or the Dutch practice in New York—almost
from the outset the legal institutions, practices, and procedures of the colonists tended to duplicate English practice at
the time. Many colonial cases even went to English courts, and
colonial lawyers had to be aware of English law in order to
prosecute those cases adequately. Even after the American
Revolution, when governmental institutions were replaced by
native-grown varieties not subject to English rule, American
judges and, under their instruction, juries continued to regard
English case and statutory authorities as controlling legal
questions. Thus, during much of the history of this country,
American law was based on the English Common Law.

The Common Law, itself, was not based on written statutes.
Rather, the Common Law is regarded as having expressed
"the usage and customs of immemorial antiquity" common to
the people of England, though, like many other concepts in

---

*Because Chapter 1 is more discursive than the other chapters, it is set in
straight narrative, rather than outline, form.

the law, that view is partly a fiction. (Undoubtedly the law, that is, the ways in which local communities attempted to resolve disputes or public complaints of various kinds, did not represent a truly common law universally applied throughout England, and customs and usages even change in times that people can recall. They are not constant from time immemorial.)

Indeed, it was only from the time of Henry IV, when there had evolved in Britain a central government which could significantly express its will on the outlying districts, and a corresponding judicial administration, that one could speak of a law common to the country of England. (The fiction of a common law, of course, helped unify the country politically, as well as give credibility to the decisions of the courts who declared and applied it.) It was only from the time that court decisions began to be recorded that usages and customs could be articulated as an organized body of law, in which customs and usages could be somewhat consistent.

The early records of court decisions were kept in the "yearbooks." It is clear from them that the great English courts, the Common Pleas, the King's Bench, and the Exchequer,* regarded themselves as interpreters of the unwritten law and that they regarded their own interpretations as being extensions of the previous interpretations of other judges.** The courts both believed themselves and declared themselves to

---

*A subsequent English body, the Chancellor's Court (Chancery) evolved into the tribunal of Equity jurisdiction, now treated in most American courts of general jurisdiction with other civil matters, although with a few special rules. Equity resembles the common law but supposedly provided for cases which the common law courts were too rigid to handle, and tended to be more discretionary in application than the presumedly fixed legal principles the common law has been envisioned to be. Probate courts jurisdictions are also an outgrowth of the Chancellor's Court.

**It has, in fact, been a traditional myth among common law judges that they merely interpret the law, which impliedly exists independently. Ostensibly, serving a legislative function is anathema to a judge. Actually, however, the nature of the cases presented to courts has frequently demanded that judges, by deciding specific cases at all (an unavoidable function for a court), create new law. The court, in effect, decides such cases on its view of social policy and hardens that policy into law. Of course, as will be seen later, one case decision does not create immutable law; nevertheless, such a decision from a court (for example, the U.S. Supreme Court) has a significant impact on what is regarded as "the law.")

be mandated to follow decisions made previously by their predecessors or even by themselves. Because of the need in what was to be a stable society for predictability of legal decisions, this self-constraint, a fundamental necessity for any real system of justice, formed the seed of the common law both in America and England. Indeed, early reported decisions show that the Massachusetts courts felt constrained not only to follow their own decisions, but also to continue adhering to precedents established by English courts in times past.

The decisions to which judges on both sides of the Atlantic referred were the determinations of the English courts in particular cases, based on particular facts, resulting from particular applications. The decision principle, or ratio decidendi, of a case represented an inference from the application of law to the facts in the specific case.

The tailoring of decisions to specific cases leaves much room for modification of the law, a necessity as society changes and new types of decisions are required. It is a tribute to the ingenuity of common law attorneys and judges, in fact, that the fiction of a common law based on settled practices could be preserved, despite the exponential increase in types of cases decided. This preservation of the myth has occurred in that, in challenging and novel legal situations, creative attorneys have been able to argue successfully that because cases in point have uniquely different facts from previous cases, the legal principles should be applied differently. This means the law should be qualified and extended, thus, requiring new legal principles cloaked in the language of the "old tradition." (Note that the English decisions and the decisions of American courts after them were and still are opinions, usually engendered when the outcome of a case was appealed. The opinions were generally discursive, typically beginning with a statement of the facts that were proved at the trial, and then explicating the rationale for the decision. Generally, though not always, the opinions are those of appellate judges who "determine" what is the "proper" application of law to the facts of the specific case.)

Conceptually, it is important to realize that, in a sophisticated community, law does not have to be derived from case decision source. In continental Europe, for example, "the law" is predominantly derived from a written code of laws, and the critical watershed of legal history is far easier to pick out— namely, the development of the Code Napoleon, arising out of the French Revolution.

In contrast, American law during the 1800's took pride in its being a common law arrangement. The most prominent American judges and teachers were distinguished common law scholars who had mastered the English precedents and those of the courts of this country. Noted American jurists include Chief Justice Lemuel Shaw of Massachusetts, Chief Justice Charles Doe of New Hampshire, Justice Joseph Story of the United States Supreme Court, and Chancellor James Kent of New York, each of whom left a legacy of opinions with broad impact.

The fashion in which one case governs another is elusive of description. In retrospect, the process is seen to constitute a form of logic, but a logic which often deals with principles that are imperfectly expressed, even in the court's opinion in the case at hand. Indeed, merely because a case has been decided in a given direction and because a legal principle applying to the case has been enunciated, the law on the point is, by no means, necessarily established. The saying, "Hard cases make bad law," illustrates a common failing of judges to overgeneralize a legal principle in rationalizing a case which, because of its one-sidedness, is easy to resolve. But one case does not establish the law; others come along which test declared legal principles and, consequently, lead to refinement.

Typically, case law originates with a case, for example, in Oklahoma; the Supreme Court in that state formulates a legal principle that will be considered binding in Oklahoma (until it is successfully challenged). But the lawyers in an adjoining state might say that they are from Missouri and that they, themselves, have to test such a finding in their own courts. (A precedent in a neighboring state is bound to carry some weight in a jurisdiction, but it is not binding as precedent.) Missouri, with a somewhat similar fact situation as that in the Oklahoma case, will be likely to deal with the Missouri facts in the light of the decided case from Oklahoma, but may find different conclusions and somewhat different case law. Ultimately, several states, and perhaps even the courts of the Federal system, will formulate principles dealing with the same type of related cases, and a "weight of opinion" will have been achieved. The weight of opinion, expressed in differing ways and perhaps binding with somewhat differing nuances in different states, is considered to be law. (If an original decision on a case, as in Oklahoma, should, in retrospect, be seen as countering the trend of opinions, it is likely that that viewpoint will be challenged in the original state. The highest appellate court may overrule its original opinion, usually in some face-saving manner, or the state may continue in a maverick status with respect to that particular legal point. The trend is for some homogeneity to evolve over the various states and over Federal jurisdictions. The process of this evolution takes place over time and over several regions.)

Note also that the social utility of law is, in cases of first impression, one of the cardinal test points considered by judges. If the rigid application of a mechanistic logic with respect to a legal principle leads to a socially maladaptive situation, ultimately qualifications of the logic of application of the principle to the situation will develop. Otherwise, the original principle, however it may have been regarded as a fixed star in the firmament, will, itself, be modified in the light of experience. Over time, the courts must consider most strongly the social effect of their opinions, in addition to the strict logic of those opinions. (It is this sense of the situation that led Justice Oliver Wendell Holmes in his celebrated, but extreme, epigram, "The life of the law has not been logic—it has been experience.")

In the course of the 1800's, and with acceleration in the 1900's, legislation often modified the common law, still more often supplemented it. Patterning themselves on English parliamentary experience and embodying the democratic principles of the Revolution, the constitutional structures of each of the states left the legislatures theoretically the "sovereign." Although the common law dealt with such large areas of civil matters as sales, wills, negotiable instruments, etc., and such criminal areas as homicide, theft, and embezzlement, the relative inflexibility of the courts in applying the precedents of legal authority, and the further circumstance that the common law was less than comprehensive in dealing with any subject, motivated all the states to adopt statutory provisions mending inconsistencies and filling gaps and breaches. Among significant developments were a uniform Negotiable Instruments Law, a Sales Act, statutes of wills (in fact patterned after the English Statute of Wills), and many statutes treating particular crimes.

This legislative development was visualized by many scholars as an overlay of the common law. John Chipman Gray, a professor at the Harvard Law School in the early 1900's and a founder of the still existing Boston firm of Ropes & Gray, declared that even a statute was not a law in the philosophical sense until it had been applied to a set of facts by a court. Inevitably statutes, of necessity formulated in general terms, had to be construed in judicial proceedings. The result was that American law retains a common law base, fundamentally composed of American case law (often derived from the precedent of English cases), with a superstructure of statutes, frequently of great complexity. The entire legal edifice is in continual process, covered with a mosaic of ongoing judicial decisions which interpret and adjust both case law and statutory concept, and by a parallel ongoing process of legislation, which modifies previous case decisions as well as previous statutes or even previous constitutional principles.

An excellent illustration of the evolution of a legal principle, which spans a time more than a century in duration, is that of the so-called "product liability" cases. These commence with the Exchequer decision in 1842 of *Winterbottom v. Wright*.[1] The plaintiff, a passenger, was injured because of a defect in a carriage negligently repaired for the owner by the defendant. The Court, in ruling that "privity of contract"* between plaintiff and defendant was a condition of tort liability for negligence in the manufacture or repair of goods, relied strongly upon common law, but at the same time used sociological reasoning which was appropriate enough in the early hey-day of the industrialization of Europe: "There is no privity of contract between these parties; and if the plaintiff can sue, every passenger, or even any person passing along the road, who was injured by the upsetting of the coach, might

---

*See Chapter 10, Contracts

bring a similar action. Unless we confine the operation of such contracts as this to the parties who entered into them, the most outrageous and absurd consequences, to which I can see no limit, would ensue."

The product liability cases of much later decades, after much searching in successive cases for the logical underpinnings of liability, dispensed with the requirement of privity, initially in cases where a negligently made product would place life and limb in peril. The landmark case is Judge Cardozo's opinion allowing recovery in *McPherson v. Buick Motor Co.*[2] This involved a person injured in a car accident, arising out of a defective wheel, which the defendant had been negligent in inspecting during manufacture of the car.

The cases culminate in holdings in the last 20 years which dispense with the requirement of proving negligence in the design or manufacture of the defective product. *Greenman v. Yuma Power Products, Inc.*[3] Without much doubt, the growing availability of liability insurance, together with less apprehension of scaring prospective manufacturers away from making new products, tended to encourage such changes.

Over the course of 120 years, the concept of product liability has thus progressively broadened, in accord with changes in economic, social, and moral conditions. More people have recourse to legal remedies for losses suffered in connection with items. Manufacturers and vendors have become much more vulnerable to adversity which results at a great distance from their activities. The law has much more of a social insurance flavor now, as contrasted with the manufacturers' protectionistic emphasis in the nineteenth century, and at the same time, the involvement of the courts, themselves, in social and political situations has also increased.

The changes have materialized gradually, and subtly, but by degrees, a view which was originally anathema has become of general acceptance. That phenomenon has been repeated in many areas of law, and of course, is still ongoing. As society changes, the law inevitably changes. In fact, it seems to be that even though the law changes society, the factors which determine social order are more pervasive than law. In the long run, social organization determines the shape of law to a far greater extent than occurs in the opposite direction.

It is, thus, apparent that despite declarations by judges implying fixed legal principles, the law, that is, the judicially declared outcome of a given case, is not predictable entirely in terms of precedents and statutory enactments. Furthermore, the law, both written and unwritten, in the sense of the predisposition of judges, lawyers, and juries to make judicial decisions, appears to change with the times, mostly as an obvious reflection of underlying social changes, but, occasionally, without any clear connection being manifest. Over time, however, the needs and conflicts of society do manifest in the kinds of cases that are presented for resolution to courts, and a context of rationalized principles of decision-making evolves. In the broad sense a litigant, who is ultimately a member of society, cannot quite predict how any given lawsuit will turn out. There is always an element of uncertainty of the legal consequences of action, somewhat as there is uncertainty in predicting the consequences of any action. But the uncertainty that is faced when the law is involved pales in contrast to the uncertainty which would exist in the absence of legal structure. Given the principles which have evolved over time, conflicts can be decided in a peaceful and in a somewhat rational manner, and there actually is a great deal of predictability about the legal system and its decisions. Without such a large edifice of law encompassing so many details of life, our social system would be reduced to anarchy. The influence of the law is felt throughout society; that people complain about the law as much as they do suggests aspirations for the law and a feeling of importance of the law in the preservation of social order. Indeed, a social order like ours without a superstructure of law is truly unthinkable.

Text References

1. *Winterbottom v. Wright,* 10 Mees & W. 109
2. *McPherson v. Buick Motor Co,* 217 N.Y. 382, 111 N.E. 1050 (1916)
3. *Greenman v. Yuma Power Products, Inc.,* 59 Cal.2d 57, 377 P.2d 897 (1963)

General References

Holmes, O. W. *The Common Law* (Ed. by Howe, M.D.). Orig. pub. by Little Brown, Boston, 1881, reissued by Harvard Univ. Press, Cambridge, 1963

Questions on Chapter 1,
The Origin and Functions of American Law

1. The common law is not based on written statutes. On what is it regarded as being based?
2. What were the three major English Courts?
3. What is Chancery? Into what jurisdictions did Chancery develop?
4. What is the major difference between English and Continental (European) law?
5. If there is no specific precedent for a case in New Hampshire, where might a lawyer there seek justification for his position?
6. What is "product liability?"
7. The strict doctrine of interpretation of the law is that the judge merely follows past decisions. Is that the case in practice, or do judges tend to take the social consequences of their decisions into account?
8. a. Is the manufacturer of an automobile with a gas tank that catches fire in rear-end collisions likely to be held liable for a defective product? b. Would this have been the case in 1850?
9. What is the significance of Holmes' saying that law is not logic but experience?
10. What were the year-books, and what was their significance?

CHAPTER 2

Ethics

Nathan T. Sidley

Ethics

Nathan T. Sidley

"Human behavior ... is the circuitous technique by
which human genetic material has been ... kept intact.
Morality has no other demonstrable ultimate function."
—Edward O. Wilson

I. Basic approaches to the study of ethics.

A. Introduction.

Mankind shares with many species such tendencies as
etiquette, cooperative labor, incest taboos, and cleanli-
ness training. But mankind, alone, engages in speculation about ethics. In man's speculating about ethics,
three paradoxes have repeatedly been pondered.

1. Man is rational; yet, all-too-frequently, he acts knowingly and deliberately against his own best interests.
2. Man is intrinsically self-centered; yet, he is capable of
   the highest acts of altruism.
3. Man's behavior is determined by many causes; yet, he
   is treated by authority as if he has freedom of will.

In addition, the problem of what is the *summum bonum*,
the "highest good," has long occupied men's minds.
For if the principle of the highest good is known, the
other principles of conduct or of organization of life
can, at least in theory, be derived from it.

Practically, as well as speculatively, everyone must deal with ethics, for in the broadest sense ethics deals with choices; making choices, selecting one alternative action from many, concerns every area of life. Ethics involves the principles of evaluation of alternatives.

B. Systematic ethics. The study of the bases of evaluation of different choice possibilities and the rules that men use to guide behavior with respect to those possibilities.

   1. Ethics can be studied prescriptively, that is, learning about the rules that one "should" follow—or, "what are the values which determine how I should act?"

   2. Ethics may be studied descriptively. Examples include broad issues, for example, what are different sets of rules and value systems that people have, and how do those relate to other aspects of their lives? An issue not quite as broad is; what values, if any, are different in men from in women?

   3. Ethics may be studied as a conditional field. For example, if one wishes to raise children who don't take drugs, what should one do?

   4. Prescriptive ethics is generally approached from the subjective point of view, that is, of the actor, while the other aspects of ethics are studied from the viewpoint of the objective, outside observer.

C. Ethics, in the sense of the grounds of choices, is often related to the notion of "values."

   1. In the simplest sense, ethics can be abstracted into two values, namely "good" and "bad" or equivalently, "right" and "wrong." In a more complicated analysis, various degrees of good and bad are conceptualized, and more relative values of given situations, actions, or phenomena can be contemplated.

   2. Ethics is also related to the idea that individuals "should" (or "ought" to) do certain things. The concept "should" has no straightforward psychological meaning as do ordinary psychological concepts. (Most people, of course, take the concept for granted. The

mind, in its own way, learns to form a "should" concept. But to define the notion in a manner susceptible to analysis requires more subtlety.)

a. Ordinarily, the notion of "should" or "ought" is more like an order than like a description. An order is a statement which indicates a psychological state on the part of the speaker, as if to say, "I want and expect that you will act in accordance with the order." An order usually implies, even though it does not say explicitly, "if you do not obey, you will be punished." (Ordinarily of course, orders aren't given unless they are likely to be obeyed. It is a problem for both the parties if an order is not obeyed.) The person giving the order and the person receiving it have learned that the verbal form used, that is, the order, implies a psychological state of the orderer and an "if-then" consequential expectation regarding the potential response of the person being ordered. The pattern is ingrained in both persons so that the full implications of the order almost never rise to the surface.

b. The concepts of "should" and "ought", are undoubtedly, learned similarly to learning about orders; they contain the same implications of psychological states and of "if-then" consequential expectations as do orders. "Should" and "ought" are at times more abstract than orders because there may be no specific individual responsible for making the directive. The fundamental principle of "if-then" consequences is the same, however.

3. Values relate to the goals of behavior. In any ethical system, that which is valuable is regarded as "good" or as desirable (whatever names are used). Furthermore, by means of "should" and "ought" notions, ethical systems direct people to perform actions, which bring about what is regarded in the system as something good.

a. The term "values" is related to individuals in a similar manner. A person's choices are related to his values. The preferred choice has, at least at the time of choice, a higher value than other alternatives. Insofar as a per-

son's tendencies to choose are consistent, he may be
said to have a "value system."

b. A person's value system, as determined by his choices,
may not agree with his value system as he might view it
to himself. An individual might have an actual value
system as indicated by his choice behaviors; he might
have an overt value system as indicated by how he describes himself to others. (Indeed, he may describe
himself differently to different others, and may have a
third value system according to the way he sees himself. It is, obviously, difficult to ascertain what are the
concepts by which a person defines himself.) Finally,
he may have values which appear inconsistent in that
they vary according to the situation or his state of
mind. This kind of inconsistency is more difficult to
conceptualize as a value system and may represent per-
sonality instability or handicap.

D. Problems in studying ethics
   1. Ethical terms are used in ordinary language in many
      ways. Those terms have not been defined scientifically
      in a way which unambiguously relates to observable
      phenomena, nor in such a way as to lead to homogene-
      ity of interpretation by scientists. Unless terms are
      used unambiguously by students in a field, confusion
      results.

   2. Emotions are aroused in studying ethics.
      a. Ethics relates to human behavior and its evaluation.
         The student of ethics will be likely to have strong emo-
         tions aroused when he studies ethics.
         1) Everyone relates his perceptions to his own experi-
            ence.
         2) Relating anything to experience gives rise to emo-
            tions similar to those occurring under the previous
            experience conditions.
         3) Ethical concepts in a person's life are often related
            to experiences with strong emotions.
      b. The arousal of emotions usually results in distorted
         perceptions of the situation which gives rise to the
         emotional arousal. In order to perceive and compre-

hend ethical concepts adequately, the student must recognize the emotions which are aroused in himself, and he must then compensate for them. To recognize such emotions and to compensate for them requires the ability to observe one's own emotional reactions, a talent not possessed by all. It also requires the ability to compensate. (Indeed, if the emotions are strong enough, no one can make proper allowances for them.) Compensation for the distorting perceptual effects of emotion requires that the individual not have overly strong emotional reactions, a characteristic also not universally possessed. Training at self-recognition and at compensatory mastery of emotions is a help in dealing with them. But such training, at least in a formal and systematic sense, is not common.

3. A person who studies ethics objectively and systematically may be subject to pressure from those who regard their interests as threatened by such objective scrutiny.

   a. Though severe examples of such people are officials who have vested interests in preservation of a specific status, essentially everyone with a high degree of emotional involvement in a given ethical system tends to be intolerant of those with different systems or of those who may be potentially critical. (And virtually everyone has a high degree of emotional involvement in his own ethical system.)

   b. There is a further problem that people with a strong feeling of investment in an ethical system may be dishonest in discussing, evaluating, or otherwise conceptualizing it. Such people might pervert a forum, ostensibly set up to study a system objectively, by propagandizing, misrepresenting, etc.

4. Problems in conceptualizing fact patterns.

   a. Ethics involves relating ethical principles to behavior in given situations. But even if individuals agree on ethical principles, they may disagree in their interpretation as to what are the facts and the potentialities for behavior of a given situation. Often real-life ethical situations are so complex that there is no way of resolving such differing interpretations. Science usually can be objective only about relatively simple observations, such as what number is indicated on a dial. Human behavior is generally too complex for definition precise enough to be universally acceptable to diverse observers.

b. Just as there are often strong emotions aroused in relation to ethical systems, so are there strong feelings often aroused in interpreting what are the facts of a situation. Again, efforts to recognize the emotions and to compensate for them can be helpful. But often, even the utmost of goodwill and effort may not resolve emotion-driven differences of perception and of interpretation people give to a fact situation. People may be able either to agree or disagree about the facts or to agree for the sake of expediency; those are, in the broad sense, political decisions rather than purely cognitive or scientific decisions, however.

c. Ethical phenomena and ethical behaviors relate to a set of psychological concepts. Differing psychological notions or models give rise to different expectations of the potentialities of behavior and, consequently, to different judgments about the "rightness" or "wrongness" of any given behavior. For example, two people may agree that a person has a broken finger and that he is suffering from it. They may even agree on the amount of pain. But they may disagree as to whether that amount of pain would be enough to impair the person's job performance. They may also disagree on the degree of performance impairment which should be sufficient to warrant being excused from job duties. (The latter, however, is a question of values, not of psychology.)

The kind of ethical disagreement regarding psychology usually relates to the higher integrating psychological functions. The question usually involves what people are ordinarily capable of doing, particularly when under stress. For example, it is recognized that certain psychological stresses or passions impair a person's ability to obey the law. Some people assume that there are many situations in which such psychological impairments are crippling, and they tend to be indulgent.

Others assume that people can control their behavior, even under stress of great magnitude, and that they should be held responsible (that is, subject to sanction and punishment) for any and all of their actions.

People can also differ in their concepts about the degree of stress presented by different situations. A person might feel that the stress of discovering an unfaithful spouse in flagrant deliction might be more severe than the stress of feeling persecuted by an employer. Some may, thus, be forgiving of a homicide committed under the first circumstance but not the second; others may take the opposite view. But ultimately, the implicit differences in the two attitudes relate to differences in conceptions regarding functioning of the human mind. (Differences in psychological concepts may themselves be products of other factors, such as social group memberships or economic interests. In any case, however they are obtained or derived, people's attitudes regarding psychology influence their ethical views.)

5. Another difficulty of studying ethics is a twofold difficulty, related to the complexity of the field.

    a. The first is that of defining what behavior constitutes ethical behavior. There is much agreement among people regarding ethical evaluation of behavior in given situations. For example, most people would agree that under normal circumstances, stealing from others is wrong. There are situations, however, in which there is profound disagreement as to what constitutes right and what constitutes wrong behavior. A common medical and political situation is that of abortion, a situation which has tended to polarize people. What is the right way for some is absolutely the wrong way for others. And such differing ethical views about politics may be held by people who are regarded by others as morally and ethically steadfast and who also regard themselves as such.

    b. The second difficulty, obviously related to the first, but with additional features of its own, is that of determining how ethical a person is. Many types of behaviors performed by an individual can be related to choice and right-wrong considerations, but there is no necessary correlation among the different types of behaviors that can be classified as ethical. By one set of criteria, a person might be regarded as highly ethical; by another set of apparently equally appropriate criteria, the same person might be considered unethical. Also an individual is not necessarily consistent in his ethical behavior, at least according to common categories of classifying behavior.

  c. These differing ethical phenomena can be evaluated in an individual:

    1) Statements as to what he regards as right or wrong;

    2) Statements as to what an individual should do in a hypothetical problem situation;

    3) What the person actually does in given situations;

    4) The person's psychological reaction after he does something seen as wrong (or even seen as right);

    5) How the individual responds to knowing or observing others performing various right or wrong actions.

  d. Definition of the right and wrong in specific situations is often difficult for a person:

    1) If his ethical system does not explicitly cover the facts of that situation. (Most ethical systems don't because they are very general.)

    2) If there are conflicts among different principles relevant to the choice situation.

    3) Even though situations are highly similar, a person may not give consistent judgments about them.

    4) People usually act intuitively in situations and are not always able to rationalize explicitly why an action should be taken.

E. The functions of ethics.

  1. Survival of the community.

    If, in the past, there have been groups which have placed a value on self-destruction, those groups tend no longer to be with us. It is axiomatic that in the long run, no ethical system which is employed by a group can conflict with survival, or the group will disappear. Insofar as the choice of values made by a group influences the destiny of that group, ethical systems may be said to operate on a basis of natural selection. Ethics, which are survival-enhancing for the groups employing them, are more likely to be preserved than ethics which are survival-detracting. (This is the case on the group level. It may be, however, that ethics, which under some (necessarily rare) occasions tend on an individual level to suicide, or are tantamount to suicide, are, in fact, survival-enhancing to the group.)

2. Survival of the individual.

Learning what is "right and wrong" can often give a person guidance in conducting his life. As a result of that guidance, by following an appropriate set of rules, a person might survive better than he could without following such rules. (This is not necessarily true for individual survival. But it is probably statistically true. On the whole, people who follow the rules tend to survive better than those who do not.) Following the rules to the letter is particularly useful for those whose mental capacities are limited so that they cannot use appropriate flexibility when the situation calls for it. A limitation of mental capacity is always costly, but it tends to be less costly when the rules are followed rigorously.

3. Influencing behavior of others.

a. Ethics relates to self-image, which relates to one's status in the community and to one's internalized reward-punishment system. Generally, people have a more rewarding self-image when they view themselves as good people who do right things than when they view themselves as bad people who do wrong things. After all, people are rewarded, often concretely, in their interaction with others if they are "good," and they are punished if they are "bad." (In fact, viewing oneself as having done something bad often makes a person feel bad. The word "guilt-feelings" has been applied to such situations.) As every child learns in dealing with his parents, people's behaviors can often be influenced by operating on their ethical concepts and, thus, affecting their self-image and their emotions.

   b. Ethical principles can be used as a guise to rationalize the actions of a clever person, to conceal or divert attention from his real motivation for the actions.

   c. Ethical statements can be employed as a simple rallying cry to attract support for partisan political efforts.

4. Other reasons for studying ethics.

   a. Curiosity. Understanding different ethical phenomena and ethical points of view can be intrinsically rewarding intellectually.

   b. Relieving anxiety and reassuring those in doubt.

Insofar as people can reward and punish themselves by internal mental operations involving how they look at themselves, there will be internal psychological pressure on a person to see himself as "good," (often, in fact, as better than he is) and to avoid seeing himself as "bad." Indeed, motivation to see oneself accurately frequently tends to be weaker than motivation to see oneself inaccurately.

Concern over oneself and one's self-image may give rise to self-doubt and to feelings of inadequacy. Thinking about ethics helps one to compare one's own actions and characteristics against others or standards and is often reassuring to one's concerns.

At times, learning about how others conduct themselves or how they feel they should conduct themselves, gives a person a feeling that he is ethically superior to others or confirms a previous self-image that he is ethically superior. For internal psychological reasons that, too, is rewarding to people.

F. Naïve ethics and absolutism of unchallenged ethical views.

To a person who has, throughout his life, been enveloped in a simple cultural system of good and bad, particularly if that system is relatively consistent and followed to a significant degree, there is no such thing as a comparative study of ethics. Such a person considers that

there is "good" and there is "bad," and he does not conceptualize his notions any more subtly or deeply than
that. If the individual does not know what to do in a giv-
en situation, he can usually appeal to some authority who
will tell him what to do in the situation.

It is only when an individual's ethical system is challenged, by exposure to contrary views and to alternative
ways of action in various types of situations, that the person learns that there are multiple ethical systems and
that different people judge actions differently. He learns,
in effect, that notions of "right" and "wrong" are not in-
trinsic properties of actions, but that, rather, they are
judgments which have been placed on those actions by
people, especially people who are acting in their capacities as members of groups. For example, it is only when
challenged by seeing alternative systems and viewpoints
that a person learns that a determination that the action
of *A* killing *B* is judged by some individuals as good and
by others as bad, depending on who are the *A* and *B*,
what are the circumstances of the homicide, and what are
the relationships to *A* and *B* of those making the determination.

It is easy to see how in the case of a young and unsophisticated person, an ethical naïveté and absolutism can occur. More sophisticated persons often maintain similar
absolutist moral views, but usually when there is some
concrete interest, often political or institutional, involved
in the preservation of that ethical absolutism. Without
such an underlying institutional interest, increasing
knowledge of the ethics of others, by the basic perceptual process of identifying oneself with a perceived situation, probably leads to greater ethical tolerance. Of
course, everyone has a certain degree of institutional interest, but with increasing age, and knowledge which involves depth and breadth of experience, that basic bias is
somewhat overcome.

G. Ethical systems.

   1. A system of ethics is a set of abstract definitions of situations with the judgments of "good" or "bad" that
   go with the situational definitions.

A system of ethics may be rationalized as flowing from some metaphysical or religious premises or assumptions, or the system may be declared valid in its own terms.

2. A system of ethics may be said to be different from law in the following respects:
    a. Laws tend to have a formal staff devoted to their enforcement. Ethical systems tend to have more informal enforcement mechanisms.
    b. Laws tend to deal with objective behavior. The law cannot go beyond conformity of visible behavior to the legal standard. Ethical systems not only are concerned with objective conduct, they tend to deal also with subjective perceptions, including self-perceptions and private behavior. Many behaviors, which do not have immediately and directly visible adverse effects and are not the subject of laws, are, nevertheless, dealt with by ethical systems. Many intangible aspects of personal behavior, such as drug use, sexual behaviors, personal reputations emerging from interpersonal relations, etc., are considered to be appropriate for consideration by many ethical systems. In ordinary contemporary environments, those areas are not easily handled by the law and may even be considered inappropriate for consideration by the law.
    c. Ethical principles are abstract and general. Because of an absence of enforcement sanctions, there is seldom a great need to resolve a specific ethical dispute, and ethics can remain abstract. Because of the distinctions and qualifications involved in applying a given principle of law, the law has developed elaborate methods of analysis of cases. A brief devoted to a single case could run hundreds or even thousands of pages. There is nothing comparable for ethical principles, since there is an absence of a problem-resolving body of record such as a court. (An exception is certain issues dealt with by ecclesiastical judicial bodies. These bodies use quasi-legal methods of dispute resolution, however.)
    d. The law is a limited agency. It can only punish, and it punishes those whose behavior falls below the mini-

mum standard of acceptable community behavior.
(When the law works as it is formally stated to work,
that is. There are perversions of law perpetrated in the
name of the law, and there are also informal punishments often meted out to people who are selected for
punishment merely because those individuals are
members of certains groups. The purpose of these
punishments serves as a reminder of dominant group
power.)
Ethics deals more than does law with subjective intentions and other phenomena that may not be measur-
able. It rewards, both internally and externally.
Sometimes, individuals are even given special recognition for their ethical achievements. In ethics, the effort
is to reach 100 percent in order to be rewarded. In law,
it is to avoid failing so that one will not be punished.

3. Ethical systems and the law frequently interact.
   a. It is common for people to evaluate the law in terms of
   an ethical system, with the implicit assumption that the
   law, as an influence on human behavior with enforcement powers, should promote what is regarded as righ-
   teous, good, or just. Those evaluations are frequently
   accompanied by actions to influence the legal system to
   conform with the ethical judgments.
   b. At times and places, the law has displayed a marked in-
   tolerance for ethical opinions, especially for ethical
   opinions differing from those predominant among individuals who occupy positions of authority. This is
   true because law enforcement authorities often either
   lack understanding of views other than their own, feel
   so deeply and strongly about their own views, or, of
   course, selfishly use their offices for private purposes,
   they do not tolerate any other views. Unfortunately, legal power is often directed severely against those who
   express ethical dissent from some dominant position.
   c. Ethical issues often become legal issues. Many areas of
   medical ethics, for example, abortion, allowing people
   to die, etc., have entered the legal arena and are subjects of both statutory and case law in addition to being
   ethical issues.

4. Systems of ethics differ among themselves as to the areas they emphasize.
   a. Some systems focus on political behavior and the state. Such systems often relate to overall action programs which constitute an ideology.
   b. Some focus on individual lifestyles.
      In the broad sense, for example, the Greeks tended to define what a person is when he leads a good life. Nietzche, a more recent philosopher, used a similar focus but came to some different conclusions about a good life.
   c. Some systems focus on the evaluation of acts. There are two major emphases.
      1) Deontology—the study of duty.
         a) In general the concept of deontology is that in a given situation, one should always follow the rule. For example, one should always tell the truth, even if other actions might lead to more desirable outcomes.
         b) Deontology can at times become an absolutistic, inflexible, simple-minded and naïve ethic, especially when enforced by fanatic authorities.
         c) Kant's "categorical imperative" is an important example of deontological ethics.
      2) Teleology—the study of purposes.
         a) Teleologists tend to assert that the evaluation of an action depends on the consequences of the action.
         b) Two problems with teleology.
            1)) The far-reaching consequences of an action cannot be determined. Only some immediate consequences can be foreseen. Also, it is difficult, without a good deal of thought, to predict even short-term consequences of some acts. A true teleologist would be forced to do a great deal more thinking than people usually do.
            2)) There still must be some kind of overall values judging the consequences of actions.
         c) Utilitarianism—the doctrine that the ultimate moral principle is the greatest happiness for the

greatest number, and situation ethics, which does not state an overlying ethical principle but judges actions on the foreseeable consequences, are important examples of teleological systems.

3) Even a system based on duty, however, ultimately relates to purposes. The practical justification for following the rule, even when it gives a result which appears bad, is that, in the long run, if everyone were always to follow the rules, society would be better off than under any other system. (Theoretical justifications of duty-oriented systems may not always give lip service to that practical consideration, but it is almost always implicit.)

4) Systems which focus on acts tend to emphasize the intentions behind acts (in relation to foreseeable consequences) almost more than the actual outcomes of the actions.

5) There is a fourth ethical paradox which is related to the deontological versus the teleological approach. No matter how thorough a set of rules is devised, there are always situations in which the rule appears inappropriate if applied completely. The rule must, therefore, be modified or qualified, in the interest of group survival, justice, etc., which are important to the deontologist. Thus, everyone must evaluate situations and outcomes and must make a unique decision. But if decision-making is left up to everyone,, there will be anarchy and lack of order, an uncomfortable situation for the deontologist. Independent thought, in addition, reveals the inadequacies of the authority and the rules themselves, thus, destabilizing the entire system and rendering it nonuniform. Fortunately, there are not many situations in ordinary life which are not predictable in advance and which cannot be appropriately covered by some rule. This eliminates the need to think about what the best course of action is.

6) Teleological systems are often related to considerations of practical ordinary social intercourse in time of peace. Compared to them, deontological systems

are often more mystical and denying of practical considerations (that is, more ascetic), tend to emphasize obedience rather than thought, and relate more to high emotion as in times of strife and war.

   a) Systems emphasizing intellectual contemplation tend to emphasize being content with life's limitations and adversities, if not resigned to them.

   b) Systems emphasizing mystical experiences lead to continual striving for unusual experiences and a more intense life.

d. Ethical relativism and ethical analysis.

   1) These are two related philosophical schools, which hold, fundamentally, that the notions of right and wrong are not relatable to observable phenomena as are scientific concepts, but rather they represent emotions and feelings about behaviors. In their view, there is no ultimate criterion which can establish that one system of right and wrong is any more "valid" objectively than any other view. Therefore, disagreements regarding ethical values cannot be resolved by appeal to observation. Rather, they must be resolved by attempting to change feelings and attitudes, or, in some cases, by stimulating change by indicating inconsistent values. (For example, a person cannot place a high value on preserving health and at the same time place a high value on indiscriminate use of drugs like heroin and cocaine.)

e. Many systems of ethics have been proposed. Only a few have been adopted by significantly large groups of people and have survived in a viable way.

   1) For a system of ethics to survive, it must accomplish the following:

      a) Be fulfillable by a group of people large enough to survive as a unit.

      b) Be comprehensible by such a group of people.

      c) Seem appropriate to the group of people in terms of their lives, interests, and goals.

   2) A system which fails in any of those is unlikely to win the allegiance of enough people for survival of a group living by the system.

The fifth ethical paradox. Any ethical barrier that prevents people from doing what they are motivated to do, even if that motivation is against their best interests, and even if the people understand that, is resented if it is promulgated as legislation. (Some people will not understand; some people cannot understand. Many will actively struggle against the restriction if there is any possibility of avoiding it.) Those irrational resistances mitigate against a stable social order, based on systematic ethics, even though adherence to such a system would seemingly benefit all.

3) Because of those limitations, an ethical system can generally relate only to short term group goals. Considerations of long-term survival of the group are usually lost because of pressing short-term factors.

4) Because of the time and education factors involved, a system which can appeal to a large fraction of a population must be simple in concepts. Human behavior is complex, however, and understanding it requires complex concepts. That is a basic limitation of any viable ethical system.

f. Ethical conflicts within a system.

A situation in life may be complex enough so that each alternative action available for implementation has multiple effects, for example, deciding how to vote. Some of the effects are likely to be categorized in the system as good and some categorized as bad. Some of the good outcomes are regarded as better than others, while some bad outcomes are regarded as worse than others. Choosing from among alternatives, all of which represent different mixtures of outcomes of different degrees of goodness or badness (most of which are unpredictable anyway), is a far cry from making a decision on the basis of a simple principle. Most important life situations, however, represent that kind of complexity and are not simple decisions.

In addition, no matter how much effort is put into the process of weighing and balancing different alternatives, there is always an irreducible, usually large, uncertainty involved in a decision. There is no "right answer" in such circumstances, and there is an unavoidable risk that the outcome of an action will not at all be what was desired or predicted by the decisionmaker.

No ethical system can deal in more than a rudimentary way with those true ethical conflicts, which are inherent in virtually all of life's major decisions. It is a fact with which anyone seriously interested in ethical behavior must contend, and in this writer's opinion, if truly recognized, is bound to lead to a position of ethical humility.

II. Some ethics-related empirical facts.

A. Ethical development and the epidemiology of ethical behavior.

Given that standards of behavior are valuable to a group, there are interesting questions as to how those standards become operating influences both in the community, as a whole, and in the individuals in the community. There are also questions as to the failures of appropriate standards to be incorporated, as in the case of criminals or in the cases of societies that are unable to take requisite measures to protect themselves and are overwhelmed, either by internal dissension or by a foreseeable external attack.

Not much is known about any of these questions. A brief synopsis of some of the empirical data and theories is presented.

1. Moral behavior.
   a. The most difficult question is determining how to apportion moral considerations as a factor in action. A person may do something which would be considered as highly moral in itself for reasons which are completely expedient and nonmoral. People often act for the most immoral of motives in doing immoral things, but they attempt to justify them on the basis of moral

considerations. And even for truly moral motivations a person may do something which appears to be heinous immorality.

Because of multiple factors in the background of any behavior, it is impossible to ascertain what are a person's motives for any given action. Over a period of time, observing consistent trends in the behaviors of a person, one can formulate hypotheses as to what his motives are, in general; but those, too, are highly subject to error. The task is an uncertain one. And with respect to practical issues, how many people can actually be observed in multiple situations, anyway?

b. The problems of determining what is moral, in general, and what are a given person's moral motivations are the limiting issues in studying moral development. Since those cannot be studied definitively or directly, a compromise approach has been to study children's and adult's understanding of moral issues and to ascertain the ways in which people conceptualize those issues.

2. There are various conceptions of "stages of moral development." Some are based on the notion that a person must understand a basic issue before he can understand a refinement of that issue. (For example, a person who does not understand addition cannot understand multiplication.)

a. Between the ages of six and nine, a child's sense of his own continuing identity begins. (A six-year-old recognizes that a boy remains a boy even if he dresses and acts like a girl.)[1]

Under age six or so, a child believes that everyone sees things exactly as he himself sees him. When a little older, he realizes that things look different, according to where one is standing, etc.[2]

A young child believes in "immanent justice," that is, a person who does a forbidden thing will be punished by nature, for example, hit by lightning, etc., if he is not punished by an authority.[3]

Young children see the outcome of an act as the only criterion in its goodness or badness; the older child recognizes good intentions as mitigating bad out-

comes. By age seven a child comes to believe that "punishment should fit the crime."[4]
A young child cannot conceive of changing the rules of a game; changing the rule is not differentiated from breaking it.[5]

b. A child's earliest response to morality is in terms of being sensitive to an authority person's actually being there. At an older age, children respond to conventional rules and modes of dealing with situations. Subsequently, more sophisticated children think in terms of abstract mental concepts like "fair play" or "justice."[6]

c. It is agreed that education and training, as well as the moral atmosphere of the home and the community, affect children's moral development. How they do, and how one can raise children to be moral citizens, are still largely unknown.

d. The following characteristics have been regarded as correlated with moral behavior:

   1) Intelligence.
   2) Ability to maintain attention.
   3) Ability to anticipate future events.
   4) Ability to delay gratification.
   5) Autonomic nervous system stability.
   6) Low level of internal fantasies of aggression.
   7) Satisfaction with oneself and one's environment.

e. The foregoing are not much different from the characteristics related to morality by Aristotle, that is, good birth, good family, good looks, and sufficient material goods.

B. Postulated biological correlates in immoral behavior (that is, crime).

  1. Hypothesis. Criminal psychopaths are persons with a highly reactive emotional system and with a high requirement for stimulation from the outside environment, in order to prevent boredom. The emotional reactions represent changes in state of arousal of the autonomic nervous system; the stimulus-seeking represents a state of low arousal of the cortex of the cerebrum of the brain (the highest processing centers).[7]

2. It is also hypothesized that there is a group of psychopaths who are biologically much like schizophrenics in that they have a low hold on reality.[8]

C. Two interesting sets of experiments.
   1. Social influence leading to immoral behavior (Milgram).
      At the urging of an experimenter, who said it was necessary for an experiment and, therefore, "all right," individuals frequently administered seemingly painful shocks to a subject even though they were under the impression that the shocks might be severely harmful to the subject. People were much less willing to administer the shocks when they had to hold the victim's hand than when they were in an adjoining separated room.[9]
   2. Influencing children's inhibitions (Aronfreed).
      Children punished while reaching for an attractive toy delayed reaching for it when no adult was around for a longer time than did children who were not punished until after they had picked up the toy. (The implication is that punishing the intention is more effective than punishing the deed. A person who has done the deed has received some reward from it; thus the reward-punishment balance is different from when the deed is not consummated.) When the punishment was accompanied by a conceptual rule (for example, saying, "You shouldn't touch that bad toy."), there was an even longer delay in reaching for the toy.[10]

D. Some other facts of morality.
   1. Females seem to be more sensitive to moral considerations than are males, but they probably cheat as much as males do.[11]
   2. An honor system tends to reduce the incidence of cheating in a school.[12]
   3. Even though older children are more consistent in their behavior than younger children, older children, themselves, are quite inconsistent in different aspects

of moral behavior, for example, cheating as compared with doing other forbidden things.[13]

E. Analysis of an ethical problem.

  1. There are typically three types of ethical issues that involve health care professionals.

    a. Ethical decisions in their own lives, especially involving how honest and how charitable they should be, when to do so conflicts significantly with their own interests;

    b. General public policy concerns in their functioning as citizens; for example, how much of community resources should be devoted to education, crime control, highways, etc.?

    c. Policy issues in the health care area; these generally involve economic issues or patient care issues.

      1) Examples of economic issues. What is an appropriate fee to charge a given patient for a given procedure? Is it appropriate to go on strike over financial issues?

      2) An example of a patient care issue: When should one discontinue life-prolonging treatment?

      3) An example of a mixed issue: How much of a hospital's resources should be allocated to dialysis units for incurable patients?

  2. Stages in the rational analysis of an ethical problem.

    a. The first step is a tentative one, namely looking grossly at the facts and trying to ascertain what there is about the situation which makes it one requiring action. What motivates a need for decision? Usually, the origin is that someone is suffering and is looking for relief.

    b. The second issue is to look carefully at the facts, especially to ascertain whose interests are involved in the situation and how they are involved. Usually in a health care problem, there are at least four, and probably five, separate sets of interests that are involved. They include: the suffering individual, his family, "society" (including the law and probably including an insurance company), and the health care professional (and colleagues in various fields). In institutional practice, the interests of the institution and of its influential personnel will also be involved and must be considered in decision-making.

Unfortunately, there is no experience-based classification scheme for decision-making. This is in contrast with medical treatment, in which for each diagnostic classification there tends to be a corresponding set of known treatment possibilities with more or less known potential outcomes, both good and bad, for each treatment in relation to that diagnostic category. Since only a few treatment possibilities are sensible to use in relation to a given diagnostic situation, the decision-making problem is far simpler and far more reliable than it is for ethical questions, where speculation must play a far more important role; systematic experience is almost nonexistent, and there are many alternative action possibilities with different kinds of consequences. Thus, in an ethical decision situation, it is almost impossible to be "wrong" in one's decisions, provided one has given them due consideration.

c. After the facts are considered, the more difficult issue of considering alternative courses of action occurs. Generally, a creative solution occurs to a person by a process of mental evolution, that is, after long thinking about possible approaches in the light of balancing of the interests involved. (Usually, that means trying to satisfy everyone partially and being able to satisfy no one completely. Much of the time, especially where one deals with interests which are in conflict, there is no solution which satisfies anybody. The problem is to find a solution which is least dissatisfying. Note that in balancing interests, one does not, in fact reasonably cannot, consider all parties' interests as of equivalent value. For example, in the ordinary patient-doctor encounter, the interests of the patient and doctor are uppermost, because they are the most heavily involved in the situation. No course of action which severely compromises either the patient's or the doctor's interests will truly resolve the problem. If there is a true, intense, irreconcilability of interests, even the cleverest of approaches to a problem will fail.) One must, of course, consider how ordinary, simple ethical rules apply to the facts of the problem.

The process of evolving the most creative solution involves a significant amount of cogitation and of comparing of different possibilities against different interests. It is often only after one has explored many possibilities that an action-possibility with real potential for optimizing among the different interests, occurs to the decision maker.

It is apparent that the evolution of a creative, optimal solution is a time-consuming process and can only be applied to a few problems that arise. Fortunately, most decision problems can be dealt with by simple ethical rules of thumb in a relatively expeditious manner. The less common ones, however, can be taxing.

    d. Once a solution has been defined, one can try to implement the action.

It is important to monitor the implementation, however. A solution determined *a priori,* to be best, may, in its implementation, demonstrate shortcomings which require reconsideration of the selected approach. (An attempt to impose one's solution, without monitoring for a possible need for reevaluation, is likely to be unsuccessful because of authoritarian inflexibility.)

    e. No problem-solving method will guarantee successful adaptation for the person who employs it. The above is a somewhat systematized common sense or rational method. The rational method is not always the best method in a situation. On the whole, however, experience suggests that rational methods of decision-making usually work more effectively and more consistently than do nonrational methods.

F. The ultimate paradox—ethics and human evolution.

The human brain has evolved in such a way as to conduce to human adaptation to the environment, given the biological constraints of the evolution of the body and of the brain itself. That is, the basic evolution of the human brain has followed from that of the mammalian brain in general. There are vestiges of mechanisms of adaptation of, say, shrews and mice in the functioning of the human brain.

The environments which have resulted in the behavior tendencies of contemporary humans are not the same as today's environment. And it is likely that many brain-founded behavior mechanisms which were adaptively productive in prior environments are detractive of adaptation in today's environment. In particular, certain propensities for aggression, which have contributed to the survival of humanity until today, may lead to its destruction tomorrow. Today's environment, with its technically oriented mutual interdependence, depends more than yesterday's on mankind's ability to anticipate long-term survival interests and adapt behavior to them. But adaptive behavior is likely to be in conflict with emotionally motivated behavior, which tends to be short-term, situation-oriented. It is difficult for people to overcome such emotional motivations.

Since mankind now has the capability of destroying itself, a capability not available hitherto, if the balance between rational control and emotional destructiveness goes in the wrong direction, the whole human race will suffer. It is to be hoped that common sense will prevail, and humanity will survive in spite of itself.

Text References

1. Lickona, T. Research on Piaget's theory of moral development. Ch. 12 in Lickona, T., infra
2. *Ibid.*
3. *Ibid.*
4. *Ibid.*
5. Epstein, R. The development of children's conceptions of rules in the years four to eight. Unpublished; cited in Lickona T., infra
6. Kohlberg, L. Moral stages and moralization: The cognitive-development approach. Ch. 2 in Lickona, T., infra
7. Eysenck, H.J. The biology of morality. Ch. 6 in Lickona, T., infra
8. *Ibid.*
9. Milgram, S. Behavioral study of obedience. *J. Abn. Soc. Psychol.* 67, 371–378, 1963, cited in Lickona, T., infra
10. Aronfreed, J. Aversive control of internalization. In Arnold, W.J. (Ed.). *Nebraska Symposium on Motivation* (v. 16). Lincoln, Univ. Nebraska Press, 1968, pp. 271–320; cited in Lickona, T., infra
11. Burton, R.V. Honesty and dishonesty. Ch. 10 in Lickona T., infra
12. Canning, R. Does an honor system reduce class cheating? An experimental answer. *J. Exper. Educ.* 24; 291–296, 1956; cited in Lickona, T., infra

General References

Aristotle. *Nicomachean Ethics* (Tr. by Rackham, H.). Harvard Univ. Press, Loeb Classical Library, Cambridge, 1934

Eysenck, H.J. and Wilson, G.D. *The Psychological Basis of Ideology.* University Park Press, Baltimore, 1978

Frankena, W.K. *Ethics* (2nd ed.). Prentice-Hall, Englewood Cliffs, 1973

Gilligan, C. *In a Different Voice: Psychological Theory and Women's Development.* Harvard Univ. Press, Cambridge, 1982

Lickona, T. (Ed.). *Moral Development and Behavior: Theory, Research, and Social Issues.* Holt, Rinehart and Winston, New York, 1976

Wilson, E.O. *On Human Nature.* Harvard Univ. Press, Cambridge, 1978

Questions on Chapter 2,
Ethics

1. In this chapter, the concept, "should," is related in psychological development to what kind of interpersonal situation?
2. What problem relating to emotions is involved in studying ethics?
3. What two fundamental conceptual areas are involved in every specific ethical decision?
4. What are the three main functions of becoming conversant with ethical principles?
5. What are four major differences between ethics and the law?
6. What two classes of ethical systems focus on acts?
7. What is the inherent paradox in any ethical system?
8. True or False: An emphasis on mystical experiences tends to be more related to deontology than teleology.
9. True or False: Practical ethical choice is almost never between right and wrong but, rather, from among greater or lesser degrees of good and evil.
10. Young children and some very unsophisticated adults seem to have a concept of "immanent justice." Explain.

CHAPTER 3
Constitutional Law
Colleen Kollar-Kotelly

Constitutional Law
Colleen Kollar-Kotelly

I. Introduction.

The Constitution of the United States establishes our basic system of government. The Constitution also guarantees each American citizen certain basic rights by limiting the actions of government. The primary impact of the Constitution on health professionals is in relation to those guarantees of individual rights and limitations on governmental powers.

The first 10 Amendments to the Constitution, known as the Bill of Rights, with the Fourteenth Amendment, comprise the most important of these rights. Although these limitations on governmental action against the individual apply basically to the Federal government, the Supreme Court has determined that a number of the Bill of Rights' safeguards are also applicable to the states under the due process clause of the Fourteenth Amendment.

Included in the concept of limitations on government are the following: all the First Amendment guarantees (speech, press, assembly, right to petition, free exercise and nonestablishment of religion), the Fourth Amendment (unreasonable search and seizure), some elements of the Fifth Amendment (privilege against self-incrimination, compensation for taking of private property for public use), the Sixth Amendment (speedy and public trial by impartial jury, notice and right of confrontation, compulsory process, and the right to legal counsel in all serious criminal proceedings), and the Eighth Amendment (cruel and unusual punishment; excessive bail and excessive fines provi-

47

sions are assumed to be incorporated, but there is no precise ruling). Although these provisions of the Constitution do not specifically apply to individuals acting privately, Congress and state legislatures can pass laws restricting individual citizens from certain actions, thereby protecting other individuals; for example, the 1968 Civil Rights Act forbids individuals from discriminating in the sale or rental of homes.

What follows is a review of many of these basic individual rights, except for those relating to the criminal justice system, which will be dealt with in Chapter 4, Criminal Law and Procedure.

II. **The First Amendment:** "Congress shall make no law respecting an establishment of religion, or prohibiting the free exercise thereof; or abridging the freedom of speech or of the press; or the right of the people peaceably to assemble, and to petition the government for a redress of grievances."

A. Freedom of speech. Speech is the communication of thoughts and ideas through verbal communication or through conduct, for example, "symbolic speech."

A state or the Federal government may punish or restrain a wide range of activities essential to the processes of communication. In doing so, the following broad principles apply:

1. All speech is conveyed through physical action, whether that action is talking, writing, distributing pamphlets, picketing, or wearing an arm band. The fact that conduct is intended to communicate does not preclude it from reasonable government regulations. This regulation, however, must further an important government interest, unrelated to the message being communicated, and the restriction must be no greater than what is necessary to further the government interest involved.

Reasonable restraints by the government on the time, place, or manner of pamphleteering or picketing are allowed, if necessary to achieve the state's purpose. Regulations must be especially narrow, however, if a public forum is affected.

Conduct, such as wearing armbands or burning draft cards, may be a substitute for verbal communication. Governmental attempts to regulate such conduct, when they have the effect of suppressing its communicative content, are construed by the courts as if the efforts were aimed at directly suppressing the content of the message conveyed by the conduct.

2. If a less restrictive alternative of regulation of speech is available than the method proposed in a law, the law is overly broad and therefore void.

3. Laws receive great scrutiny if they restrict the dissemination of political, philosophical, or religious ideas.

4. Laws which give officials broad discretion to decide which speech-related activities to permit, are carefully scrutinized by the courts.

5. A law which allows prior restraint on speech-related activities is less likely to be upheld by the courts than one providing for punishment after the fact of the speech.

6. In deciding when free speech should be protected under the First Amendment, courts use a balancing test. Circumstances involved are examined, and an attempt is made to balance the interests of society against the interests of the individual in expressing the ideas. For speech or related activities to be restricted because of content, at least one of the following bases must be present:

   a. The communication creates a clear and present danger of imminent lawless action (not just unrest, dissatisfaction, or anger).

   b. The communication constitutes "fighting words" (personally abusive epithets, which, when addressed to ordinary citizens, are likely to lead to immediate physical retaliation) as defined by a narrow, precise statute. It should be noted that statutes of this type are rarely upheld by the courts.

    c. The speech, film etc, is obscene.

    d. The speech constitutes defamation.

    e. The speech violates regulations against false or deceptive advertising. Commercial speech is protected by the First Amendment. It cannot be restricted in order to aid private interest.

B. Freedom of the press.

Freedom of the press covers newspapers, books and other writings, movies, television, and radio. The government may either try to restrict material prior to its being printed or shown (prior restraint), or it may try to interfere with the distribution of material by confiscation or punishing the person who wrote, produced, or sold the publication. Any prior restraint on speech is suspect under the First Amendment, that is, is probably violative of the Amendment.

There are, however, certain types of publications which the government can confiscate and for which a person can be punished for having written, produced, or sold.

1. Libel and slander. Libel is publishing false written statements about someone and, thereby, damaging his reputation. Slander is the same, but involves verbal communication. (Communicating the truth is not libel nor slander.)

   Defamatory speech directed at public figures has a greater degree of First Amendment protection than such speech directed at a private citizen. (A public figure is defined as one who commands substantial public interest because of voluntary activity designed to thrust himself into public controversy and attention.)

2. Obscenity. Obscenity is not protected by the First Amendment. The following test to determine whether material is obscene has evolved from Supreme Court cases.[1] (All four must be present.)

   a. Its dominant theme appeals to a prurient interest in sex.

   b. It is patently offensive to contemporary community standards.

   c. Its depiction of sexual conduct meets the definition set in the local state obscenity law.

   d. As a whole, it lacks "serious" literary, artistic, political, or scientific value.

It should be noted that the Supreme Court has held that the First Amendment forbids a criminal penalty merely for the knowing, private possession of obscene material. For example, a person may legally possess such materials in his home, even if he is legally prohibited from selling or publicly exhibiting them.[2]

C. **Freedom not to speak or act.** The essence of the First Amendment is to allow each person to think or believe anything. This freedom includes the right to refrain from speaking or endorsing beliefs with which an individual disagrees.

D. **Freedom of religion.** There are two clauses involving religion in the First Amendment.

  1. **Establishment clause.** This clause prohibits the government from establishing a "state religion" or supporting any one religion, or even all religions impartially. There must be a separation between church and state. Problems arise with this clause when the government supports religious activities directly or indirectly.

    a. An example of a prohibited activity. A state law requiring that the Bible be read for 30 minutes every day in all public schools.[3]

    b. An example of a lawful activity. States may provide bus fare (but not free transportation) to parents whose children go to private or parochial schools, on the grounds that this is aid to taxpayers and not aid to religious schools.[4]

  2. **Free exercise clause.** This clause prohibits the government from restricting the practice of religion unless the impact actively interferes with the rights of others or is inimical to the public's health, safety, or morals. A balancing is required between "legitimate state in-

terest" and the extent to which state regulation impinges on the free exercise of religion.

    a. An example of unlawful government restriction. A state of Wisconsin requirement that children attend school until age 16 was held to be an unconstitutional burden on the free exercise of religion by Amish parents, whose religion forbade their children from obtaining formal education beyond the eighth grade. Instead, the Amish require Bible study and training at home for those aged 14–16.[5]

    b. An example of lawful government restriction. Prohibiting polygamy.

E. Freedom of assembly and the right to petition the government for redress of grievances. Peaceful assembly is protected. The state may control parades, processions, and other gatherings in public places by narrowly drawn requirements, incorporating precise, objective, and reasonable criteria as to time, place, size of group, and duration, in the interest of public safety and convenience.

III. **The Fourth Amendment.** "The right of the people to be secure in their persons, houses, papers, and effects, against unreasonable searches and seizures, shall not be violated, and no warrants shall issue, but upon probable cause, supported by oath or affirmation, and particularly describing the place to be searched, and the persons or things to be seized."

A. The right to privacy. The phrase, "right to privacy," is not found in the Constitution. This right seems to be based primarily on the Fourth Amendment (unreasonable searches and seizures), although courts have also cited the First, Fifth, and Fourteenth Amendments.

    1. Privacy at home. Probably the strongest case on the right to privacy in the home involves the freedom to read obscene material in an individual's place of residence. The Supreme Court found that an individual has the right to think, observe, and read what he chooses, especially in his own home.[6]

Conversely, in another case, the Supreme Court held that an individual's right to privacy had not been violated by a New York law which required that in order to qualify for welfare, a person had to allow a social worker to visit the person's home during working hours without advance notice.[7] The Court tried to balance the interests of the state against those of the individual's privacy, and decided that the government's valid interest in monitoring welfare payments justified the invasion of privacy.

2. Privacy in public. An individual's right to privacy is diminished when the individual is on the street or in other public places.
   a. An individual is not permitted to possess obscene materials in public, although as indicated above, he may possess them at home.
   b. Although police cannot forcibly enter an individual's home without first obtaining a warrant, under certain circumstances an individual may be stopped and frisked on the street.
3. Privacy relating to one's body.
   a. The right to privacy was invoked to hold unconstitutional Connecticut's ban on the use of contraceptive devices.[8]
   b. The Supreme Court has ruled that a woman has a right to have an abortion to end her pregnancy during the first three months thereof.[9]
   c. It is illegal for police to have a suspect's stomach pumped against his will or to induce vomiting and consequently recover drugs.[10] Courts, however, have allowed intrusions into the privacy of a person's body in the case of vaccinations for children without a parent's consent[11] and in the case of forced blood tests in order to determine whether a person has been drinking while driving.[12]
   d. To date, the Supreme Court has not used the right to privacy to establish a right to choose one's own "life style". It has, however, denied the right of policemen to wear long hair,[13] while it upheld the right of "unusual" but nondangerous persons to remain at liberty rather than be committed to mental institutions.[14]

4. Gathering of private information by the government. The government's need to have certain information is still accorded deference by the courts.

a. The Supreme Court upheld a statute requiring the recording in a centralized computer file of the name and addresses of all individuals who have obtained, by prescription, certain drugs, such as narcotics, for which there is an unlawful market.[15] This statute was upheld as a reasonable exercise of a state's broad police powers. (Note that Congress has enacted specific legislation to safeguard an individual against invasion of privacy by Federal government agencies. Pursuant to the Privacy Act of 1974, Federal agencies are required to disclose records kept on individuals and to allow individuals to correct or amend such records. The agencies must also keep such information confidential.)

IV. The Fifth, Sixth, and Fourteenth Amendments.

The Fifth Amendment. "No person shall be held to answer for a capital,* or otherwise infamous** crime, unless on a presentment*** or indictment of a grand jury, except in cases arising in the land or naval forces, or in the militia, when in actual service in time of war or public danger; nor shall any person be subject for the same offence to be twice put in jeopardy of life or limb; nor shall be compelled in any criminal case to be a witness against himself, nor be deprived of life, liberty or property, without due process of law; nor shall private property be taken for public use without just compensation."

The Sixth Amendment. "In all criminal prosecutions, the accused shall enjoy the right to a speedy and public trial, by an impartial jury of the State and district wherein the crime shall have been committed, which district shall

---

*Where the penalty may be death.
**Where the penalty may be imprisonment.
***An uncommon form in which a grand jury initiates a criminal charge based on its own knowledge.

have been previously ascertained by law, and to be informed of the nature and cause of the accusation; to be confronted with the witnesses against him; to have compulsory process for obtaining witnesses in his favor, and to have the assistance of counsel for his defense."

The Fourteenth Amendment. "All persons born or naturalized in the United States, and subject to the jurisdiction thereof, are citizens of the United States and of the State wherein they reside. No State shall make or enforce any law which shall abridge the privileges or immunities of citizens of the United States; nor shall any State deprive any person of life, liberty, or property, without due process of law, nor deny to any person within its jurisdiction the equal protection of the laws."

The three Amendments quoted above are concerned with insuring that questions relating to a person's rights or property are determined through fair methods and proceedings. "Due process of law" includes both procedural and substantive considerations. The Fifth and Sixth Amendments protect the citizen from unfair procedures by the Federal government. The Fourteenth Amendment protects citizens from unfair procedures by state governments.

A. Procedural due process. Fair procedure in a court or similar action requires, at minimum, both an opportunity to object to the proposed action and a fair, neutral decision-maker (not necessarily a judge). Procedural safeguards are required before a government agency can take a person's "life, liberty or property"; however, no comparable procedural protection is required when a person is subjected only to general rules or legislation. Even when government action forces an individual to bear unfavorable treatment, no hearing is due unless life, liberty, or a property interest is involved. It should be stressed that this right is merely to a hearing; the decision criteria used and the final actions taken are governed by substantive, not procedural, constitutional rules.

1. Procedure regarding deprivation of life or liberty as criminal sanctions is discussed under Criminal Law and Procedure, Chapter 4.

2. Property interests protected include all the traditional property interests, such as real property, personal property, intangibles, and future interests. (See Glossary.) It should be noted here that government benefits (welfare) or employment are recognized as property when the governmental unit, by law or administrative action, creates a claim of entitlement to the benefit.[16] There is only an expectation and no property, however, if the government has indicated that the benefit or employment is terminated at the will of the government.[17]

3. Liberty interests to be protected are the most difficult to define. They usually include any governmental act that deprives a person of physical freedom (example: mental hospital commitment) or that imposes physical punishment on the individual. In the case of a prisoner already in prison, liberty includes the freedom from more severe incarceration, but only if the state's rules assure that more severe incarceration will not occur unless specified misconduct occurs. Transferring a prisoner from one jail to a more secure jail is not a deprivation of liberty, but the Supreme Court has held that transfer to a mental hospital of a prisoner is a deprivation likely to require due process.[18]

4. Some interests qualify as both "liberty" and "property." State laws provide that children of a certain age are entitled to public schooling. If a student is suspended for alleged misconduct, the deprivation of "property" created by the schooling entitlement and the deprivation of "liberty" (diminished reputation due to the allegations of misconduct) both require due process safeguards.[19]

5. Government procedures which deprive persons.
   a. Commercial taking:
      1) Garnishing (See Glossary) wages. Usually, a hearing is required before a wage garnishment order can be issued.

2) Garnishment, replevin, (See Glossary) or attachment (See Glossary) of property other than wages. These are actions used prior to a civil trial. They allow a creditor to gain possession of property or prevent an alleged debtor from using the property. Unless the debtor will remove or destroy the property, there must be an opportunity for a hearing prior to the issuance of the writ; alternatively, procedure for the issuance of the writ must include a prompt subsequent hearing, a creditor bond,* a written statement of a prima facie claim, and a neutral magistrate to review the statement and to issue the writ.

b. Noncommercial taking. This includes all other government acts such as government benefits, employment, etc.

6. Requirements for due process include.
   a. A neutral trier of the claim.
   b. Other safeguards, such as a chance to offer evidence, the opportunity for confrontation of the opposing parties, access to counsel, and records of the proceeding. A balancing process takes place. The greater the potential deprivation to the party, the more stringent is the requirement for procedural safeguards at the hearing.

7. "Taking" and "just compensation." The Fifth Amendment applies. ". . . Private property . . . (shall not) be taken for public use without just compensation." In the Constitution, there is no specific and explicit grant of Federal power to take private property. Therefore, such a "taking" must be valid under one or more powers ascribed to Congress in the body of the Constitution.
   a. "Public use." This phrase is liberally construed by the courts to include the entire social, economic, moral, physical, aesthetic, and political well-being of the public concerned. It even includes a government-authorized taking by private enterprise (for example, railroads and public utilities), if it is to the public benefit.

---

*A creditor bond is a security bond posted by the creditor as insurance against loss or damage of the debtor's property.

b. Taking.
  1) A "taking" may occur without formal exercise of the power of eminent domain when an act of government directly impairs the use or value of private property. Such an act, however, is regarded as a taking only if it involves "affirmatively appropriating" an interest in property. (For example, forbidding building in an area zoned as "wetland," an undesirable and unsafe location to build, is not affirmatively appropriating an interest. Forbidding building on an area adjacent to a road, a prime location for building, however, would be regarded as an affirmative appropriation.)
  2) Government regulation which impairs the use or value of private property but is otherwise a reasonable police power measure, for example, zoning laws, is not regarded by the courts as a taking.
c. Just compensation. The owner is entitled to the reasonable value (that is, fair market value) of his property at the time of the taking. The important issue is the loss to the owner and not the gain to the taker. Due process guarantees include notice and a hearing on the amount of the compensation. (The hearing need not necessarily precede the taking.)

B. Substantive due process. The due process clauses of the Fifth and Fourteenth Amendments assure that certain governmental acts are invalid no matter what procedure is used. Where government action is an arbitrary limitation of liberty, it transcends the legitimate exercise of government power. Under due process guarantees courts review the legitimacy of governmental acts which are without clear guidelines in the Constitution. The courts generally consider whether there is a "rational basis" for finding that the law relates to a legitimate end; this involves "minimal* judicial scrutiny." The courts,

---

*The terms, "minimal" and "strict", refer, in this context, to the criteria, or tests, used by courts to determine whether a law is constitutional, not to the amount of care the court devotes to looking at the case.

however, will use a "strict scrutiny" if the law or action encumbers a fundamental right.

1. If a law limits a fundamental right (interstate travel, privacy, voting, speech, religion, or other First Amendment rights), the law must be necessary to promote a compelling or overriding state interest.

2. A law must rationally relate to a legitimate end of government. (Most laws pass this rationality test).

C. Equal protection of the laws. Pursuant to the explicit equal protection clause of the Fourteenth Amendment and the implicit due process provisions of the Fifth Amendment, governmental acts which classify people improperly may be invalid. (A substantive due process question is raised if the law limits the liberty of all persons to engage in a particular activity. An equal protection question is raised if the law limits the liberty of some persons but not of others.)

1. The tests for the validity of governmental classifications are parallel to those used in relation to due process of law.

   a. Strict scrutiny, or compelling interest. When a classification relates to those who may exercise a fundamental right, or when it is based on a "suspect" trait, (that is, a classification which on its face seems illegitimately discriminatory and has been used in an improperly discriminatory manner), the classification will be valid only if it is necessary in furtherance of a compelling state interest.

   b. Minimal scrutiny or conceivable basis. This classification, relating only to economics or social welfare, is valid if there is any conceivable basis that the classification relates to a legitimate governmental interest.

   c. Intermediate approach. In a constitutional attack on a governmental rule classifying persons, the courts require that a "fair and substantial" relation to "important government objectives" actually motivated the promulgation of the challenged rule. That motivation must also expressly be set out in defense of the rule.

Laws involving "sensitive," though not "suspect," classifications (for example, gender, legitimacy) or affecting "significant," though not "fundamental," rights (for example, sexual relations or childbearing) are subject to intermediate scrutiny. In such situations, laws which classify people are considered to be arbitrarily discriminatory under these conditions:

1) The underlying basis for the law is tenuous.
2) The law has no objective beyond efficiency or ease of administration.
3) An acceptable goal of the law is offered as afterthought rather than being the purpose for original passage of the law.
4) The law can be rationalized, but not in terms of the legitimate interests expressly articulated in the law's defense.

2. Suspect classifications. Race, national origin, alienage (status of citizenship).
   a. A law is subject to strict scrutiny as discriminatory on grounds of race or national origin if the following conditions are present:
      1) Racial discrimination is explicitly provided by the law.
      2) The law is applied in a discriminatory manner; for example, state officials use different standards for enforcement of the law for different groups.
      3) The law has a deliberately discriminatory impact.
   b. Any racial motive for a law triggers scrutiny to determine if the impact is discriminatory; a discriminatory impact of a law triggers scrutiny to determine if the motive is racial.
   c. If no neutral explanation is available to validate a discriminatory impact, the law is subject to strict scrutiny.

3. Birth-legitimacy and sexual gender are "almost suspect" categories if individuals classified on such a basis are discriminated against because of a law.

4. Wealth and age have not been considered to be suspect classifications. A minimal rationality usually has sufficed to sustain governmental rules which explicitly disadvantage the poor or the elderly.

Text References

1. *Roth v. U.S.*, 354 U.S. 476 (1957), as modified by *Miller v. California*, 413 U.S. 15 (1973)
2. *Stanley v. Georgia*, 394 U.S. 557 (1969)
3. *Engel v. Vitale*, 370 U.S. 421 (1962)
4. *Everson v. Board of Education*, 330 U.S. 1 (1947), *Wolman v. Walter*, 433 U.S. 229 (1977)
5. *Wisconsin v. Yoder*, 406 U.S. 205 (1972)
6. *Stanley v. Georgia*, supra
7. *Wyman v. James*, 400 U.S. 309 (1971)
8. *Griswold v. Conn.*, 381 U.S. 479 (1965)
9. *Roe v. Wade*, 410 U.S. 113 (1973)
10. *Rochin v. Calif.*, 342 U.S. 165 (1952)
11. *Jacobson v. Mass.*, 197 U.S. 11 (1905)
12. *Schmerber v. Calif.*, 384 U.S. 787 (1966)
13. *Kelley v. Johnson*, 425 U.S. 238 (1976)
14. *O'Connor v. Donaldson*, 422 U.S. 563 (1976)
15. *Whalen v. Roe*, 429 U.S. 589 (1977)
16. *Goldberg v. Kelly*, 397 U.S. 254 (1970)
17. *Bishop v. Wood*, 426 U.S. 341 (1976)
18. *Vitek v. Jones*, 445 U.S. 480 (1980)
19. *Goss v. Lopez*, 419 U.S. 565 (1975)

Questions on Chapter 3, Constitutional Law

1. Guarantees pursuant to the Bill of Rights and the Fourteenth Amendment are *absolute*. True or False?
2. None of the safeguards of the Bill of Rights applies to the states. True or False?
3. Verbal communication is the only form of communication protected by the First Amendment. True or False?
4. Which of the following speech or related activites can be restricted by law because of its content without violating the First Amendment?
   a. religious material.
   b. political material.
   c. obscene material.
   d. medical research material.
5. An individual's right to privacy is diminished when the individual is on the street or in other public places. True or False?
6. Procedural due process is required before a government agency can take a person's life, liberty, or property. True or False?
7. If the law limits the liberty of some persons but not others, an equal protection question can be raised. True or False?
8. In reviewing laws for discrimination, which of the following are considered suspect classifications:
   a. wealth and age.
   b. race or national origin.
   c. legitimacy and gender.
9. There is no property or liberty interest requiring protection if a student is suspended from school. True or False?
10. An amendment to the Constitution would be required to allow prayers in public schools. True or False?

CHAPTER 4
Criminal Law and Procedure

Ann O'Regan Keary

Criminal Law and Procedure

Ann O'Regan Keary

I. Introduction.

Criminal law is one of the oldest branches of the English common law. Even today, the major body of criminal law in most states is the basic common law. Every state, however, has enacted its own criminal laws in a code; many states have also modified and supplemented the traditional common law of crime.

Although the basic purposes of criminal law are similar to those of other branches of law, that is, to promote social order and to provide a system of dispute resolution, criminal law differs from other branches of law in one significant feature. The ultimate remedy for harms inflicted in violation of criminal laws is punishment of the violator in the name of the state. (In civil law, the remedy is some compensation, usually monetary, to the victim.)

II. Definition and classification of crimes.

A. Definition. A crime is an act or omission prohibited by a law enacted to protect the public. The violation of such a law is prosecuted by the state itself and is punishable by imprisonment or other sanction.

B. Classification of crimes.

1. Felonies. Generally, a felony is any offense punishable by death or imprisonment for more than one year, or,

in some states, by imprisonment in a state prison. (Examples: murder, manslaughter, rape, mayhem, robbery, arson, burglary, etc.)

2. Misdemeanors. Any crime which is not a felony; usually those crimes which are punishable by imprisonment for less than one year, or by imprisonment other than in the state prison. (Examples: larceny (petit), simple assault)

III. Elements of a crime.

In order to establish that a crime has been committed, the "corpus delicti"* must be complete, that is, there must have been a specific act which was prohibited by law, and some person must have committed or caused the act, that is, it was not accidental. The corpus delicti of a crime consists of the two basic elements: a criminal state of mind, and the commission of a criminal act.

A. Criminal state of mind ("Mens rea").

The law makes use of various terms referring to states of mind. Because there is no objective manner in which to determine states of mind, however, the law uses such terms in an inferential manner. Thus, for example, "intent" is inferred on the basis of a presumption, namely that every person intends the predictable outcome of his actions, given the circumstances under which the actions take place. Knowing the circumstances of an individual's conduct and knowing what he did, one infers the intent to produce the outcome. (It is irrelevant whether the person has a subjective wish for the expected outcome. For example, leaving a baby on a doorstep in a blizzard is likely to lead to the death of the baby. However much the person leaving the baby might hope that someone will find and save the child, the inferred intent is to cause the infant to freeze to death.)

---

*The body of the crime, that is, the factors which make the event a crime.

As an additional example, "malice," another word used in connection with the elements of a crime, merely connotes an intent to do something which is forbidden by law. There can easily be situations in which there is malice within the legal meaning, but not malice as in common usage, that is, an evil intent toward another.

Another presumption of the law is that a person is capable of making a choice in a situation in which he has alternative courses of action. The notion of holding a person responsible for his behavior is reasonable *only if the person has the capacity for choice.*

1. Mens rea is the "nonphysical" part of the crime, usually described as "criminal intent." There are basically three types of mens rea: general, specific, and criminal negligence. Each crime has its owns mens rea requirement.

   a. General intent (or general mens rea). The mental element of a crime, which requires no special state of mind; it is merely the intentional, volitional doing of an act which is criminal. This requirement is met as long as the accused intended to do the thing which he did. (Examples of general intent crimes: manslaughter, murder, and rape.)

   b. Specific intent (or specific mens rea). A particular wrongful state of mind is required, in addition to general intent, to constitute certain other crimes. For these crimes, the accused must have intended not only to do the act, but also to do some further act or accomplish some additional consequence. (Examples of specific intent crimes: burglary, which is defined as breaking and entering a house with the intent to commit a felony, robbery, and all attempt crimes.)

   c. Criminal negligence. Although an act may not have been intended, it may have been done with such a gross lack of care that it constitutes "criminal negligence." (Examples of criminal negligence crimes: negligent homicide or involuntary manslaughter.)

2. Doctrine of transferred intent. When an accused undertakes a criminal act with the requisite wrongful state of mind, but the act results in a harm different

from that intended, the accused is still considered to have the necessary criminal intent for the resulting crime and will be held responsible under the doctrine of transferred intent. (Example: If A intends to kill B and accidently kills C, A is guilty of the same kind of crime as if he had killed B.)

B. Criminal act ("Actus reus").

  1. In addition to criminal intent, a criminal act is necessary to constitute a crime. (Criminal intent, mere criminal thoughts, or the intention to commit a crime are not, by themselves, punishable.) Such requirement of an actus reus is met by any act or omission in furtherance of the intended crime, as long as the act is volitional and conscious.

C. Causation. The requirement that the accused's actions be the legal cause of harm which was prohibited by the law, may be considered an additional element of a crime. For an accused to be held criminally responsible:

  1. His act must have been the cause of the harm (The harm would not have happened, but for his act.); and

  2. There must have been no unforeseeable intervening act which became a superseding cause of the harm.

    (Example: A approaches B on the sidewalk and strikes B, knocking him to the sidewalk. Before B gets up, driver C loses control of his truck, hits the sidewalk and kills B. A may not be held responsible for B's death; his only crime is assault, since the truck accident is an independent force and unforeseeable. [If B had hit his head on the sidewalk and died, A could be held responsible for the death, because it is, at least within reason, foreseeable.])

IV. Parties to crime.

Criminal culpability is not confined to the person who actually commits the act. It extends to anyone who knowingly encouraged the crime or impeded the apprehension of the perpetrator of the crime. Such persons are considered parties to the crime along with the person who actually commits the crime.

A. The traditional common law classifications of parties to crime are as follows:

1. Principal in the first degree. The actual perpetrator of the crime.

2. Principal in the second degree. Anyone who incites or abets the crime, and who is actually or constructively present at the time of the crime, but who does not actually commit the elements of the crime. (Example: a lookout posted near the scene of a crime.)

    a. The distinction between principals in the first and second degree is minimal, since generally they are subject to the same penalty.

3. Accessory before the fact. Anyone who incites or abets the commission of a crime by another, but who is not present actively or constructively at the commission of crime. (Example: *A* provides *B* with a key to *C*'s safe. If *B* then uses this key to steal from *C*, *A* is an accessory before the fact.)

4. Accessory after the fact. Anyone who receives, comforts, or assists someone, with the knowledge that the person has committed a felony, in order to impede his apprehension. (Example: *A* shelters *B*, keeps him, and hides his weapon after *B* comes to *A* and tells her of his murdering a neighbor.)

B. Modern statutes in many states have modified these classifications. The trend is to treat as principals all persons who are involved in the commission of a crime, including accessories before the fact, but excluding accessories after the fact.

V. Crimes. Definitions and descriptions.

A. Preparatory crimes (inchoate offenses).

Certain crimes are committed prior to or in preparation for other offenses. They are, nevertheless, in and of themselves, offenses. Those offenses are solicitation, conspiracy, and attempt.

1. Solicitation. Counseling, inciting, or inducing another to commit or to join in the commission of any crime. Usually, solicitation to commit a crime carries a lesser sentence than the crime itself.

2. Conspiracy. An agreement between two or more persons to accomplish an unlawful purpose.
   a. Conspiracy requires an intent to agree, plus a specific intent to achieve the unlawful goal.
   b. Under common law, as well as under many state codes, the only act required is the agreement or combination of the persons to accomplish the unlawful act.
   c. Some states now require some overt act in furtherance of the conspiracy to be performed by one of the conspirators.
   d. A significant feature of the crime of conspiracy is that any co-conspirator may be held criminally responsible for any crime committed pursuant to the agreement by any other co-conspirator.

3. Attempt. An attempt to commit a crime is, itself, a crime. The elements of an attempt are:
   a. A specific intent to commit a particular crime.
   b. A step taken toward the commission of that crime. The step must be something "beyond mere preparation to commit the crime."

   (Example: *A*, intending to kill *B*, purchases a gun and bullets. Later, he takes the gun and hides near *B*'s place of work and waits for him to pass by. When *B* appears, *A* shoots at him but misses. *A* is guilty of an attempt when he shoots; however, he is also guilty of an attempt when he takes the gun and hides in ambush to await *B*. The purchase of the gun, however, would only be considered preparation.)

B. Crimes against the person.
   1. Homicide. The killing of a human being by another human being. There are two basic types of criminal homicide.

a. Murder. The unlawful (that is, unjustified and unexcused) killing of a human, by a human, with malice aforethought. (Malice aforethought may be shown by the intent to kill, intent to inflict serious bodily injury, intent to commit a dangerous felony, or intent to do an act which has a high risk of death or serious injury.)

1) In most jurisdictions, for purposes of the definition of murder, if the death of *A* occurs within a year and a day following the causal act of *B*, *B* is considered to have killed *A*.

2) Most states' codes break down murder into two degrees:

   a) First degree murder. All killings with malice aforethought which are willful, deliberate, and premeditated, or (in most states) killing in the perpetration of a serious felony such as arson, armed robbery, or rape (the "felony murder" rule).

   b) Second degree murder. All killings with malice aforethought other than those classified as first degree murder (that is, homicides which are not willful, deliberate, and premeditated).

   (Example: *A* and *B* decide to play "Russian roulette" with a partially loaded revolver. *A* positions the revolver next to *B*'s head and pulls the trigger. The gun fires and *B* is killed. *A* has committed second degree murder because, although his actions do not indicate a deliberate and premeditated killing, they show a reckless disregard for a known and serious risk, that *B* could be killed. This is the so-called "depraved heart.")

b. Manslaughter. The unlawful (unjustified and unexcused) killing of one human by another without malice aforethought. Such killing may be of two types.

1) Voluntary manslaughter. An intentional killing done in a sudden heat of passion caused by a reasonable provocation. Because of these mitigating circumstances, the killing, which would otherwise be murder, is reduced to the lesser offense of manslaughter.

(Example: *A* learns from his daughter, *B*, that she has just been raped and beaten by *C*. *A*, enraged, goes immediately to *C*'s home and, while still in a "heat of passion," kills him.)

2) Involuntary manslaughter. An unintentional killing committed without excuse or justification and also without malice aforethought. It applies to:

   a) Unintentional killings in the doing of unlawful acts.

   (Example: *A* approaches *B* in a threatening manner, intending to strike *B* in the face. *B*, who happens to have a serious heart problem unknown to *A*, has a heart seizure due to the threatened attack and dies. *A* is guilty of involuntary manslaughter.)

   b) Unintentional killings which are the result of criminal negligence.

   (Example: *A* uses the butt of his loaded pistol to crack ice at a picnic. The gun discharges and kills *B*. *A* is guilty of involuntary manslaughter.)

2. Rape. The unlawful carnal knowledge (penetration, however slight, of the vagina) by a male of a female, without her consent.

   a. Consent is normally deemed to be lacking when:

   1) The woman submits as a result of force or threats.

   2) The woman is incapable of giving consent because she is mentally impaired, is unconscious, or has been drugged.

   3) The woman's consent is obtained by fraud or deception as to the nature of the act or the identity of the man.

   4) The female is under a statutorily specified age (usually 18). Carnal knowlege of such a female is rape, whether or not she consents ("statutory rape").

3. Assault and battery.

   a. Battery. The unlawful, intentional, and unconsented to touching of another.

   1) Any offensive touching will suffice; no injury need result.

      2) Unless aggravated, it is usually classified as a misdemeanor.

      (Examples: *A*, despite *B*'s remonstrations, kisses her. *A*, a doctor, gives *B* an injection, or performs a surgical operation on *B*, without *B*'s consent.)

  b. Assault. An attempted or threatened battery. It is characterized by:

      1) The accused's intent to commit a particular battery, with a substantial act toward its commission, or

      2) Alternatively, by the accused's intent to place the victim in apprehension of a battery, with some act which creates a reasonable apprehension in the victim.

C. Crimes against a habitation.

  1. Arson. At common law, the willful and malicious burning of the dwelling house of another. Modern statutes have expanded the scope to include other buildings and property as well as dwellings.

  2. Burglary. At common law, the trespassory (unauthorized) breaking and entering of the dwelling house of another, in the nighttime, with the intent to commit a felony. This definition has been somewhat expanded by modern statutes.

D. Crimes against property.

  1. Larceny. Trespassory taking and carrying away ("caption and asportation") of the personal property of another with intent to deprive the owner of such property permanently. (Example: A store customer intentionally takes merchandise out of the store without paying for it.)

  2. Embezzlement. Fraudulent conversion (a taking, as if one owned something) of the property of another by one who is already in lawful possession of the property. (Example: A cashier at a bank, receiving money for the bank, converts it to his own use, rather than turning it over to the bank.)

3. False pretenses. The obtaining both of possession and of title to the property of another by false representations. (Example: *A* falsely tells *B* that he has discovered a diamond mine and that he needs $10,000 to develop it. After offering *B* a partnership in the mine, *A* is given $10,000 by *B*, and then disappears. *A* is considered guilty of false pretenses.)

4. Robbery. An unlawful taking and carrying away of the personal property of another, from his person or in his presence, by use of force or the threat to immediately use it, with the intent of depriving the owner of the property permanently. (Example: *A* confronts *B* on the street and says: "Give me your money, or I'll kill you." *B* complies and *A* runs away with the money.)

VI. Defenses to a criminal accusation or charge.

A. Excuses for the defendant's act.

1. Infancy. At common law, no child under seven could be held responsible for any crime, due to the presumption of the child's incapability.

2. Insanity. A person is excused from criminal responsibility for his act if, at the time of his act, his mental condition was such that he is deemed legally "insane." In such cases his act is deemed nonvolitional, since he is considered incapable of forming the necessary criminal intent. Various courts have adopted differing legal tests for insanity.

   a. The "M'Naghten Rule."

      1) The "M'Naghten rule" is the traditional test developed in an early British case. The rule still remains the standard in many jurisdictions.

      2) Under M'Naghten, a person is excused from responsibility if, by reason of the condition of his mind, he was unable to understand the nature of his act or, even if he knew what he was doing, he lacked the capacity to distinguish whether his act was right or wrong.

b. Irresistible impulse test. Some states have supplemented the M'Naghten test with this test, which would allow
an accused to be excused from criminal responsibility,
even if he had the capacity to distinguish right from
wrong, if he was "irresistibly impelled" by his mental
disease to commit the criminal act.

c. Durham test. Some states have adopted the Durham
test, which excuses a criminal act if it was the "product
of a mental disease or defect." The test, which was
originally adopted in New Hampshire in 1869, was utilized for approximately 20 years in the District of Columbia. It was ultimately rejected there in the
mid-1970's.

d. *Model Penal Code* (American Law Institute) "substantial
capacity" test.

1) This test, which has been adopted in many Federal
circuits, as well as in several states, and which represents a prevailing trend, provides that a person is
not responsible for criminal conduct if at the time of
such conduct, as a result of mental disease or defect,
he lacked substantial capacity either to appreciate
the criminality (wrongfulness) of his conduct or to
conform his conduct to the requirements of law.

2) One feature of this test is its excluding from the definition of "mental disease or defect" any abnormali-
ty evidenced only by repeated criminal or antisocial
conduct. (That is, psychopaths are not deemed to
have mental disease or defect.)

e. The customary disposition of an accused who is found
not guilty by reason of insanity is court-ordered commitment to a mental institution, the subsequent release
from which usually requires court authorization.

f. The doctrine of diminished capacity. In a number of
states, evidence of a mental disorder which is legally insufficient to establish insanity is still admissible on the
issue of whether an accused has the requisite specific
mens rea for the offense. (That is, when the crime
charged is one which requires specific intent, for example, burglary, this evidence can be used to show that
the accused was incapable of forming the necessary

specific intent and is, therefore, not guilty of that crime.)

1) This doctrine can serve to reduce the crime charged to a lesser offense which does not require a finding of specific intent. (That is, a person may be acquitted of first degree murder, but convicted of the lesser offense of manslaughter.)

2) Diminished capacity is no defense to general intent crimes.

g. "Guilty but mentally ill." Some states have passed legislation creating an alternative jury finding of "guilty but mentally ill" in cases in which the defendant's mental condition is at issue.

1) It would ordinarily be applied in cases in which the jury concludes that the defendant was mentally ill at the time of the offense but was nevertheless still legally responsible for his actions.

a) In jurisdictions where this alternative verdict is available, the jury could find a defendant 1) "not guilty by reason of insanity," 2) "guilty but mentally ill" or, of course, 3) "guilty" or 4) "not guilty".

b) A defendant found "guilty but mentally ill," receives a sentence like other convicted persons, but might receive treatment in a hospital until no longer in need of any hospital treatment. He could then be returned to prison to continue serving the remainder of his sentence.

2) A criticism of this disposition has been that, by appearing to guarantee hospital treatment as a disposition, it may give juries a convenient alternative to avoid facing the real question of determining whether the defendant was legally responsible at the time of the offense. It is expected that some defendants who might otherwise be exonerated of penal consequences under the insanity defense might be kept in prison inappropriately by being declared guilty but mentally ill, and that they would then not receive proper treatment.

h. In a small minority of states the jury is not allowed to reach a verdict of "not guilty by reason of insanity"; that is, the insanity defense has been legislatively abolished. (At the time of the writing, such a restriction of the insanity defense has not been fully tested constitutionally.)*

3. Intoxication.
   a. Involuntary intoxication. When a person is drugged or forced to consume intoxicants against his will and becomes so completely intoxicated that he does not know what he is doing, he will not be held responsible for his act.
   b. Voluntary intoxication. When a person has intentionally consumed a substance which he knows, or should know, will intoxicate, subsequent intoxication will not be held a defense to a crime charged. Voluntary intoxication can be raised, however, to rebut a charge of a crime which requires specific intent. (The "doctrine of diminished responsibility.")

---

*Editor's note

The law cannot yet fully comprehend and resolve problems of crimes which arise from human behavior pathology. Mental illness is uncommonly manifested by violent crime; conversely, individuals who commit violent crimes are seldom grossly psychotic (though, of course, they may be mentally ill according to other criteria). Nevertheless, there are some terrible criminal actions done by flagrantly psychotic persons. However, the question as to what the law should do in relation to such cases, each of which is unique, and none of which can be analyzed nor understood with precision, has never received, and probably will never receive, a resolution that provides justice for all parties.

Yet our legal system does make an attempt to deal justly with those issues, and considering the multiple problems involved, on the whole the effort seems reasonable. Perhaps an appropriate attitude on the part of a health professional who is a student of legal phenomena is that of calm detachment and an effort to evaluate each case in its own terms. Society must exist with its laws over a time. Though a dramatic event may result in strong motivation for a quick improvement in an issue like mental illness and crime, sudden change made in a long-standing scheme of doing things, even when all the purposes of the system are not accomplished completely satisfactorily, seldom leads to a real improvement in the overall situation. When a radical method is proposed to deal with a chronic problem, circumspection is more useful than enthusiasm.

    c. If an accused's condition is a settled and permanent one from long-term use of intoxicants, it may rise to a level which can be treated as insanity.

4. Ignorance or mistake of fact. This may be used as a defense when it negatives the existence of a mental state essential to the crime charged.

    (Example: *A*'s cattle stray from their pasture and become mixed with *B*'s herd. *B* sells his herd (including *A*'s cattle), unaware that some belong to *A*. This mistake of fact would be a defense to a charge of larceny.)

5. Ignorance or mistake of law. It is not a defense that an accused was unaware that his acts were prohibited by law, or that he was mistaken in a belief that his acts were not prohibited.

6. Duress. A person can be excused from criminal responsibility for a criminal act (other than homicide or other capital offenses) if he was under duress due to a threat of imminent infliction of death or serious bodily injury.

7. Entrapment.
    a. If a law enforcement officer or his agent entraps an accused into committing an act which the accused was otherwise not predisposed to, it will act as a defense to all but the most serious crimes.
    b. It must be shown that the police officer instigated the offense, that is, that he induced the accused to commit an act which he would not otherwise have committed.

B. Justification for a defendant's acts.
  1. Self-defense.
    a. Usually, an individual who is without fault may use such force as reasonably appears necessary to protect himself from the imminent use of unlawful force upon himself.
    b. A person may only use "deadly force" when he is:
      1) Without fault.
      2) Confronted with "unlawful force."
      3) Threatened with imminent death or great bodily harm.

   c. Self-defense is generally not available as a defense to a
      party who is the aggressor in a situation.
 2. Defense of others. A person is considered justified in
    using non-deadly force in the defense of any third per-
    son and justified in using deadly force where the third
    person is a member of his family or household.
 3. Defense of property.
    a. A person is justified in using non deadly force to pre-
       vent an unauthorized taking or entry of his property.
    b. A person is not justified in using deadly force in de-
       fense of his property except to prevent a felony at-
       tempted by surprise, and/or violence, or in defense of
       a crime against the dwelling.

VII. Introduction to the rights of an accused person.

Much of the law relating to criminal procedure stems
from the development of numerous constitutional limitations on the manner in which a criminal suspect may
be handled in the criminal justice system. These constitutional limitations are based on Amendments to the
U.S. Constitution, in particular, the Bill of Rights.

VIII. Investigation and the obtaining of evidence. Legal limitations.

 A. Search and Seizure.
    1. "Unreasonable" searches and seizures are prohibited
       by the Fourth Amendment, which guarantees citizens
       a certain expectation of privacy in their actions and
       possessions.
    2. Lawful (that is, reasonable) searches or seizures fall
       into three main categories:
       a. Searches pursuant to warrants granted by judges or
          magistrates upon a finding of the existence of "proba-
          ble cause."
       b. Searches incidental to (contemporaneous with) a law-
          ful arrest. The scope of such searches is usually limited

to the arrestee's person or areas within his immediate control.

c. Searches undertaken with the voluntary consent of the accused.

d. Searches under certain special circumstances have also been considered lawful:

1) Emergency searches may be upheld where a compelling urgency justifies the failure to obtain a warrant. (Example: Evidence might be lost or destroyed by delay.)

2) Limited "stop and frisk" searches may be conducted by a police officer who reasonably believes a suspect may be armed or dangerous. Such a "frisk" is limited to a pat-down of the outer clothing (to feel for weapons). A police officer is only privileged to reach inside a suspect's clothing if the frisk discloses a weapon-like bulge.

3) Vehicle searches are usually considered lawful because of "exigent circumstances" (that is, the mobility of the vehicle).

4) Border searches of persons or things crossing international borders are considered lawful under a relaxation of the "probable cause" requirement, in light of the significant traffic of illegal and stolen items crossing international borders.

3. Under the "exclusionary rule" (a judicially created remedy to compel police compliance with the Fourth Amendment protection from unreasonable searches), evidence obtained by a search or a seizure which is unlawful cannot be used in a criminal proceeding against the person searched.

B. Interrogations and confessions.

1. Only statements voluntarily made by an accused to the police may be admissible against him in a criminal trial. The Fifth Amendment provides that, "No person shall be compelled in any criminal case to be a witness against himself."

2. In order to assure that the privilege against self-incrimination is safe-guarded and that an accused is

guaranteed his basic rights, the Supreme Court has developed certain requirements for the appropriate procedure to be followed by the police in obtaining statements from an accused.

   a. Prior to any "custodial interrogation" of an individual he must be advised that:

      1) He has a right to remain silent.

      2) Any statement he makes may be used against him.

      3) He has the right to have an attorney present, either retained by the individual or appointed for him if necessary.

   b. Failure to follow the procedure of giving these "Miranda"[1] warnings will make statements from an accused inadmissible at trial.

C. Identification procedure.

   1. It has been determined that it is not violative of the Fifth Amendment privilege against self-incrimination for the police to:

      a. Compel an accused to appear in a lineup, to utter specified words, or to put on an item of clothing in a lineup.

      b. Secure fingerprints, handwriting samples, or blood samples from an accused.

   2. An accused has a right to counsel at a lineup held after he has been formally charged; however, there is no right to counsel when an accused's fingerprints, blood, or handwriting samples are taken, as these are not considered "critical stages" of the proceeding.

IX. The criminal justice process prior to trial.*

A. Arrest.

   1. An arrest is the taking into custody of a person so that he may be held to answer for the commission of some offense. (The temporary detention of a person for questioning or a weapons search (a "stop and frisk")

---

*The procedures described are generally in use in Federal jurisdictions and the District of Columbia. They may vary slightly from those used in other state jurisdictions, depending on the court structure and rules in that state.

does not constitute an arrest, since the person is not taken into custody for criminal prosecution.)

2. An arrest may be the initial step in the criminal process, or it may occur after a person has been indicted.

3. Types of arrest.
   a. Arrest by warrant. A lawful arrest can be made with a warrant issued by a magistrate on finding "probable cause" for the arrest of the accused.
   b. Warrantless arrests. An arrest without a warrant is lawful if:
      1) The police officer has probable cause to believe a felony has been committed.
      2) The police officer has probable cause to believe a misdemeanor is being committed in his presence.
   c. Because "stop and frisk" is not an arrest, it does not require probable cause; however, it does require more than a mere suspicion or hunch.

4. Pursuant to an arrest, the police record on their log book, or "blotter," the facts of the arrest and the charges that they will seek to have placed against the individual when he appears in court. The process is often called "booking" an arrestee. Police usually file as many charges as might possibly be prosecuted ("throw the book" at the arrestee). Such a procedure gives more of a safety margin for procedural errors which might subsequently be noted, or for new findings which might be developed through further investigation, and it gives the prosecution maximum leverage in subsequent plea bargaining with the defendant.

B. Appearance before a judicial officer.
   1. Arresting authorities are required to bring an arrested person before a court "without unnecessary delay."
   2. At this stage several things take place.
      a. The accused is informed of the charges against him.
      b. The accused is informed of his right to counsel, and that counsel will be appointed for him, if necessary.
      c. The accused may enter a plea of "not guilty," if he has been formally charged at that point.
      d. Bail is set.

C. Pre-trial release. The Eighth Amendment prohibits the setting of "excessive bail." This has been traditionally interpreted to mean that bail should be set no higher than is necessary to assure an accused's presence at trial.

1. The potential danger that the accused will commit further crimes is not a legitimate basis for setting a high bail. The imposition of high bail is justified only to prevent flight of the accused from the jurisdiction.

2. Bail may be required for an accused to be released at any stage of a criminal proceeding.

3. Bail is something of value pledged to the court with the purpose of ensuring that the accused appears in court at a designated time. If the defendant fails to appear, the posted bail money may be forfeited to the court.

   A "surety," such as a relative or friend, often posts the money (or a house deed, etc.) with the court so as to enable an accused to be released. In the absence of such a relative or friend, an insurance company, for a fee, through a "bail bondsman," will act as surety by "posting a bond" with the court. Any surety is obviously motivated to make sure the defendant appears in court at the appointed time.

4. The amount of bail is set by a judicial officer authorized to do so.

5. Some jurisdictions have "preventive detention" statutes which permit absolute denial of bail to certain defendants who are found likely to commit serious offenses if released, or who are found very likely to flee. An accused detained under such statutes usually has additional due process protections, including a guarantee of an early trial date.

D. Preliminary hearing.

1. If the crime is a felony, a person usually will be entitled to a preliminary hearing before a judge or magistrate shortly after his initial appearance before the court.

2. The purposes of such a hearing, which often includes testimony and cross-examination of prosecution witnesses, are to allow some examination of the prosecution's case and to determine whether there is probable cause to believe the accused committed the crime charged.
   a. When the court does not find probable cause, the accused is released.
   b. When the court finds probable cause, the accused is "bound over for grand jury action."

E. Accusatory pleadings. The actual commencement of a criminal prosecution occurs with the filing of an accusatory pleading.
   1. In misdemeanor cases, the pleading is called a "complaint."
   2. In felony cases, the pleading is usually an "indictment," which is a product of a grand jury proceeding.

F. Grand jury proceedings.
   1. A grand jury is a group of laymen summoned to meet during a session of court. Its usual function is to issue formal accusations of crime, based on evidence it hears.
      a. With exceptions in some states, the common law size of a grand jury is between 12 and 23 people.
      b. The grand jury's decisions require 12 votes (with some state exceptions).
   2. At common law, a grand jury indictment was necessary for any felony prosecution.
   3. Today, the use of grand jury proceedings is somewhat more limited; felonies are charged in some of the states simply by an "information" (a pleading filed directly by the district attorney); however, grand jury hearings are still required for all Federal felony cases.
   4. At grand jury hearings, the prosecutor presents evidence to the jury. (It is an investigative, not a judicial proceeding.)

5. If the jury believes the evidence would warrant a conviction of the crime charged, it returns a grand jury indictment.

G. Arraignment.
 1. After the accusatory pleading is filed, the defendant appears before the court for the arraignment.
 2. At this hearing:
   a. The accused is informed of his rights, including the right to counsel.
   b. The pleading is read to him.
   c. He enters a plea (usually "not guilty" at this stage). (He may subsequently change his plea to "guilty" at any stage of the proceeding prior to the rendering of a finding by the court. To plead "not guilty" initially gives the defendant some leverage in plea bargaining.)
   d. The defendant is asked whether he wishes trial by jury.
   e. Bail is set, or it may be reviewed if previously set.

H. Discovery.
 1. An accused has no constitutional right to obtain pretrial discovery (that is, inspect physical evidence or obtain names and statements of witnesses who will be called to testify against him).
 2. The prosecution, however, is under an affirmative duty to disclose to the accused evidence known to it, which is favorable or exculpatory to the accused. Failure to make such a disclosure after a defense request for such evidence is a violation of the defendant's due process rights.
 3. Federal practice under the *Federal Rules of Criminal Procedure* allows very broad discovery. The defense may obtain from the prosecution pre-trial:
   a. Any statements by the accused.
   b. The accused's prior criminal record.
   c. The results of any scientific tests conducted.
   d. Any relevant physical evidence (weapons, etc.).
   e. There is no requirement that the government disclose its witnesses' statements prior to trial. Once a govern-

ment witness has testified at trial, though, before cross-examination of the witness, the accused is entitled to inspect any of the witness's prior statements ("Jencks Rule")[2].

I. Guilty pleas.
  1. Any guilty plea must be made voluntarily and with an understanding of the nature of the charge and the consequences of the plea of "guilty."
  2. Pleas made with the inducement of promises or threats are considered involuntary. (Nevertheless, "plea bargaining," based on the defendant's expectation that the prosecutor's sentencing recommendation and the court's sentence will be more lenient than if there is a full trial, is the most common disposition of criminal cases.)
  3. A guilty plea is a waiver of:
     a. The right to trial by jury.
     b. The right to confrontation of accusers.
     c. The privilege against self-incrimination.

X. The trial: Process and safeguards for the defendant.

  A. Competency to stand trial.
    1. As an accused person has the right to be present at his trial, it follows that it would violate his rights to subject him to trial if he were mentally incompetent to understand the trial or participate in it.
    2. A defendant is incompetent to stand trial if, because of his present mental condition, he either:
       a. Lacks a rational and factual understanding of the charges and proceedings against him; or,
       b. Lacks sufficient ability to assist his lawyer in his defense.
    3. If a defendant is determined by the court to be incompetent to stand trial, that is a bar to proceeding with a trial. Such a defendant may be committed to a mental

hospital for a period of evaluation and treatment to help him become competent. (He may later be tried for the offense, on becoming competent.)

  a. The defendant cannot be hospitalized indefinitely, merely because of incompetency to stand trial, however.

  b. If it is determined that the accused will not attain competency within the foreseeable future, the state either must release him or institute commitment proceedings through the normal statutory civil commitment process.

4. It is crucial to remember the distinction between insanity and incompetency. Insanity is a defense to a criminal charge, and relates to the defendant's mental condition in the past, at the time the crime was allegedly committed; incompetency depends on a defendant's mental condition in the present, the time of trial; incompetency bars a trial until the defendant is found competent.

B. Sixth Amendment rights at trial.

1. The Sixth Amendment provides that, ". . . the accused shall enjoy the right to a speedy and public trial, by an impartial jury of the state and district wherein the crime shall have been committed."

2. The right to a trial by jury exists for every case in which the charge against the accused carries a potential sentence of more than six months.

  a. Such a jury, ordinarily consisting of 12 laymen, is called a petit jury.

  b. Usually, a unanimous verdict is required to convict a defendant of a crime.

3. The right to a speedy trial. This right attaches after a person has been accused or arrested.

  a. Violation of this right is not established by delay alone. A balancing test is used to weigh the length of the delay, the reason for it, the defendant's assertion or nonassertion of his right to a speedy trial, and any prejudice to the accused.

b. The remedy for an accused's having been denied his right to a speedy trial is dismissal of the case.

4. The right to a fair and impartial trial. A defendant is entitled to have a trial free from prejudicial publicity or other undue influence on the trier of fact (the jury or judge).

C. The right to counsel.

1. The Sixth Amendment provides that an accused has the right to have the assistance of counsel for his defense in any criminal prosecution. Counsel must, therefore, be appointed to represent indigent defendants who are unable to hire their own attorneys.

2. The right to counsel applies in any case where a defendant is charged with an offense punishable by imprisonment.

3. The right to counsel arises once the accused has been formally charged (that is, arraigned), or, of course, if he is subjected to a custodial interrogation prior to being formally charged.

4. Once charges have been filed, an accused has the right to the assistance of counsel at all critical stages of the proceeding (every stage where substantial rights of the accused may be affected).

5. Denial of the right to counsel automatically vitiates any conviction from such a trial.

D. The right of confrontation. The Sixth Amendment provides that the accused in any criminal prosecution has the right to be confronted with the witnesses against him.

1. In essence, this is a right to cross-examine the witnesses against him.

2. This includes the accused's right to be physically present at the time the testimony is being given against him. The accused may implicitly waive this right, however, by improper, disruptive courtroom conduct.

E. The right of the accused not to testify. The Fifth Amendment privilege against self-incrimination means that the accused in a criminal proceeding can refuse to testify, and the prosecution cannot force him to take the witness stand.

XI. Some post-trial procedural aspects.

A. Double jeopardy.
1. The Fifth Amendment provides that no person shall be "put in jeopardy" twice for the same offense.
2. After a defendant has been prosecuted for a criminal offense, any further prosecution of him for this same offense is barred by this double jeopardy clause.
   a. One effect of this is that the prosecution cannot appeal a defendant's acquittal.
   b. The state, however, is not barred from a second prosecution of a defendant who, after conviction, appeals the conviction and succeeds in having it set aside by an appellate court. Such a defendant is viewed as having waived the bar of jeopardy.
   c. Note that the same act may occur in two jurisdictions. (For example, a kidnapping may be a Federal crime and also a crime in the state in which the kidnapping took place.) It is not regarded as double jeopardy for the individual to be tried in both jurisdictions for the same act, although it is uncommon for that to occur.

B. Conviction and sentencing.
1. Conviction results from a jury's (or, in a nonjury trial, a judge's) verdict of guilty. (The actual judgment of conviction is not usually entered until sentence is imposed.)
2. Sentencing.
   a. An accused has the right to counsel at sentencing.
   b. It is usually required that a sentence be imposed without unreasonable delay.

    c. Sentence is imposed by the court (the judge) although some states permit the jury to make recommendations.

    d. A sentence may consist of death, incarceration, imposition of a fine, or probation.

    e. Cruel and unusual punishment.

      1) The Eighth Amendment prohibits the imposition of cruel and unusual punishment.

      2) Punishment which is deemed to be either barbaric or excessive for the particular crime has been held to be violative of this prohibition.

      3) The death penalty has not been held to be cruel and unusual punishment (unconstitutional) per se. Capital punishment is considered permissible under circumstances which appropriately provide for giving consideration to various factors about the crime and the defendant.

C. The right to appeal.

  1. The right to have an adverse verdict reviewed by a higher court is fundamental to defendants and is included in all states' statutes.

  2. Appellate review is limited, however, to errors of law, not to conflicts in the evidence.

  3. Appellate courts do not reverse a lower court merely because of the existence of erroneous legal rulings in the trial. Reversal will only occur if it is likely that the defendant was prejudiced by the error.

XII. Juvenile offenders.

A. Individuals under the age of 18 who are charged with criminal offenses are generally dealt with in juvenile court systems, whose goals are rehabilitation and treatment, rather than in adult criminal courts. Some states, however, permit juveniles who are above a certain age and charged with serious felonies to be tried as adults in criminal courts.

B. Although juvenile proceedings are considered "civil" rather than "criminal" in nature, juveniles charged with crimes must still be afforded most of the same constitutional rights as adult criminal defendants. These rights are considered necessary to assure fundamental fairness in the fact-finding process. They include the rights to counsel, to confront and cross-examine witnesses, to have the case proven "beyond a reasonable doubt" (the standard of proof in adult criminal proceedings), and the privilege against self-incrimination. Due to the informal and confidential nature of juvenile proceedings, however, a trial by jury is not constitutionally required.

Text References

1. *Miranda v. State of Arizona*, 384 U.S. 436 (1966)
2. *Jencks v. United States*, 353 U.S. 657 (1957) (See also 18 U.S.C.A. §3500)

General References

Kadish, S. and Paulsen, M. *Criminal Law and its Processes.* Little Brown, Boston, 1969

LaFave, W. and Scott, A., Jr. *Hornbook on Criminal Law.* West Publishing, St. Paul, 1972

Model Penal Code (Draft). American Law Institute, St. Paul, 1962

Perkins, R. M. *Criminal Law* (2nd ed.). Foundation Press, Mineola, N.Y., 1969

Questions on Chapter 4, Criminal Law and Procedure

Choose one answer in each of the following three questions:
1. In order for a crime to have been committed, there must have been:
   a. a criminal intent.
   b. a criminal act or omission.
   c. an injury to a person or property.
   d. (a) and (b).
   e. (a), (b), and (c).
2. *A* throws a hand grenade into a crowded bus, on a dare from one of his friends. *B*, a rider on the bus, is killed.
   The killing of *B* is:
   a. first degree murder.
   b. second degree murder.
   c. voluntary manslaughter.
   d. involuntary manslaughter.
3. *B* sees *A*'s bicycle parked in the carport of *A*'s home and decides to steal it to replace his own, which is broken. *B* approaches the bicycle and tells *C*, *A*'s six-year-old daughter who is playing in the carport, that he is going to borrow the bicycle and return it. *B* rides off and does not bring the bicycle back.
   B has committed the crime of:
   a. larceny.
   b. robbery.
   c. false pretenses.
   d. burglary.
4. A police officer sees *A* breaking into a store. *A* has burglars' tools in his possession. He is arrested and, when taken into custody, is searched. The search reveals a large quantity of illegal drugs in his coat pockets. The state may use the illegal drugs as evidence in a trial of the defendant for illegal drug possession since the search was a lawful and "reasonable" one. True or False?

Choose whichever answers apply in the following question:
  5. Defendant D is charged with assault on a police officer. At the time of trial, his court-appointed attorney withdraws from the case, and the court informs D that since it would cause further delay of the case to appoint a new attorney, he will have to proceed pro se* without an attorney. When the jury is selected, it includes three members of the police force, one of whom knows the assaulted officer (who will be the chief prosecution witness). When the testimony finally begins, D becomes ill and asks the court to discontinue the trial. The judge excuses D to go to the doctor but continues the trial in D's absence. The next day when D returns, the prosecutor calls D to testify. Subsequently, he is convicted. On appeal, which rights should he assert were denied him?
     a. the right to a trial by jury.
     b. the right to an impartial and fair trial.
     c. the right to a speedy trial.
     d. the right to counsel.
     e. the right to confront witnesses.
     f. the right of the accused not to testify.
     g. the right to be free from cruel and unusual punishment.
  6. B, a 19-year-old immigrant, is arrested and charged with rape. He is questioned by a police officer about the offense for an hour. During the questioning, the officer urges him to confess so that he will be able to get it over with. The officer does not offer to allow him to speak with an attorney, nor does he inform him that he has the right to remain silent. B, who has some language difficulty and has never been arrested before, believes that if he confesses he will be allowed to go home. B confesses to the rape, which he has, in reality, committed. This confession is legally admissible at B's trial. True or False?
  7. A and B go to a bank in order to rob it. A, who is unarmed, instructs B, who is armed, to shoot the bank teller, who is uncooperative in their robbery attempt. B shoots the teller, who subsequently dies.
     Who can be convicted of the teller's murder?
     a. B.
     b. A.
     c. B and A.
  8. The insanity defense, if properly pleaded, will usually mitigate or shorten the sentence which is ultimately imposed by the court. True or False?

---

*On his own behalf.

9. Since juvenile proceedings are not "criminal" in nature, a juvenile charged with crime need not have an attorney appointed to represent him at trial. True or False?

10. Defendant *A*, charged with assault on his mother, is evaluated by a court-appointed psychiatrist. It is determined that the defendant is suffering from paranoid schizophrenia, but that he is not currently actively psychotic. It is determined that at the time of the assault, when he struck his mother, he believed that he was striking an invader from another planet and that such action was necessary and was authorized by the F.B.I.

    Based on the above information, it is likely that a court would find the defendant to be:

    a. insane (that is, not criminally responsible for the assault).

    b. incompetent to stand trial.

    c. a and b.

CHAPTER 5
Civil Procedure
Michael J. English

Civil Procedure
Michael J. English

I. Introduction.

The rules of civil procedure present a methodology, or framework, within which claims by one party (or parties) against another party (or parties) are adjudicated before a court. The rules of civil procedure do not create rights or causes of action; they only affect the manner in which adjudication of a cause of action will occur. Application of the civil procedure rules can drastically affect the success or non success of the claim, however, because the manner of presentation of a claim often dictates its resolution.

The rules of civil procedure only apply to claims resolved by courts. There are many other methods for the resolution of disputes, for example, administrative proceedings, compulsory arbitration, etc. Furthermore, the rules of civil procedure apply only to civil litigation, that is, litigation where the remedy sought will directly benefit the party to the suit; they do not apply to criminal cases or other proceedings, such as Federal bankruptcy proceedings, which have their own procedural rules.

This outline describes general rules of civil procedure, not specific applications of those rules. (Many of the rules can be very complex when applied to specific factual situations. Also exceptions to many rules commonly exist in both state and Federal jurisdictions.)

II. Jurisdiction.
In order for the court to have the power to adjudicate a controversy, it must have jurisdiction over

the parties to the suit and/or the subject matter of the suit. Without either personal and/or subject-matter jurisdiction, the court cannot act or bind persons or property to a particular judgment.

A. Parties to litigation. In order for a court to have jurisdiction over a party, at least one of the following prerequisites must be met.

1. Presence. Presence within the jurisdictional limits of the court is the traditional grounds of personal jurisdiction. Any person served with process within the jurisdiction is subject to the power of the court, even if the person is in that locality only momentarily.

2. Residence. If a person resides within the state, the court may exercise jurisdiction over the person, even if the person is not physically within the state at the time of service of process. (Service may be accomplished at the residence of the party.)

3. Domicile. Domicile, defined as an "indefinite intent to reside in the state," has been held to be sufficient to give the court jurisdiction over the person, even if the person is not within the borders of that state. (Even if a court has jurisdiction over a person, however, statutory authorization is necessary to achieve service of process if the individual is physically outside of the state).

4. Consent. If a party consents to be subject to the jurisdiction of the court, proper jurisdiction lies. Consent generally occurs when an individual enters an appearance in the court or where a particular state statute defines certain conduct within the state as consent to jurisdiction. For example, in states having a non resident motorist statute, operation of a motor vehicle in the state constitutes consent to jurisdiction. In fact, in most states, the non resident motorist statute allows for service of process on a given official of the foreign state rather than on the individual himself.

5. Property. In certain cases where specific property within a state is the subject of a suit, the court may

have jurisdiction, (called "In Rem" jurisdiction) over the property. Although personal jurisdiction does not arise in this instance, the court is empowered to enter a judgment affecting the disposition of the property.

6. Long-arm statutes. Many states allow out-of-state service to obtain personal jurisdiction over non residents when one of the following prerequisites is met.
   a. The person transacted business in the state.
   b. The person committed a tortious act within the state.
   c. The person owns, uses, or possesses real estate within the state.
   d. The person contracts for insurance within the state.
   e. The subject matter of the suit involves product liability, and the product was used in the state, or advertised for use in the state.

B. Subject matter jurisdiction. The court must have the authority to act on the issue presented in the suit.
   1. State courts. Each state code specifies which matters state courts are entitled to hear. Unless the court is authorized by statute to hear a particular matter, it does not have subject-matter jurisdiction.
   2. Federal courts. Special rules apply regarding subject-matter jurisdiction in Federal courts.
      a. Diversity.
         1) A Federal court generally may entertain lawsuits involving the following parties:
            a) Between parties from different states.
            b) Between states.
            c) Between states and private parties.
               There must be diversity of citizenship between the plaintiffs and the defendants in the suit, that is, each plaintiff must have different citizenship from each defendant before a Federal court can take jurisdiction over the subject matter of a suit.
         2) In a case based on diversity, the amount of damages sought must exceed $10,000 in order for a Federal court to entertain subject-matter jurisdiction. The amount-in-controversy requirement also applies to

cases where a Federal question (discussed below) is involved, unless Congress has specifically provided otherwise by statute.
   b. Federal question. A Federal court has jurisdiction over the subject-matter of a suit if the issues involved arise under the Constitution, laws, or treaties of the United States.
   c. United States a party. Federal courts have subject-matter jurisdiction in all suits where the United States is a party to the suit.
   d. Pendent and ancillary jurisdiction. Where a Federal court has jurisdiction over the primary cause of action, it can also exercise jurisdiction over other issues arising in the case, even though those other issues would not themselves create jurisdiction over the subject matter.
   e. Removal. A defendant in a case brought in a state court may unilaterally have the suit removed to a Federal court if the cause of action involves subject matter over which the Federal court would have had original jurisdiction.

C. Service of process. Even if the jurisdictional prerequisites have been met, the court will not have personal jurisdiction until "service of process" has been achieved, that is, the defendant has formally been notified of the suit. In a civil action, process normally includes delivery of the complaint which initiates the cause of action and a summons to appear in court at a definite time. Personal service is controlled by constitutional principles of due process, and depending on local law, may be achieved by one of the following methods:
   1. Service by personal delivery to the party.
   2. Substitute service by delivery of process to the party's regular dwelling place within the jurisdiction.
   3. Service by registered or certified mail (controlled by principles of reasonableness, for example, service by certified mail is acceptable if it is likely to give notice to the party).

4. Service by publication in a local newspaper or other periodical (permitted in only very limited circumstances).

5. Federal personal service is achieved in ways similar to those described above, except that service may be achieved only within the territorial limits of the state where the district court sits or within a 100-mile radius of those territorial limits.

D. Subpoenas. A subpoena is a document, issued under the seal of the court, by the clerk of that court, which when served, compels attendance at the court. (In practice, subpoenas are usually issued in blank by the court and filled in and served by counsel for a party to the litigation.)

1. Subpoenas are used for one or more of the following purposes.
   a. To compel appearance of witnesses at trial.
   b. To compel a person to produce documentary evidence (subpoena duces tecum).
   c. To compel appearance at a deposition of a non party witness.

2. Sometimes, an attorney issues a subpoena calling for broader discovery than is appropriate. To avoid complying with an improper subpoena, the party on whom it is served can offer a motion to the court to either "quash" (annul) the subpoena altogether, or limit its scope in an appropriate manner.

3. It is a prudent policy to check with one's own attorney whenever one is served with a subpoena.

III. **Pleadings.** Pleadings are documents filed in court, which describe the nature of the case, set out defenses to claims, or bring before the court specific issues for the court to resolve. The major pleadings usually filed in a civil case include:

A. Complaint. A statement, filed by the plaintiff, of the claim which initiates the suit. The *Federal Rules of Civil*

Procedure and many state rules require that the complaint be a concise statement. There is no need for specific allegations of each detail of the activity giving rise to the suit. In addition, most rules allow for a complaint to be framed under alternative theories of recovery. Liberal rules for amending the complaint are also generally allowed, as facts and circumstances dictate.

B. Answer. The response by the defendant to the complaint. The answer states the defendant's defenses to the cause of action, including denials of factual allegations and affirmative defenses which the defendant has to the suit, for example, contributory negligence or lack of jurisdiction. Failure to answer a properly served complaint may result in a "default judgment," that is, judgment for the plaintiff without the requirement of strict proof.

C. Motion to dismiss. A pleading, filed by the defendant, which contains legal arguments to the court attempting to show that the suit should be dismissed without a trial. Motions to dismiss are limited to arguments of law. For purposes of a motion to dismiss, the factual statements alleged in the complaint must be regarded as true. The usual bases for a motion to dismiss are a lack of personal or subject-matter jurisdiction, or a failure to state a claim on which relief can be granted. (Under certain state rules and under the *Federal Rules of Civil Procedure*, this motion is titled, "Motion for judgment on the pleadings.")

D. Motion for summary judgment. A motion filed by either the plaintiff or the defendant, which argues that the party is entitled to judgment without a full procedural trial on the merits, because no material fact is genuinely in dispute *and* the law requires judgment. A motion for summary judgment differs from a motion to dismiss in that in the former, each party is permitted to set out facts which are alleged not to be in dispute. The party argues for summary judgment based on such a statement of facts.

E. Responsive pleadings. Because a court decision in response to a motion substantively affects a lawsuit, the rules of civil procedure in all jurisdictions allow a party to respond to any motion filed in court by the other party. Responsive pleadings present arguments in opposition to the arguments presented in the original motion.

IV. **Multi-party and multi-claim litigation.** Civil litigation may expand to involve parties other than a single plaintiff and defendant or involve claims not orginally included in the complaint. The following sections describe the methods by which additional parties and/or claims may be incorporated into a civil suit.

A. Counterclaim. Once the complaint is filed, a defendant may make a claim of his own against the plaintiff. Such a claim may arise out of the same transaction or occurrence as the plaintiff's claim. Under the *Federal Rules of Civil Procedure* such a claim is called a "compulsory" counterclaim, that is, if the claim is not brought by the defendant, the defendant loses the opportunity to bring such a claim in another cause of action. Counterclaims unrelated to the same transaction or occurrence as contained in plaintiff's claim are also allowable but are "permissive," that is, the defendant has the choice of whether or not to bring the counterclaim into the pending action.

B. Joinder. Either a plaintiff or defendant may join additional parties to the suit, if the party to be joined was involved in the same transaction or occurrence as the original plaintiff and defendant. Joinder is permissive if the activity of the party to be joined arose out of the same transaction, or occurrence, or if the activity relates to a common question of law or fact. If, however, the party to be joined is indispensable to the litigation (if adjudication of the case without the party would result in a manifest injustice), joinder must occur, or the case must be dismissed.

C. Class actions. When an individual has a claim, which is representative of claims of many individuals against the defendant, that individual can sue as a representative of a class of persons having the same legal claim.

  1. Class actions are only permissible when *all* the following requirements are met:
     a. The class is so large that joinder of all potential plaintiffs is not feasible.
     b. The issues in litigation are common to all class members.
     c. The class representative is typical of all the other class members.
     d. The class representative will fairly and adequately represent the class.

  2. Other requirements for class actions may be:
     a. There is a potential for inconsistent verdicts, which might create incompatible standards to be followed by a defendant.
     b. There is a likelihood that there would be an impairment of the rights of class members not party to individual claims.
     c. The suits are for declaratory relief (no money damages but, rather, injunctive relief*), and the injunctive relief is appropriate for all class members.
     d. Common issues of law and fact predominate, and a class action suit is the best method for resolution of the issues.

  3. Judgments in class actions are binding on all class members.
     a. In most instances, each class member must receive notice of the class action and of the opportunity to refuse to participate in it.
     b. If a class member refuses to participate, any judgment in favor of or against the class does not apply to that member.

D. Interpleader. This allows a party to a suit to bring a non party into the suit if the party has a question about

---

*"Injunctive relief" ordinarily means that the court issues an order for the defendant not to do something which harms the plaintiff.

which of two or more claimants against him has the most valid claim. The purpose of interpleader is to prevent double or multiple findings of liability against the same party for the same actions.

E. Cross-claims. Cross-claims are claims for relief asserted against a coparty, that is, against a fellow plaintiff or defendant. They are similar to counterclaims but never compulsory, that is, such claims can be litigated later; cross-claims must relate to the substance of the initial claim, to a counterclaim, or to property which is a subject of the original claim.

F. Third-party practice (impleader). A defendant to a civil suit may bring in another party where the defendant asserts that the other party is liable to him for all or part of plaintiff's claim. To implead a party, a third-party complaint must be filed and served on the additional party in the same manner that the original complaint was filed by the plaintiff against the defendant. The third-party complaint must independently satisfy all jurisdictional requirements in order for the court to have the power to review the claim.

V. **Discovery.** Discovery is the process by which the parties to a suit obtain factual information relating to the issues of the suit prior to trial. Discoverable information is essentially any obtainable information which may be relevant to the issues in the suit, subject only to limited restrictions. Rules of discovery permit wide-ranging inquiry into the factual circumstances giving rise to the suit.

A. Most states and the Federal system allow for the following methods of discovery.

1. Oral depositions. A deposition is the taking of oral testimony under oath. The testimony is recorded verbatim, usually by a court reporter, and is preserved in the same manner as testimony taken in court. Depositions are usually conducted at the offices of the attorney for the party taking the deposition. An oral deposition

may be taken from a party to the suit or from any other person subject to the subpoena power of the court. Depositions may be undertaken without prior express permission of the court.

2. Depositions on written questions. These are similar to oral depositions, except that the deponent (person being deposed) receives written questions from the deposing party and is required to answer those questions orally, under oath, before a court reporter. Depositions on written questions are most often used when the deponent is located at a great distance from the deposing party and where the deponent is a non party witness.

3. Requests for admission. Written statements of fact or combinations of law and fact are submitted to a party to be admitted or denied. Requests for admissions are statements, not questions; responses to the statements must be an admission or a denial of the truth of the statement or a statement of reasons why the party can neither admit nor deny the statements. Requests for admissions are normally used to clarify and delimit issues requiring formal proof. An affirmative response to a request for admissions conclusively establishes the truth of the facts stated therein, for purposes of the lawsuit.

4. Interrogatories. Written questions, which must be answered under oath and in writing. They are submitted only to parties to the litigation. The use of interrogatories is common in most civil litigation. The written answers to the questions usually are formulated in close consultation with counsel for the party answering the questions.

5. Requests to produce documents. Written requests to a party in the litigation, which require the party to produce original documents for inspection by the party submitting the request. Requests to produce documents are complied with either by providing the documents requested or by identifying the location of the documents and allowing the requesting party to inspect them.

6. Requests for physical and mental examinations. A party may compel another party to submit to a mental or physical examination, on a court order. The court can order a physical or mental examination only on a showing of good cause. There must also be sufficient notice to the party to be examined. The physical or mental condition of the party must be at issue in the case. The report of a physician conducting an examination ordered pursuant to this discovery rule must be made available to the party examined.

7. Documents in possession of a non party. Non parties to litigation can be compelled to produce documents in their possession if served with a "subpoena duces tecum." Failure to produce requested documents subjects the non party to the contempt powers of the court.

B. Restrictions on discovery:

1. A person otherwise subject to discovery procedures may avoid them if the information sought is protected by a privilege. Privilege is normally found to exist when the information results from a particular protected relationship, for example, the husband-wife relationship, the physician-patient relationship, the lawyer-client relationship, the priest-penitent relationship. (See chapter 6, Evidence.)

2. Discovery of information may also be avoided if the information constitutes "attorney work-product." Attorney work-product is defined as any information developed by an attorney for a party in preparation for trial. The work-product privilege can be either qualified or absolute. It is absolute if the information constitutes the mental impression, conclusions, or opinions of the attorney. The privilege is qualified, and therefore subject to a certain degree of discovery, if the information is contained in the attorney's notes of an interview with a potential witness or in reports submitted to the attorney by persons charged with investigating the action. Qualified work-product information is discoverable only when the party seeking

discovery shows it cannot obtain substantial equivalent information by other means.

3. Expert opinions are not discoverable under certain circumstances. These circumstances relate to the role played by the expert and to the availability of other opinions. Three categories of exclusion exist.
    a. For experts directly involved in the subject matter of the case, the usual rules of discovery regarding witnesses apply, and expert opinion is discoverable.
    b. For experts who have been retained specifically to testify at trial, the identity of the expert and the substance of the expert's intended testimony is discoverable by interrogatory. Discovery by deposition can only be conducted on court order after a strong showing of need.
    c. For an expert retained to give an opinion regarding the substance of the claim but not expected to be called at trial, no discovery of the expert's opinion is allowed except on court order. The court must find exceptional circumstances, such as when it is highly impractical to obtain an opinion on the subject matter from another source.

C. Compelled discovery. Except in the case of discovery by physical or mental examination, discovery is conducted without participation by the court. If a party from whom discovery is sought refuses to cooperate with discovery, the party seeking discovery can ask the court to compel cooperation by a court order. If a party refuses to obey a court order for discovery, sanctions may be imposed by the court. These sanctions include:

1. Award of costs to compel the discovery.
2. Exclusion of non discovered evidence at trial.
3. Treating the issue about which discovery is refused as admitted at trial.
4. Civil contempt.
5. In an egregious case, dismissal of the cause of action.

VI. Pre-trial conference and trial.

A. Pre-trial conference. A meeting of the court and the litigating parties' attorneys, for purposes of:

1. Simplifying and reducing the number of issues to be decided at trial.

2. Amending pleadings if necessary.

3. Obtaining stipulations regarding specific facts which are admitted as true by both parties in order to avoid unnecessary presentation of evidence at trial.

4. Identifying and limiting the number of witnesses to be called.

5. Reaching a settlement of the case, if possible. The pre-trial conference is intended to avoid a trial by reaching negotiated settlements, or to streamline the presentation of proof if a trial does take place.

B. Trial. The specific method of conducting a civil trial is not outlined in the rules of civil procedure. The rules of civil procedure, however, do affect certain aspects of the trial of a civil case. Also, most of the conduct of the trial is dictated by the rules of evidence. (See Chapter 6, Evidence.) The major procedural aspects of a trial which relate to rules of civil procedure are these:

1. Burden of proof (two senses).

   a. First sense, how strong must the proof be: The burden of proof in civil cases is preponderance of the evidence. The preponderance of the evidence means that the party with the burden must show that it is more likely than not that the set of factual circumstances underlying his claim occurred.

   b. Second sense, who has to prove what: The burden of proof in civil cases initially rests on the plaintiff, and the burden remains with the plaintiff until he/she has presented sufficient evidence to establish a prima facie* case. Then the burden of proof shifts to the defendant, who tries to rebut the plaintiff's evidence.

---

*A prima facie case is one which is sufficient to prove an issue, unless contrary evidence is presented by an opposing party.

2. Juries.
   a. Trial juries, (that is, petit juries) typically are comprised of twelve individuals selected from a panel of eligible citizens. Their responsibility is to hear the evidence presented and to reach a verdict. (Note that the right to a jury trial in a civil case is not absolute, nor is the number of jurors required to be 12. Both matters are determined by state statutes.) Traditionally, a jury verdict has been required to be unanimous. Indeed, in criminal cases, unanimity is constitutionally required. Now, however, some states allow for a non unanimous or even a majority verdict in civil cases.

   In order to have a jury trial in a civil case, there must be a jury demand by one of the parties. A jury trial may be waived. (In certain circumstances, there is never a right to a jury trial, for example, Federal Tort Claims Act litigation against the United States.)
   b. Voir dire. An examination of potential jurors by counsel for the parties to the litigation or in some instances by the presiding judge. The voir dire is intended to determine if potential jurors have a bias which would interfere with the juror's ability to evaluate the case objectively.* In most states, each party is allowed to prevent certain potential jurors from sitting on a jury. Where bias or prejudice has been shown, potential jurors can be dismissed for cause; in addition, most states allow parties to make peremptory challenges, that is, the exclusion of a juror without a showing of cause.

3. Use of discovery information at trial. Information obtained through discovery (for example, depositions, answers to interrogatories, etc.) can only be admitted if the evidence meets the general rules for admission of that evidence. Information obtained from discovery is normally utilized to:
   a. Impeach a witness, that is, show the witness has made contradictory statements in the past.

---

*The term, "voir dire," is also used to describe the process of qualifying expert witnesses.

    b. Introduce prior statements of a party to the litigation.

    c. Present the testimony of a witness who is unavailable to testify at trial (for example, the witness is deceased; the witness is not obtainable by subpoena; the witness is too ill to testify, or the witness lives more than 100 miles away from the court, etc.)

4. Directed Verdict. A request or motion for directed verdict is, in effect, a request that the case be taken from the jury and that the judge decide in favor of the moving party. It is appropriate when the evidence presented is such that no reasonable man could find other than for the party moving for the directed verdict. After the plaintiff's evidence has been admitted, a defendant may move for a directed verdict. After all the evidence has been admitted, either party may make this motion. A judge will enter a directed verdict only rarely in civil cases, usually when undisputed testimony which undermines the plaintiff's case has been presented on a controlling issue.

5. Judgment notwithstanding the verdict. (Judgment *"non obstante verdicto"* or n.o.v.). Either party may move that the court reverse the verdict of the jury and enter a judgment in the party's favor, on the grounds that the judge can find no sufficient legal basis for the verdict of the jury. (That is, on its face, the presentation of the party to which the jury granted the verdict was defective in that it gave no legal basis for the verdict.)

6. Jury instructions. In any civil case where a jury sits to assess the evidence, the judge is required to instruct the jury regarding the legal precedents and criteria which apply to the facts of the case.

7. Findings of fact and conclusions of law. In any case where the judge sits as the trier of fact instead of a jury, most rules of civil procedure require that the judge enter his verdict in writing. He also submits a written statement which identifies the facts on which he relied in reaching the verdict and which presents the basis for his legal conclusions.

VII. Post-trial procedure.

A. Appeal. Details of appellate procedure are not included in this outline. Usually, however, an appeal is a request that an appellate court change some aspect of the outcome of a case tried in a court of initial jurisdiction. Usually, the grounds for appeal are that errors of law occurred in the lower court proceeding and that those errors were of sufficient importance to have improperly prejudiced the outcome against the appellant. The appellate court rules on whether the law was appropriately adhered to by the trial court. The evidence, that is, the facts, is considered only insofar as to determine whether proper legal decisions were made concerning it.

B. An additional remedy for the losing party is a motion for new trial. Judges in both state and Federal jurisdictions have substantial discretion to grant a new trial on the following grounds:

1. Judicial error occurred, for example, the court erroneously instructed the jury on an important matter of law.

2. There was a prejudicial occurrence, that is, misconduct by a participant. A new trial may be granted for prejudicial occurrence only when there is substantial risk that the misconduct resulted in an unfair verdict. (Jury misconduct involving outside influences or concealing bias or prejudice on voir dire, might constitute such a prejudicial occurrence.)

3. The verdict was against the weight of the evidence. (Wide variation in application of this standard exists from state to state.)

4. There is newly discovered evidence. A motion for new trial on newly discovered evidence, however, is only permitted when all the following occur:
   a. There is a clear showing that the evidence was, in fact, discovered after trial.
   b. The evidence could not have been discovered earlier by due diligence.

c. The evidence is material to a substantive issue in the case.

C. Effects of judgments. Rules of procedure dictate the effect judgments will have as they relate to future claims. The three most important principles relating to this issue are:

1. Res judicata. The principle that an issue litigated between the same parties cannot be relitigated in another suit stating the same cause of action. This principle prevents a losing party from suing the same party in another case in an effort to get a different judgment.

2. Collateral estoppel. This principle mandates that an issue litigated between parties cannot be relitigated between the same parties (and in certain instances by either party against another different party), even when the party attempts to litigate the issue in an unrelated cause of action. Collateral estoppel is similar to the principle of res judicata except that its applicability extends beyond suits alleging the same cause of action. (In order for collateral estoppel or res judicata to take effect, the issue must actually have been litigated in the prior case, that is, dismissals based on lack of personal or subject-matter jurisdiction, improper venue, or failure to join an indispensable party do not give rise to collateral estoppel or res judicata).

3. Full faith and credit. The principle that each state must give to judgments of any other state the same effect that the judgment would have had if it had been rendered in the state. In other words, one state must give full effect to the judgments of another state, even if it might be evident that the first state misinterpreted its own laws.

D. Execution of judgment. If a judgment is obtained against a party in a case and if he doesn't pay the judgment, the judgment lien holder (the winner) can initiate further legal proceedings (supplementary process) to enforce the judgment. The loser may be forced to sell various possessions, or he might be forced into bankruptcy. (In the past, imprisonment was even a possible consequence for non payment of a judgment.)

If the loser delays payment so that supplementary process is required, the overall costs usually increase by virtue of interest charges as well as because of additional legal fees.

Reference

Federal Rules: Civil Procedure; Evidence; Appellate Procedure. West Publishing, St. Paul, 1982

Questions on Chapter 5,
Civil Procedure

1. A witness in a civil case, who is not a party, cannot be compelled to answer written interrogatories properly served upon him. True or False?
2. A court cannot exercise jurisdiction over real estate unless personal jurisdiction over the owner of the property can be obtained. True or False?
3. A motion to dismiss may only be granted if there are no material facts genuinely in dispute. True or False?
4. On a vacation trip to Maine, John, from Vermont, is in an auto accident involving William, who is from Maine. William believes John is at fault and that he has suffered $1 million worth of harm. What kinds of laws enable William to sue John in a state court in Maine?
5. Horace believes that Dr. Smith has committed malpractice on him and sues for $1 million. Wishing to document that Dr. Smith has done similar things to other patients, Horace subpoenas all of Dr. Smith's patients' records for the last 10 years. Dr. Smith is very reluctant to give out those records. What may he do?
6. A paint manufacturer has changed his manufacturing process to one which emits a foul odor over a one-half-mile-radius residential neighborhood. What is the type of suit which would be filed on behalf of the neighborhood to get the company's plant to stop emitting the odor?
7. John, an owner, sues Henry, a builder, for the costs of repairs to a crack in the foundation. Henry wishes to have Sam, the foundation digger, and Alfred, the foundation pourer, included in the suit. Which process does he use to get them included?

   a. Cross-claim b. Interpleader c. Third party practice
8. Despite the absence of sufficient proof of negligence, out of sympathy for the defendant, the jury awards damages to the plaintiff. What remedy is available to the defendant against that kind of jury irresponsibility?
9. A jury verdict must always be unanimous in a civil case. True or False?
10. What are two senses of the expression, "burden of proof"?

CHAPTER 6
Evidence
Michael J. English

Evidence

Michael J. English

I. Introduction.

The rules of evidence constitute a set of standards that control the admission of proof at the trial of a lawsuit. Rules of evidence describe which proof is admissible in a trial and methods by which the proof shall be presented. Evidence or proof can include the testimony of witnesses, writings, physical objects, or anything else which is presented to a judge or jury for consideration during the trial.

The purpose of rules of evidence is to ensure that evidence is accurate and, in presentation, conforms to public policy. These rules also ensure that evidence is presented in the most expeditious manner.

In most states, the rules of evidence are derived from the application of principles of common law and statutes, although some states have enacted comprehensive statutory rules of evidence. *The Federal Rules of Evidence* constitute a codified, comprehensive outline of the rules relating to introduction of evidence in a Federal trial. Since these rules represent common applications of the rules of evidence throughout the United States and are usually indicative of modern trends, this outline will reflect the principles established by the *Federal Rules of Evidence*. The rules outlined below usually apply in both civil and criminal cases.

There is no series of rules which can be applied in all instances. Application of the rules of evidence varies, to some extent, from state to state; indeed the practical application of these rules may vary when they are applied by different individual judges in the same jurisdiction. Experience in participating in trials in a particular jurisdiction is necessary to determine specifically how the rules of evidence will be applied in that jurisdiction.

II. Types of evidence.

A. Direct or circumstantial. Direct evidence is any evidence which relates to facts in dispute and which is presented by testimonial or other proof which directly describes the facts. Direct evidence is communicated by those who have actual knowledge of a fact, for example, a witness to a crime.

Circumstantial evidence is evidence which relates to a fact in dispute by implying the existence of the fact, rather than directly establishing its existence. Normally, circumstantial evidence is evidence of the existence of a set of facts from which one could deduce another fact. (For example, testimony of a witness that he saw the defendant near the scene of the crime carrying a television set is circumstantial evidence on the issue of whether the defendant stole the set.)

B. Testimonial evidence. Oral evidence given by a witness under oath or affirmation.

C. Documentary evidence. Evidence in the form of written documents.

D. Real evidence. Concrete objects as distinguished from assertions by witnesses about objects or events. Real evidence would include any physical object relevant to an issue in the suit.

III. Requisites for admissibility.

A. General.

1. Relevance. Evidence is admissible only if it is relevant to an issue in the case. Evidence is relevant if it tends

to show that such an issue is more probably true or untrue than it would be without the evidence.

2. Materiality. Evidence is admissible only if it is material, that is, if it relates to one of the substantive issues in the case. (The distinction between materiality and relevance is difficult to make and in most instances, objections to the admissibility of evidence relate to relevance as a term which encompasses both concepts of relevance and materiality.)

3. Relevance outweighed by policy issues (See also section on Privilege, infra). In some cases, evidence which would be both relevant and material may still be excluded from evidence for certain policy reasons, usually because such information would be too likely to prejudice the jury in the case at hand. (See also Real evidence, infra.)

   The most common examples of such policy exclusions are:

   a. Evidence of the existence of liability insurance. (There seems to be a temptation among juries to be more likely to make awards, or to make higher awards, if they believe that an insurance company, rather than the defendant, is paying.)

   b. Evidence of subsequent remedial measures, for example, road repairs after an accident. (It is too easy to suggest an attitude of liability on the part of the defendant if he makes repairs after the fact; admissibility of such evidence would tend to discourage taking remedial measures in a timely manner.)

   c. Evidence of offers of settlement, that is, an offer by a party to pay an amount of money in lieu of trial. (Again, the jury may infer liability or self-blame if the defendant offers to settle. Other possibilities, including pure economic considerations, could lead to a settlement offer.)

   d. Evidence of similar acts of a party.

   e. Evidence of prior contracts or course of conduct.

   f. Evidence of habit, unless it can be shown that the habit is automatically, instinctively, or invariably adhered to in all similar situations.

B. Real Evidence. In order for real evidence to be admissible, it must not only be material and relevant; it also must have the following characteristics.

1. Authenticity. Such evidence must be proved authentic. Authentication can occur through the testimony of an individual who recognizes the real evidence or by proof establishing "chain of custody." Proof of chain of custody occurs when the proponent of the evidence proves that the object has been held in a substantially unbroken chain of possession without any chance of substitution. (For example, a custodial chain extending from seizure to testing to exhibiting of the sample must be established before evidence of drug possession will be admitted.)

   a. If the real evidence is an illustration (map, chart, drawing, etc.), it must be authenticated by testimonial evidence showing that it is a faithful reproduction of the object depicted. (In many cases, the parties will agree the evidence is authentic and eliminate the need for introducing evidence of authenticity at trial.)

2. Introduction of real evidence must not create a prejudice which outweighs its relevance. (For example, a gruesome picture of a murder victim may be held inadmissible because of its inflammatory nature when viewed by a jury. The jury may be so upset that the defendant might be inappropriately convicted.)

C. Documentary evidence. In addition to general rules of materiality and relevance, a document must be proved to be authentic in order to be admissible.

1. External evidence of authenticity may include:

   a. Evidence that the party against whom the writing is offered either has admitted its authenticity or has acted on the writing.

   b. Testimony of a witness who has seen the document executed or has heard it acknowledged.

   c. Verification of the genuineness of handwriting by expert testimony or by testimony of a lay person who has personal knowledge of the handwriting of the purported writer of the instrument.

d. Circumstantial evidence which leads to the inference that the document can be presumed genuine (for example, by showing the content of the writing and that it contains information known only to the purported author).

2. Self-authentication. Some documentary evidence is presumed to be admissible without formal proof of authenticity. Such evidence includes:
   a. Certified copies of public records.
   b. Official publications.
   c. Newspapers and periodicals.
   d. Trade inscriptions (signs, tags, or labels) indicating ownership, control, or origin.
   e. Commercial paper.

3. Best evidence rule. This rule states a preference for admission of original documents rather than copies or reproductions, when introduced to prove the terms of the documents. The rule is usually only applicable to legally operative or dispositive documents (contract, deed, will, etc.), or where knowledge of a witness is based on reading the document. Secondary evidence (copy) is generally admissible if authenticated and if the original is unavailable for any reason other than misconduct of the party presenting it.

4. Parole evidence. If an agreement (normally a contract) is reduced to writing, the writing is the only admissible evidence regarding the substance of the agreement. This rule is *not* applicable in certain situations.
   a. Where the agreement is incomplete or ambiguous on its face.
   b. Where allegations of any of the following are made:
      1) Mistake.
      2) Fraud.
      3) Duress.
      4) Lack of consideration.
      5) Illegality of subject matter.
      6) Non delivery of the contract service or the contract product.
   c. Where the terms of the written document have been modified subsequent to its execution.

D. Testimonial evidence.
  1. Competence.
     a. In order to testify, a witness must be competent. Competence means the witness has:
        1) The ability to observe (perception).
        2) The ability to remember (memory).
        3) The ability to communicate.
        4) An appreciation of the obligation of an oath.
        5) (Federal rules simply state that the witness must have personal knowledge of the subject of testimony. He must also declare, by oath or affirmation, that he will testify truthfully.)
     b. Some common disqualifications from testimony are:
        1) Infancy: There is no definite age; it depends on the intelligence and perception of the individual child.
        2) Insanity: This is not a blanket disqualification; to be disqualified one must be shown to have actual mental incapacity.
        3) Being judge or juror automatically disqualifies individuals from testifying in cases in litigation before them.

  2. Opinion testimony: Subjective opinions or inferred conclusions are generally inadmissible as evidence because such remarks are not the province of a witness. It is preferred that the jury form its own conclusions based on the facts. There are two major exceptions to this rule:
     a. Opinion by lay witness based on sense perceptions: A lay witness may express an opinion based on perceptions available to any lay person; these opinions are generally descriptive. (For example, a person appeared "elderly", "ill", "weak", et cetera.) Other permissible expressions of lay opinion would include:
        1) State of emotion, for example, "He was angry."
        2) Sense recognition, for example, "The box was heavy."
        3) Identity and likeness of appearance, voice or handwriting, for example, "The voice I heard was John's."

4) Estimated speed of a moving vehicle (if there is some showing of ability).
5) Value of the witness' own services.
6) Rational or irrational nature of another's conduct.
7) Apparent state of intoxication or sobriety.
  b. Expert testimony: An expert may give opinion testimony if the following prerequisites are met:
    1) The witness is qualified as an expert with special knowledge, skill, experience, education, or scientific, technical, or special qualities enabling him to provide better information relating to an issue than could a lay person.
    2) The subject matter must be appropriate for expert testimony, that is, the subject is of a nature which is beyond the ability of a lay person to form an informed opinion without specialized knowledge.
    3) The opinion can be expressed with reasonable certainty, that is, the opinion must be more than mere speculation or guess.
    4) The opinion is supported by a proper factual basis. The opinion must be formulated on the basis of the personal observation of the expert, or upon facts admitted into evidence and made known to the expert at the trial (the basis for the traditional "hypothetical question"). Under the Federal Rules, an opinion may be made on the basis of facts made known to the expert, not within his personal knowledge but of a nature usually relied upon by experts in the particular field. Examples are medical histories or reports of consultations. Under the Federal Rules, a factual basis need not be stated prior to giving the opinion, because the basis may be explored on cross-examination.
    5) Opinion on an ultimate issue. Traditional rules of evidence forbid opinion testimony on an ultimate issue, that is, an issue that enables resolution of the case. For example, "Did the defendant know right from wrong?" is an ultimate issue in an insanity defense to a criminal charge, because the answer to that question would establish the disposition of the

case. For a witness to express such opinions is regarded as an invasion of the responsibility of the jury.

One reason for this is that ultimate issues, as in the preceding example, are, in effect, value and policy questions for community decision-makers to decide. They should not be left to an expert witness to decide.

The rule has been repudiated in many jurisdictions and under the Federal rules.

  c. Character testimony. Testimony concerning the personal character of a party or witness is usually inadmissible, particularly if the purpose is to prove conduct. There are certain specific circumstances in which character evidence may be admissible:

    1) In civil cases, character evidence only may be admissible to prove character where character itself is an ultimate issue in the case, for example, defamation cases.

    2) In criminal cases, character evidence may be admissible if:

      a) Character evidence is introduced by the defendant to infer innocence. (If the defendant introduces evidence of good character, the prosecution may then introduce evidence of bad character).

      b) Character evidence is introduced by the defendant concerning the character of the victim, where conduct of the victim in conformity with his character would show the defendant's innocence, for example, showing the victim's own assaultive character in an assault case in which the defendant asserts self-defense.

      c) Character evidence in the nature of prior crimes may be introduced by the prosecution to show motive, intent, absence of mistake or accident, or a common scheme or plan in the criminal activities.

IV. Hearsay. In addition to the prerequisites for admissibility described above, evidence is inadmissible if it constitutes hearsay and fails to come within any exception to the hearsay rule.

A. Definition. "A statement, other than one made by the declarant while testifying at trial, offered in evidence to prove the truth of the matter asserted" (Fed. Rule 802). Examples of hearsay evidence are:

1. Oral statements made by another. (For example, the witness testifies that somebody else said ". . .".)

2. Writing. Any document written by someone other than the witness, offered in evidence to prove its content.

3. Conduct substituted for words. (For example, the witness testifies that somebody else "nodded yes.")

4. Application of the general rule against admission of hearsay has been extremely difficult and has resulted in complicated and confused interpretations nationwide.

B. Common exceptions to the hearsay rule. The following hearsay statements are usually admissible.

1. Prior testimony, or statements made under oath, where the declarant is presently unavailable.

2. Prior admissions of a party to the case concerning an issue in the case.

3. Declarations against interest, that is, statements by a person, now unavailable as a witness, which are against that person's interests. Examples would be pecuniary, proprietary, community reputation, legal, etc.

4. Dying declarations, where the declarant knew his death was imminent (usually admissible in homicide cases only).

5. Declarations of physical or mental condition; excited and contemporaneous utterances ("res gestae"), where the declarant makes the statements simultaneous with an incident.

6. Business records, admissible when the record offered in evidence is kept in the regular course of business

and is required to be kept to accomplish the business activity (The recording individual must have a duty to record.), for example, hospital medical records.

7. Past recollection recorded. When a witness relies on a written record for the substance of his testimony, the record itself is admissible.

8. Official records, for example, records of a public agency, birth certificates, etc.

9. Ancient documents. An authenticated document, if it is more than 20 years old (or of lesser age if the document affects an interest in property). For example, a deed or will, etc., is admissible.

10. A learned treatise, if relied upon by a testifying expert and if established as a reliable authority. (This rule is of recent vintage, and many courts still refuse admission of learned treatises.)

V. Methods of presentation of evidence.

A. Direct examination. The eliciting of testimony from a witness by counsel for the party who is the proponent of the witness. Direct examination must be limited to issues relevant and material to the case. Common problems encountered in the presentation of direct examination are:

1. Leading questions are not permissible. A leading question is any question which suggests an answer (for example, "Isn't it true that . . .").

2. Misleading or argumentative questions are impermissible. A question is misleading or argumentative if it assumes a fact not in evidence or a conclusion not supportable by the evidence, or if it tends to trap a witness (for example, "When did you stop beating your wife?").

3. Recitation of testimony from notes is impermissible. A witness may not testify directly from notes but must rely on personal recollection except in two circumstances.

a. Present recollections revived. A witness may refer to notes to refresh his memory, if the notes are identified and if the jury and the court are aware that the witness's memory is being refreshed. (When notes are used to refresh memory, those notes must be shown to opposing counsel for use on cross-examination.)

b. Past recollection recorded. A witness may read from notes if he has no independent recollection of the subject matter and if the notes are the witness's own. These notes are independently admissible.

4. Opinion testimony is impermissible, unless it comes within the opinion rules described previously.

5. Sometimes, a witness called on direct examination turns out to be a handicap to the attorney who has called the witness, usually because his testimony in court is different from what was expected by the attorney. In such a case, the witness might be qualified as a "hostile witness." To do so, the proponent of the witness must show the following:

a. The testimony is necessary.

b. One of these:
1) The witness has a bias or prejudice against the party.
2) The witness is clearly uncooperative.

c. If a witness, on direct examination, is qualified as a hostile witness, the attorney examining the witness may use leading questions.

6. Bolstering or accrediting a witness' testimony by eliciting prior consistent statements is impermissible. (The introduction of such testimony may occur on redirect examination, if the witness has been impeached.)

B. Cross-examination. This is the eliciting of testimony from a witness by counsel for the party against whom the witness was called to testify. The opportunity to cross-examine witnesses presented against a party is constitutionally required. Cross-examination is usually limited to issues raised on direct examination. Some common principles associated with the presentation of cross-examination are:

1. Leading questions are permissible.

2. Testimony may be elicited which reflects on the credibility of the witness, that is, impeachment testimony. All impeachment testimony must be preceded by a proper foundation, which adequately identifies the subject matter, time,, and place of the statements to be impeached. A witness may be impeached on cross-examination (or on direct examination if the witness is a hostile witness or has given true, surprise testimony) in the following ways:

a. Introduction of prior inconsistent statements by either:
   1) Confronting the witness with the statement, or
   2) Independently introducing the inconsistency through a rebuttal witness. (The inconsistency must be relevant to a direct issue in the case and not to a merely collateral matter.)

b. Introduction of testimony showing bias, prejudice, personal interest in the matter, or hostility.

c. Introduction of evidence of a prior conviction of a crime. (But that is only permissible where the crime is a felony which relates to the witness' truth or reliability.) Evidence of an acquittal of a crime is never admissible.

C. Objections. Non examining counsel may object to questions, based on any grounds which may challenge the admissibility of the evidence.

1. Objections are entered after the question is posed and before the answer is given. If it becomes apparent from the answer that the testimony is inadmissible, it can only be removed from the record by a motion to strike. (Of course, in a jury trial, such testimony is likely to have an impact on the jury even if it is stricken from the record.)

2. Objections must be specific, that is, "objection because . . ." in order to preserve the issue on appeal if overruled. If an objection is non specific and is sustained, it is presumed the court sustained the objection on permissible grounds.

3. Additional rules concerning objections are:
   a. A party who "opens the door" by offering evidence regarding a particular topic cannot object to another par-

ty's admitting evidence concerning the same topic by asserting irrelevance.

 b. Introduction of evidence concerning a portion of a particular "transaction" makes other evidence regarding the transaction admissible. (For example, if a portion of a conversation is admitted, the rest of the conversation may be admitted.)

 c. Offer of proof. Evidence which has not been allowed for admission because of objection can be preserved for an appeal by an "offer of proof," outside the hearing of the jury. An offer of proof can consist of placing the actual testimony in the record, a description of the evidence by the attorney offering it, or submission of an item of tangible evidence for the record which goes to the appellate court for its consideration.

D. Exclusion of witnesses. A witness may be prevented from observing the testimony of other witnesses upon request of a party. This is called the "rule against witnesses" and is strictly enforced. A party to the litigation, however, may never be excluded from the trial even if he will be a witness. An expert, whose presence is requested so that the testimony he observed can be included as the basis for opinion testimony, may not be excluded either.

VI. Judicial notice. Some forms of evidence need not be formally admitted at trial, if the court takes "judicial notice" of the fact or of the conclusion, based on its own unique knowledge or on general public knowledge. Judicial notice may be taken of:

A. Matters of common knowledge in the community, for example, that the White House is located in the District of Columbia.

B. Facts capable of certain verification in well-accepted sources, for example, that February 13, 1977, was a Sunday.

C. Well-established scientific principles or testing techniques, for example, that an object filled with air will float.

D. Law applicable to the case. Judicial notice of applicable legal principles is fundamental to the judicial system.

VII. Privilege. The importance of the intimacy and trust in certain relationships between people has been recognized as being so crucial that policy considerations dictate against compelling a party to testify about information derived from that relationship. Thus, even if such testimony would be admissible under all other rules of evidence, it is inadmissible on the sole grounds that it is derived from a special relationship. Note, however, the holder of the privilege is always able to waive the privilege.

Privilege is established either by common law principles or by statutory enactment. The following are the relationships most commonly protected by testimonial privilege:

A. Attorney-client. A privilege held by the client, which prevents an attorney from being compelled to testify about information given the attorney by the client. This privilege is not the same as the work-product rule. (Work-product relates to immunity from discovery procedures described in Chapter 5, Civil Procedure.) In order for the privilege to be exercised, the following criteria must be met:

1. The relationship must exist at the time the communication is made.

2. The communication must be confidential, that is, not intended by the client to be communicated to a third party.

3. The communication must be made during a professional consultation.

B. Physician-patient. A privilege held by the patient, not by the physician, which prevents a physician from being compelled to testify about information given to the physician by the patient.

1. In order for the privilege to be exercised, the following criteria must be met:
   a. The patient actually must be seeking treatment when the communication is made.
   b. The information must be necessary for the treatment.
2. The privilege is not recognized in any of the following situations:
   a. The patient puts his physical or mental condition in issue.
   b. The case is a criminal case.
   c. The communication is in aid of wrongdoing.
   d. The case involves a dispute between the physician and the patient.

C. Husband-wife. A privilege held by either a husband or a wife, which prevents the other from being compelled to testify about communications between the two. In order for the privilege to exist, the following criteria must be met:

1. In criminal cases no spouse can testify against another. More than privilege, this is a matter of legal incapacity and can be exercised by either spouse. For the privilege to be exercised in a criminal case, there must be a valid marriage and the communication must have been made during the marriage.
2. In all other cases, the privilege may be execised if a valid marriage exists and the communication was intended to be confidential between spouses.

D. Other privileges. The following privileges also exist:

1. Clergyman-penitent. An absolute privilege where the communication is made when the clergyman acts in the capacity of spiritual advisor.
2. Accountant-client. A statutory privilege found in some jurisdictions. It is similar to the attorney-client privilege.
3. Psychologist, psychotherapist, or social worker and client. A statutory privilege adopted in many states which

applies the principles of the physician-patient privilege to these relationships.

4. Journalists' privilege. A privilege, also known as a "shield law," which protects a journalist from being compelled to identify his sources. This privilege has been reduced by recent Supreme Court decisions.

5. Governmental privileges. Two types:
   a. Identity of informer in criminal cases. The government cannot be compelled to disclose his identity, unless the informer has potentially exculpatory information. Then, it must be disclosed, or no evidence from the informer is admissible.
   b. Official information concerning internal operations of government, usually, but not always, limited to national security or foreign relations, is privileged.

Reference

Federal Rules: Civil Procedure; Evidence; Appellate Procedure. West Publishing, St. Paul, 1982.

Questions on Chapter 6, Evidence

1. Under the Federal Rules of Evidence, an expert witness must give the factual basis before he can give an opinion. True or False?
2. A hospital medical record is inadmissible because it constitutes hearsay. True or False?
3. Under the Best Evidence Rule, a photocopy of a document is never admissible in court. True or False?
4. Oral testimony may be presented regarding the substance of a written agreement if the plaintiff alleges fraud. True or False?
5. May an attorney ever ask leading questions to a witness he, himself, has summoned?
6. Peter is the defendant in an auto accident case. Would this statement by him be admissible: "I was a passenger in George's car. As soon as he hit the truck, George said, 'Oh, am I dumb! I didn't even see him coming because of that windshield wiper.' "
7. Dr. Smith is testifying as plaintiff's expert witness regarding his examination of Mr. Jones. He brings his clinical record with him, and refers to it for the exact value of one of the laboratory findings. Defense counsel, who has already seen Dr. Smith's official report, demands to see the entire raw clinical record. Must Dr. Smith comply?
8. In a trial, the judge has refused to allow certain materials to be admitted as evidence for the jury's consideration. Counsel attempting to introduce the materials intends to appeal if he loses the case. What can he do in order to let the appellate court know about the materials and their roles in his case?
9. A psychiatrist refuses to testify about a patient's mental state even though the mental state is at issue and the patient wishes for him to testify. May the psychiatrist refuse on the basis of physician-patient privilege?
10. Joseph is being sued for slander by Arthur. Joseph's wife, Catherine, was present when Joseph made the slanderous remarks to her and to third persons, now living outside the country. Will she be allowed to testify about the remarks?

CHAPTER 7

Torts

Michael L. Perlin

Torts

by Michael L. Perlin

> "Civil liability . . . is a redistribution of . . . loss. Sound policy lets losses lie where they fall, except where a special reason can be shown for interference."
> —Justice Oliver Wendell Holmes

I. Definition.

In broad contour, a tort is a civil wrong (not including contractual violations) which is usually remediable by an award of monetary damages. It is not a crime (although some criminal activity may also be tortious: for example, sexual attack may give rise to criminal rape charges and civil assault charges); it does not arise out of a contractual relationship (although many relationships which have their genesis in a contract may lead to tort actions: for example, a sales contract may lead to a tort claim if there is a warranty breach); it usually does not involve governmental action (although there is a discrete body of tort law dealing with special questions of governmental liability and immunity), and it is usually not concerned with strict property rights concepts (except for cases such as those involving an unlawful taking of land or an unlawful conversion of goods, for example). Prosser uses a broad definition: "A tort is a wrong from which compensable harm has resulted, stemming from some sort of breach of duty owed (either explicitly or implicitly) by one party to the other."[1]

II. Negligence: First tort category.*

A. History: Negligence came into prominence as an independent basis of tort liability in the early 1800's, emerging with the technological expansions of the Industrial Revolution. Winfield writes: "Early railway trains, in particular, were notable neither for speed nor for safety. They killed any object from a Minister of State to a wandering cow, and this naturally reacted on the law."[2]

B. Basic elements. In all cases, there must be proof of the following in relation to the defendant:

1. Act (or omission).
2. Duty of care.
3. Breach.
4. Causation.
5. Damage suffered.

C. Basic elements (expanded).

1. Act (or omission). The actor (defendant) must do something (or not do something which he is under an affirmative duty to do).
2. Duty of care. There must be a legal obligation requiring the defendant to conform to a certain conduct code so as to insulate others from unreasonable risks.
   a. The standard of duty is that of the "reasonable person of ordinary prudence"**or what such a person would have done under similar circumstances.

---

*Traditionally discussed second, but of greater importance in this overview.
**Reasonable man of ordinary prudence. "An ideal, a standard . . . who invariably looks where he is going and is careful to examine the immediate foreground before he executes a leap or bound; who neither star-gazes nor is lost in meditation when approaching trap-doors or the margin of a dock . . . who never mounts a moving omnibus . . . and will inform himself of the history and habits of a dog before administering a caress . . . who uses nothing except in moderation, and even while he flogs his child is meditating on the golden mean. (He) stands like a monument in our Courts of Justice vainly appealing to his fellow-citizens to order their lives after his own example. (In all that mass of authorities which bears upon this branch of the law there is no single mention of a reasonable woman.)"—Alan Patrick Herbert

1) An objective standard—not what an individual defendant may have believed, but how an average, reasonable person would have acted.

2) Even though the type of care may vary with circumstances, the test stays the same: what the average reasonable person would have done under those circumstances. Even if the situation is an emergency, the standard is how the reasonable person would have acted if faced with that emergency.

   a) Thus, the standard is always subject to proof of all the attendant circumstances. (For example, were the facts such as would lead a reasonable person to assume that an emergency actually did exist?)

   b) In determining the standard of duty, evidence as to such matters as custom or compliance with statute may be admissible, but is not conclusive. Example: In at least one case, the defendant's manufacture of drugs in accordance with governmental regulations would not be enough to absolve negligence if the regulations were minimal and a reasonable person would have exercised greater care under those circumstances.[3]

   c) Application to special groups.

     1)) Children are generally held to a standard of the "average, reasonable child" of the same age and intelligence, except when they engage in an adult activity (for example, operation of a power boat).

     2)) A physically disabled person's conduct is judged by the reasonableness standard in the light of the person's knowledge of his infirmity; thus, an epileptic who has not taken medication may be negligent in choosing to drive a car.

     3)) Interestingly, lack of mental capacity is usually not factored into this equation, so that mentally deficient adults are generally judged by the average reasonable person standard. Although a handful of cases have suggested that mental deficiency may be so gross as to prevent a person from comprehending or avoiding danger, the reasonable person standard still predominates.

4)) Of special interest. When an actor provides service in a recognized field or profession, he is held—at minimum—to the standard of care customarily exercised by members of that trade or profession. A rule of thumb: If the work calls for special skills, the actor must not only excercise reasonable care, but he must possess a standard minimum of special knowledge in the specialty.[4] At one time, a determination of that "standard minimum" was governed by the "locality rule"—that a practitioner's skill need only be as high as other practitioners in the same community. This rule has been progressively eroded, and a national standard of care is now usually applied to cases involving medical specialties. "If the [locality] rule is not dead, it is in its death throes."[5]

b. To whom is the duty owed? At the least, to anyone toward whom a reasonable person would have foreseen injury as a result of his conduct. Beyond this, however, there are two divergent theories, both stemming from the famous Palsgraf case,[6] the most written about case in tort history. In Palsgraf, the facts were these. X was running to catch a train operated by the defendant railroad company. When the defendant's employee helped X to board, he dislodged a package, which fell on the rails. The package contained fireworks, which exploded, and the explosion's concussive force overturned scales located at another section of the platform. The scales fell on the plaintiff (Ms. Palsgraf) and injured her.

1) In the majority of decisions regarding to whom duty is owed, it has been held that the defendant owes a duty of care to anyone who might suffer injury as a proximate result of a breach of duty.

2) The minority of decisions have held that the defendant's duty of care is only to persons within that "zone of danger" in which a reasonable person would have foreseen a risk of harm to the plaintiff.

3) The opinion of the court majority in deciding the

Palsgraf case was that of the minority of the totality of decisions on the point. Since in the court's view the defendant had no duty to her, she lacked the basis for a tort suit.

3. Breach: If there is a duty of care, there must be evidence that the defendant breached the duty (by doing something or by failing to do something) which exposed the plaintiff to an unreasonable risk of harm.

   Proof of breach may come from direct evidence, from circumstantial evidence, or in some cases, through the use of a legal doctrine called res ipsa loquitur* ("the thing speaks for itself").

4. Causation.
   a. Defendant's conduct must be the "cause in fact" of the plaintiff's injuries. If the plaintiff would not have been injured "but for" the defendant's act, the act is regarded as *the* (or at least *a*) cause of the injury.
   b. After "causation in fact" is established, the question remains as to whether defendant's actions were the "proximate cause" of the injuries, that is, the legally responsible causation nearest in time before the injury.
      1) Proximate (and legally responsible) cause requires foreseeability of outcome. This issue arises only after causation is established.
         a) "Thin-skulled plaintiff" cases. A person with an exceptionally thin skull was bumped by the defendant and died from the fall. It was unanimously held that the defendant was liable for the full extent of the plaintiff's injuries. "A defendant must take a plaintiff as he finds him."[7]
         b) Authority is split on the fact pattern where one type of injury might be foreseeable but another injury occurs. For example, an oil tanker crew negligently allowed oil to overflow in a harbor, and it was clearly foreseeable that oil would do minor damage to the plaintiff's pilings; not then foreseeable was that the oil had a peculiarly high

---

*See Glossary.

flash point which caused it to ignite when contacted by a type of waste material commonly found near docks. The plaintiff sued after his dock burned down.

It was held by the court that this was not a foreseeable risk, and the defendant was not liable.[8]

When owners of ships docked at the same wharf sued in a similar circumstance six years later, the same court found that the defendants should have been aware of the ignition risk of the oil. Since the defendants' actions in allowing oil to spill had no special justification, they could not justify neglecting even the slight risk in question.[9] (This latter decision balances magnitude of risk and gravity of harm against utility of conduct, a formula which appears to be the majority formulation at this point. This relates to the notion as to how a reasonably prudent person would act.)

2) Proximate cause and intervening causation: Is a defendant liable for an injury to which he substantially contributed when the injury itself is brought about by a latter cause of independent origin for which he is not directly responsible?[10] Key questions: Was it reasonably foreseeable at the time of the defendant's acts that the subsequently intervening force would be involved and that the final result would occur?[11] Should the defendant be relieved of liability for a chain of causation he initiated?[12]

   a) A typical example: The defendant injures the plaintiff; the plaintiff is hospitalized, and harmful negligent hospital care ensues. The defendant is held liable for the results of the medical treatment under the theory that it should have been reasonably foreseeable that the plaintiff would have to be hospitalized as a result of the defendant's negligent action, and that the possibility of receiving negligent care while hospitalized is a "normal risk" incurred in hospitalization.[13] Interestingly, this rule has been extended to cover damages for pain and suffering even resulting from proper

nonnegligent medical treatment which was neces-
sitated by the defendant's original tortious acts.[14]

b) Similarly, where the defendant's actions injure the
plaintiff only by rendering him weaker and, thus,
increasing his susceptibility to disease, the plaintiff can recover for the expenses of such an illness.[15]

c) On the other hand, if the defendant can foresee
neither damage, direct injury, nor risk from intervening causes, he will not be considered negligent, as in a case where a town could not and did
not anticipate that an unexpected huge rainfall
would flood the street on which plaintiff injured
himself,[16] or where the defendant blocked the
road, causing the plaintiff to take a detour route,
where an airplane fell on the plaintiff.[17] In cases
such as these, where both intervening force and
result are unforeseeable, the defendant will not be
held liable.

5. Damages: The final link of the chain. After negligence
and causation are established, the plaintiff must prove
he suffered some damage in order for the defendant to
be liable. There must be a showing of actual damage
in all negligence cases.

a. General damages. Costs may be assessed for pain and
suffering or for disability resulting from the injury; this
may include future disabilities as well.

b. Special damages. Recovery is allowed for out-of-pock-
et, specific expenses, such as medical bills, loss of income, diminution of future earning capacity, etc.
(Inflation may be factored in for future losses if it is
expected that the disability will continue for many
years).

c. Punitive damages. Not applicable in negligence cases,
except where a state has enacted a specific statute covering specific areas. (For example, in drunken-driving-
caused injuries, the defendant's driving may be
characterized as such "reckless conduct" as to justify
the imposition of punitive damages.)

d. Responsibilities of the plaintiff.
1) The plaintiff must "mitigate"; that is, he must reasonably attempt to minimize loss or injury. (For example, if he unreasonably refuses to submit to
medical care after an injury caused by the defendant's negligence, he cannot recover for that additional disfigurement which might have been avoided
had he sought medical care.[18])
2) Although the plaintiff may usually make full recovery, notwithstanding any independent insurance he
might have (on the theory that the defendant's liability shouldn't be lessened by the plaintiff's prudence), this has been criticized as allowing a
windfall, or double recovery. Thus, most insurance
policies now have automatic "subrogation clauses."
Where a plaintiff's own insurance company has paid
benefits to the plaintiff, any money won in a negligence case is assigned to the insurance company.
This assignment is usually limited to special damages and not the more intangible "pain and suffering" general damages.

D. Special duties. Additional duties supplementary to the
general duty of care may be imposed on a defendant.
1. Statutory duties (usually involving motor vehicle cases,
but now expanding: for example, an anti-discrimina-
tion law may specifically create a duty not to discrimi-
nate in housing rental). There are two primary issues.
a. Did the legislature intend to prevent the type of injury
suffered by the plaintiff?
b. Was the plaintiff a member of the class of persons
sought to be protected? In most jurisdictions, if a defendant has violated such a statute, "yes" answers to
the two questions will constitute a conclusive presumption of both a duty and its breach*. Some courts, how-

---

*The situation is termed "negligence per se." A plaintiff does not have to
provide any of the ordinary evidence used to establish negligence, for example, duty owed, breach, etc. The mere act of violation of the statute enables
a negligence suit to go forward.

ever, hold that it is merely some evidence of negligence or that it raises a rebuttable presumption. In any event, causation and damage must still be shown for recovery.

2. Care of the public. There will often be imposed a separate greater standard of care, demanding "the highest caution," when a party is charged with the care of members of the public. The principle is usually discussed in the context of "common carriers," that is, public conveyances for passengers or property. Persons operating such conveyances "must always choose the course of action least likely to expose passengers to harm."[19] The principle also applies in the context of persons charged with physical custody of a minor or of incompetent person. (So-called "guest statutes" have been enacted to limit recovery in similar-in-principle automobile passenger versus driver suits, in order to thwart collusion for the purpose of defrauding insurance companies, but such laws are often struck down as violative of equal protection.)

3. Duty to control others. In some instances, a defendant will be held liable for failing to control a third person whom he had power to control; someone who can control another is seen as "vicariously liable," and responsibility for the third person's act is imputed to the controlling individual.
   a. Master/servant cases. The doctrine of "respondeat superior" generally applies. An employer is vicariously liable for any tortious act commited by his employee within the scope of the employment.[20] Problems have often arisen in hospital settings. The appropriate test is the employer's right to control the performance of the employee's duties. Usually, the rule of "apparent agency" applies. If a hospital leads a patient to believe a professional person is its employee, it may be held liable for his negligence.[21] Nurses and residents clearly fall into this category.
   b. On the other hand, one who engages an independent contractor is not liable for that party's negligence, on

the theory that the employer has no right to control the manner in which the independent contractor executes his work.[22] This theory has been used in the so-called "borrowed servant" cases. A hospital employee may temporarily become an employee under the control and supervision of the attending doctor, who is an independent contractor, thus making the attending doctor liable and insulating the hospital from liability. This, however, is a dying defense, and generally, hospitals are being held liable under the respondeat superior theory for torts of all employees.[23]

Closely related is the "captain of the ship" doctrine. Older cases had held, for instance, that the surgeon in charge of an operation was the "captain of the ship" and, thus, responsible for the negligence of all others working with him in the operating room. More recently, however, this doctrine has been discarded, and, on the theory that a negligent intern can be, at the same time, an agent of both the operating surgeon and the hospital, both may be found negligent.[24]

4. The question of a duty to aid in emergent situations is an area in which the majority of the decisions have been termed, "revolting to any moral sense."[25] The law has generally refused to recognize the "moral obligation of common decency and common humanity to come to the aid of another human being".[26] For example, an expert swimmer who sees another drowning is not required to attempt to save the drowner.[27] Similarly, doctors have been held to be under no duty to answer the cry of a dying person.[28] At least one state (Vermont) has enacted a statute making one liable to aid another recognized to be in great peril, if such involvement would not greatly endanger the other, however.

When such "non feasance" (doing nothing) shifts to "misfeasance" (doing something wrong), though, there may be a basis for liability. (For example, when a person involves himself in such an emergency situation, he is under a duty to avoid any affirmative act which would worsen the situation.) Thus, to encourage passing physicians to assist the injured, many states have passed "good Samaritan statutes," exempting doctors rendering emergency aid from all liability.

E. Defenses against negligence suits.
  1. Contributory negligence.
    a. Definition. Conduct on the plaintiff's part which both:
      1) Contributes to the suffered harm.
      2) Falls below the standard of appropriate self-protection.
    b. There is always a duty of self-protection, and it can even be violated by an unreasonable lack of action on plaintiff's part when confronted with danger.
    c. The plaintiff's conduct, like the defendant's, is measured by reasonable person standards. What would the average person have done under similar circumstances? In an emergency, the question is: what would a reasonable person have done in such an emergency? Thus, when faced with an immediate peril, in an attempt to avoid the peril, a plaintiff's behavior may be riskier than it would ordinarily be. Such risk-taking would not constitute contributory negligence.
    d. Under common law and older cases, any contributory negligence on the plaintiff's part, no matter how slight, was a total bar to recovery for the defendant's negligence. Prosser's characterization of the doctrine as "a chronic invalid who will not die,"[29] seems apt.
      1) Exceptions.
        a) "Last clear chance" doctrine. The plaintiff's contributory negligence won't bar recovery if the defendant had a "last clear chance" before the accident to avoid it and did not do so. The classic case involves a plaintiff who left his ass fettered in the highway and a defendant who drove into it. The court held that the plaintiff could recover, notwithstanding his own negligence, if the defendant, by the exercise of proper care, could have avoided injuring the animal.[30]

    b) If the plaintiff's negligence places him in a position from which he cannot extricate himself, and if the defendant discovers the danger while there is time to prevent it, but nevertheless, fails to do so, the plaintiff can still recover under the doctrine of the "discovered peril."[31]

    c) If the plaintiff is not helpless, but negligently fails to discover the extent of his peril, and if the defendent remains negligent subsequent to learning of the plaintiff's dangerous inattentiveness, most courts allow the plaintiff to recover under the doctrine of "inattentive peril."[32]

  2) Recent cases have begun to address the issue of effect of mental incapacity on contributory negligence issues. The emerging trend is to hold that the plaintiff should be held to exercise only that degree of care for his own safety consonant "with the faculties and capacities bestowed upon him by nature."[33]

2. In an effort to limit some of the more draconian applications of the contributory negligence rule, most states have adopted a theory of "comparative negligence." This allows the plaintiff to recover in direct proportion to the defendant's fault. Thus, if the plaintiff suffered $100,000 worth of loss but was, himself 25 percent at fault, he can collect 75 percent of the $100,000 loss, or $75,000.

  a. Although such apportioning may seem excessively Solomonic, it reduces the harshness of the contributory negligence doctrine in a more equitable fashion.

  b. There are two formulas for assessment of comparative liability:

    1) "Pure" comparative negligence. The plaintiff recovers a fraction of his damages even where his negligence is more than 50 percent of the fault.

    2) "Partial" comparative negligence. The plaintiff can only recover if his negligence is less than 50 percent of the fault.

  c. Court decisions are mixed in cases involving multiple defendants, each of whom is partially at fault. In some states, in order to recover, the plaintiff's negligence must be less than any individual defendant's; in others, less than the sum of all defendants' negligences; in yet others, less than 50 percent of the total negligence.

3. Assumption of risk. If the plaintiff, either expressly or implicitly, consents to take his chances of harm from a specific risk created by the defendant, he is held to have assumed the risk, and recovery for negligence is barred. There are two key elements:
   a. The plaintiff must have recognized and understood the particular risk or danger.
   b. The plaintiff must have voluntarily chosen to expose himself to the risk.
      1) A typical example: A person attending a baseball game assumes the risk that he may be hit by a foul ball, a well-known risk involved in attendance at such a sporting event.
      2) On the other hand, where a patient entering a hospital had to sign a waiver on an admission form of all claims against the hospital or doctors for any subsequent malpractice claims, a court held that the patient had not assumed the risk. Such a blanket waiver of a right to sue was held unenforceable as contrary to public policy; the patient had no real bargaining power nor any real oppportunity to negotiate the admission form's terms.[34]

F. Other variables and trial issues.
   1. The burden of proof is on the plaintiff by the standard of the preponderance of the evidence.
   2. Res ipsa loquitur. In certain types of cases, it may be presumed that the defendant was at fault by the very fact that a particular harm has occured, that is, "the act speaks for itself."
      a. There are three basic elements.
         1) The event must be a kind which ordinarily does not occur absent negligence. (For example, the plaintiff swallows a rusty nail found in the defendant's canned vegetable.)

2) The event must be caused by an agency or an instrumentality exclusively within the defendant's control. (For example, the plaintiff is hit by a sign falling from a defendant-owned building.)
3) The event must not have been due to any voluntary action on the plaintiff's part.

b. Significance to health professionals. Although expert testimony is usually required to show negligence in malpractice cases, if the occurrence is so bizarre or the error so glaring that a lay person is competent to pass judgment and to conclude that such things don't happen if proper skill and care are exercised (for example, a surgical instrument left in the patient's abdomen after surgery), res ipsa may apply, and expert testimony may not be needed. This has been extended to cases where a plaintiff is unable to show how or by whom he has been injured, as long as the defendants owed a duty to guard against such injury. For example, res ipsa was applied where the plaintiff awoke from surgery deeply disfigured, even though he could not show the manner in which the injuries occurred (as he was under anesthesia at the time of the injury). The court reasoned that inferences could be drawn that each defendant was responsible for the plaintiff's injuries.[35]

3. Insurance: There has been a steady shift from third party insurance to first party ("no-fault") insurance in the automobile negligence field. It is likely that in the future no-fault concepts will be expanded to other areas in order to reduce the expenses of litigation.

III. Intentional torts. Second tort category.

A. Background. There is a definite tendency in the law to impose great responsibility on a defendant where the purpose of his conduct was to do harm or the conduct was morally wrong. The intent need not be specifically hostile nor desirous of doing specific harm; the intent in question is an intent to bring about a result which will invade another's interests in a way the law will not sanction.

An intentional act is voluntary. The concept of intent extends beyond the act's immediate consequences and includes those consequences which the actor ought reasonably to foresee will follow from what he does. (For example, if X wants to kill A and blows up a car which A, B, C, and D are riding, for tort purposes, X intended to kill B, C, and D as well.)

B. Basic types.
1. Intentional torts against the person.
   a. Battery. The concept of battery stems from one's interest in freedom from others' intentional and unpermitted contacts with one's person.
      1) Elements necessary to prove battery. An act by the defendant; intent; "harmful or offensive" touching; causation (but not necessarily actual harm).
      2) The defendant's act must be positive and affirmative.
      3) Key. Absence of consent on the plaintiff's part to the touching.
      4) "Harmful." Any infliction of pain, injury, or impairment of any bodily organ or function. "Offensive." Any touching of the plaintiff, or something associated with his person, which would offend "a reasonable person's sense of personal dignity."[36]
      5) Damages. If there is no actual harm, nominal ($1) damages may be awarded for symbolic value. If harm is suffered, damages may be awarded.
      6) Cases stemming from performance of unconsented-to operations, treatments, surgical procedures, etc., often are couched in battery terminology. A key question is whether the plaintiff gave "informed consent."
   b. Assault. The notion stems from a person's interest in freedom from apprehension of a harmful or offensive contact. (No actual contact is necessary.) Any act which might "excite an apprehension" of a battery may be an

assault,[37] for example, shaking a fist or aiming a weapon at another.

1) Elements necessary to prove assault. Intent; apprehension; causation.
2) Words alone aren't enough.
3) The defendant's act must amount to a threat to use force, and there must be an apparent ability and opportunity to carry out the threat immediately.
4) The plaintiff needn't actually be frightened, merely placed in apprehension. Moreover, it is sufficient if the defendant had the actual or apparent ability to inflict the touching. The test is a subjective one: What did the plaintiff himself believe, not what a reasonable person in the plaintiff's position would have believed.
5) Damages. The plaintiff must show apprehension. If emotional distress or physical injury are suffered, they are recoverable.

c. False imprisonment. The concept protects personal interest in freedom from restraint of movement.

1) Elements. An act by the defendant; intent; confinement; causation.
2) "Imprisonment" doesn't necessarily mean incarceration, but, rather, restraint of the plaintiff by the defendant for a period of time within boundaries fixed by the defendant.
3) Restraint may be by physical barriers, by depriving the plaintiff of his ability to leave, or by threats which intimidate the plaintiff into complying with defendant's orders. The plaintiff needn't resist by incurring the risk of physical violence, but the restraint must be against plaintiff's will. The plaintiff must also be contemporaneously aware of his confinement.
4) Damages. No special damages need be shown (The tort is complete upon the confinement.), but if damages are sustained, they are recoverable.

2. Intentional torts against property.
   a. Trespass to land.
      1) Elements. An act; intent; intrusion upon land pos-

sessed by the plaintiff or to which the plaintiff is entitled to possession; causation.

   b. Trespass to chattels.*

   1) Elements. An act; intent; invasion of a chattel interest possessed by the plaintiff or to which the plaintiff is entitled to possession (Trespass includes theft, destruction, and barring rightful access.); causation.

   c. Conversion** of chattels.

   1) Elements. An act; intent; invasion of a chattel interest possessed by the plaintiff or to which the plaintiff is entitled to immediate possession (Conversion includes dispossession, unauthorized use, etc.); causation.

C. Defenses against intentional tort suits.

  1. Defenses against intentional personal tort suits.

    a. Privilege. The defendant acted to further an interest of such social import that the interest is entitled to protection even at the plaintiff's expense (for example, warrantless arrests).

    b. Mistake. Although the act was voluntary and the result was intended, the defendant acted on an erroneous, but reasonable and good faith belief that existing circumstances justified the conduct. (For example, the defendant enters on land believing it to be his own.)

    c. Consent. Absence of consent is part of the definition of all intentional torts; thus, consent (a willingness that the act should occur) will negate liability.

     1) Consent can be actual, apparent (implied by conduct), or implied by law. (For example, an unconscious patient "consents" to surgery where an immediate decision is necessary, where there is no reason to believe the person wouldn't consent, and where a reasonable person would consent.)

     2) Consent is not a defense, however, when it results from the plaintiff's mistake as to the nature or con-

---

*A chattel is an article of property not fixed to land. It would include anything from a diamond ring to a diesel locomotive.
**A conversion occurs when a nonowner of a chattel acts as if he owns it, for example, using it, eating it, selling it, etc.

sequences of the intrusion (for example, in medical treatment cases),[38] or when consent is obtained because of duress, fraud, illegality, or incapacity.
  d. Self-defense. An attacked person can take reasonable steps to prevent harm under conditions like these:
    1) There is no time to resort to law.
    2) The actor is in reasonable apprehension of immediate harm.
    3) The actor uses reasonable means of defense.
  e. Defense of others. Like self-defense, this is valid where sanctioned by recognized social usage or by "commonly accepted standards of decent conduct."[39]
  2. Defenses against intentional property tort suits.
    a. Defense of property. Interest in peaceful possession or enjoyment justifies protection by self-help where there is no time to resort to law.
    b. Privileged invasion of another's land to reclaim chattels: If the defendant's goods are on the plaintiff's property because the plaintiff has unlawfully misappropriated them, the defendant may enter the plaintiff's property in order to reclaim them.

IV. Strict liability: Third tort category.

  A. Overview. In some instances, a defendant may be held liable—even if he is neither charged with any moral wrongdoing nor accused of departing in any way from a reasonable standard of intent or care—simply because an accident did, in fact, happen. This theory of strict liability, usually involving abnormally dangerous conditions or activities, is recognition of a doctrine "that the defendant's enterprise, while it will be tolerated by the law, must pay its way."[40] The policy is usually applied where the defendant's activity is unusual and abnormal in the community, and where the threatened danger is unduly great even when the enterprise is being conducted with every possible precaution. The rationale for liability is the defendant's intentional behavior in exposing others to risk.

1. The concept was traditionally employed in such areas as liability arising from harm from uncaged wild animals or from fires set during a dry season.

2. General rule. One who maintains a dangerous condition or activity on his premises, or who engages in an activity involving a high risk of harm to the person or property of another, may be liable for the harm it causes, even if he has exercised the utmost care to prevent such harm.

B. Factors to consider.

   1. Whether the activity involves a high degree of risk or harm.
   2. The gravity of the risk.
   3. Whether the risk can be eliminated.
   4. Whether the activity is a matter of common usage.
   5. Whether the activity is appropriate to the place where it is being carried on.
   6. The value of the activity to the community.[41]

C. Extent of liability.

   1. Scope of duty. To make safe the condition in question, consequently, liability is imposed for injury regardless of fault. Duty is owed to "foreseeable plaintiffs"; harm must arise from the "normally dangerous propensity" of the condition in question.
   2. Proximate cause. In the majority of opinions, the same rule is applied as in negligence cases. A minority of opinions allows for no absolution from liability under any circumstances.

D. Defenses.

   1. The voluntary assumption of a known risk may prevent recovery (for example, getting clawed after teasing a leopard).
   2. Contributory negligence does not apply unless it actually caused the accident in question.

V. Special tort situations.

A. Background. Some torts have multiple bases of liability. The same injury may be actionable on several theories, depending on the specific nature of the defendant's conduct.

B. Products liability. The responsibility of a supplier of a product for physical harm that occurs to a person or to property because of an encounter with the product may be based on theories of intentional act (rarely), of negligence (usually), or of strict liability (recent in development), the latter arising where there is a "grave risk of harm" in placing such a product in the "stream of commerce."[42] The concept may apply variously, to sellers, retailers, distributors, lessors, and manufacturers of defective components.
Key issues include:

1. The plaintiff's and the defendant's relationships to the defective product.

2. The nature of the product defect.

3. The degree of the defendant's fault.

4. The type of damage suffered by the plaintiff.

5. Available defenses.[43]

C. Defamation. This is defined where matter, capable of defamatory meaning and understood as referring to the plaintiff, in a sense tending to lower his reputation in the estimation of a significant minority of the community where published or involving some manner of disgrace, is published by the defendant to a third person and causes damages.

1. "Libel." A defamation published in writing.

2. "Slander." A defamation uttered orally.

3. "Defamation per se." The defendant is liable even if no special damages are shown by the plaintiff, if the published material tends to expose the plaintiff to public disgrace or ridicule, etc.

4. Frequently, there is a conflict between the First Amendment (freedom of speech) and defamation, when a person believes he has been injured by a statement in the media.[44]

D. Infliction of emotional harm. This tort may be negligent or intentional.

   1. Negligent infliction. Proof requires a breach of the duty to exercise due care not to subject others to a foreseeable risk of physical injury through impact or threat. If impact or injury occurs from such negligence, the resulting emotional distress is compensible in tort damages.

   2. Intentional infliction. Proof requires extreme or outrageous conduct by the defendant. Such conduct must be intended to cause, and does cause, severe emotional distress. Recovery may be allowed even if there are no specific physical injuries.

E. Right of privacy. Proof that the plaintiff performed an act which seriously and unreasonably invaded the plaintiff's expectations of his "right to be left alone," (for example, public disclosure of private facts, unauthorized commercial use of his name, placing him in a bad light through political "dirty tricks," etc.) as a result of which plaintiff suffers (at least) emotional distress and mental anguish. Defenses may include newsworthiness (where there is a legitimate public interest) or constitutional privilege.

F. Malicious prosecution. This tort involves the institution of a criminal prosecution by the defendant against the plaintiff. The proceeding must have terminated in favor of the plaintiff, and no probable cause for the proceeding can have been found. The proceeding must have been instituted for reasons of malice. ("Malice" in this context means to give vent to motives of ill will.)

   1. In some areas, for example, to discourage bringing frivolous malpractice suits, this has been recently ex-

panded to include areas of wrongful civil proceedings. Usually, in proving actual damages, the aggrieved plaintiff will be held to a standard similar to that for malicious prosecution, however.

G. Interference with economic relations. Liability may be imposed for the defendant's intentional interference with the plaintiff's existing or prospective economic relations with third parties. This tort may be found when the defendant actively interferes with an existing contractual relationship.

H. Misrepresentation. Sort of a catchall, consisting of a knowingly false representation made by the defendant with the intent of inducing the plaintiff to act in reliance on the false representation. The misrepresentation has to result in damage to the plaintiff. (These torts include fraud, nondisclosure of a defect, a false statement regarding quality of goods or promises, etc.)

Text References

1. Prosser, *Law of Torts,* §1 at 1 (4th ed. 1974)
2. Winfield, "The History of Negligence is the Law of Torts." 42 L.Q.Rev 184 (1926), quoted in Prosser, above §28 at 140, n. 9
3. *Stromsodt v. Parke-Davis & Co.,* 257 F. Supp. 991, 997 (D.N. Dak. 1966), cited in Gilbert, *Torts,* §186 at 35 (12th Ed. 1977)
4. *Hammer v. Rosen,* 7 N.Y. 2d 376, 198 N.Y.S.2d 65 (Ct. App. 1960)
5. Note, "Psychiatric Negligence." 23 Drake L.Rev. 640 (1974)
6. *Palsgraf v. Long Island R. Co.,* 248 N.Y. 339, 162 N.E. 99 (Ct. App. 1928)
7. *Dulieu v. White,* [1901] 2 K.B. 669, 679
8. *Overseas Tankship v. Morts Dock,* [1961] A.C. 388
9. *Overseas Tankship v. Miller Steamship,* [1967] 1 A.C. 617
10. Prosser, above, §44 at 270
11. Gilbert, above, §246 at 51
12. Prosser, above, *id.* at 271
13. *Pullman Palace Car v. Bluhm,* 109 Ill. 20 (1884)
14. *Lane v. So. R. Co.,* 192 N.C. 287, 134 S.E. 855 (1926)
15. *Hazelwood v. Hodge,* 357 S.W.2d 711 (Ky. (1961)
16. *Power v. Village of Hibbing,* 182 Minn. 66, 233 N.W. 597 (1930)
17. *Doss v. Town of Big Stone Gap,* 145 Va. 520, 134 S.E. 563 (1926)
18. *Withrow v. Becker,* 45 P.2d 235 (Cal. D. Ct. App. 1935)
19. Gilbert, above, §301 at 65
20. *Id.,* §319 at 68
21. *Seneris v. Haas,* 291 P.2d 915 (Cal. Sup. Ct. 1955)
22. Gilbert, above, §323 at 69
23. See, for example, *Matlick v. L.I. Jewish Hosp.,* 267 N.Y.S.2d 631 (App. Div. 1966)
24. See *Tonsic v. Wagner,* 329 A.2d 497 (Pa. Sup. Ct. 1974)
25. Prosser, above, §56 at 341
26. *Id.,* at 340

27. *Osterlind v. Hill*, 263 Mass. 73, 160 N.E. 301 (1928)

28. *Hurley v. Eddingfield*, 59 N.E. 1058 (Ind. 1901)

29. Prosser, above, §65 at 418

30. *Davies v. Mann*, 152 Eng. Rep. 588 (1842)

31. Prosser, above, §66 at 429

32. Gilbert, above, §423 at 94

33. 91 A.L.R.2d 392, 397

34. *Tunkl v. Regents of U. of Calif.*, 32 Cal.Rptr. 33, 383 P.2d 441 (1963)

35. *Ybarra v. Spangard*, 93 Cal.App.2d 43, 208 P.2d 445 (1949)

36. Gilbert, above, §14 at 3

37. Prosser, above, §10 at 38

38. *Canterbury v. Spence*, 464 F.2d 772 (D.C. Cir. 1972), cert. den. 409 U.S. 1064 (1972)

39. Prosser, above, §20 at 113

40. *Id.*, §75 at 494

41. Gilbert, above, §475 at 107

42. Gilbert, above, §540a at 119

43. *Id.*, §594 at 134

44. See, e.g., *Herbert v. Lands*, 441 U.S. 153 (1979)

Questions on Chapter 7,
Torts

1. Name the five basic elements which must be proven in a tort suit for negligence.
2. What major duties does the plaintiff alleging negligence have?
3. What is the general legal view regarding a person's obligation to help others in an emergency situation?
4. What does "assumption of risk" mean?
5. After drinking several beers, John sped down the street in the wrong lane and collided with Ernest, whose car had only one working headlight and a dirty windshield. What doctrine would a court be likely to invoke in awarding damages to Ernest?
6. What are the presumptions which must be fulfilled for the res ipsa loquitur doctrine to be invoked?
7. Name three intentional torts against the person.
8. Name two intentional torts against property.
9. a. George comes up to William and says, "You owe Charlie $10 and he owes me $10. I'm going to take it from you." He takes William's wallet and is counting out 10 dollar bills when William tries to wrest the wallet back. In doing so and in immobilizing George, he breaks George's arm. George sues William for damages. What defense would William likely use?

   b. Same set of facts except that after breaking George's arm and getting the wallet back, William kicks George in the head several times, leading to George's hospitalization. Is there a difference in the applicability of William's defense?
10. Smith Company, a road builder constructing a private driveway, blasts a ledge, and a large rock from the blast crashes through the roof of Jones' house. What doctrine would Jones be likely to invoke in suing the Smith Co.?

CHAPTER 8

Malpractice

Thomas E. Shea and Nathan T. Sidley

Malpractice

Thomas E. Shea and Nathan T. Sidley

"It is the duty of every artificer to exercise his art rightly
and truly as he ought."
—Anthony Fitzherbert

I. General Considerations*

A. The nature of the health professional-patient relationship and the meaning of malpractice:

1. A fiduciary relationship. The law requires the physician to exercise the utmost good faith with respect to
all aspects of the diagnosis and treatment process.

2. A contractual relationship. Courts have traditionally
held that there is a contractual relationship, which may
be either express or implied, between a patient and
health professionals, especially physicians. A physician
has a legal obligation, by virtue of an implied contract,
to act with reasonable skill and care and to comply
with other reasonable obligations of the profession.
Additionally, a physician is bound by any express
promises which he makes. By guaranteeing to a patient
that a treatment procedure or an operation will be a
success, the physician binds himself to that promise
and becomes an insurer of success. Merely expressing
an opinion, unaccompanied by a promise, does not
constitute such an express contract, however.

---

*It would be wise for the reader to review Chapter 7, Torts, before embark-
ing on this chapter. Malpractice mostly concerns the tort of negligence and
represents an application of basic tort and negligence concepts.

(Case 1; *Carpenter v. Moore,* 51 Wash.2d 795,
322 P.2d 125)

Although there was no evidence of negligence or fault
on the part of the dentist, a patient was allowed to recover in an action against a dentist for breach of contract. The dentist had agreed to make upper and lower
partial plates to the patient's complete satisfaction.

(Case 2; *Herrera v. Roessing,* Colo.App.,
533 P.2d 60)

After performing a tubal ligation, the physician made
remarks to the effect that the patient would not get
pregnant in the future. Later, the woman did become
pregnant and sued the doctor for breach of contract.
The court held for the physician, finding that the doctor had made no warranty prior to the surgery and that
his remarks after surgery were merely opinions and not
guarantees.

3. Tort liability. Most medical malpractice cases are
   based on a theory of tort liability. The law imposes on
   all a duty to act reasonably for the protection of others. A person who causes a foreseeable injury to another by a negligent act breaches that duty and is liable in
   damages. This means that the health professional
   must exercise the same degree of fundamental care for
   others as does any individual.
   In addition, by virtue of his special relationship to patients, the health professional owes to patients a special degree of protection from harm. He must protect
   others from deficiencies in the practice of his profession by adhering to the standards of the profession.
   The standard of skill and care required is a medical
   question within a legal framework. Absent a special
   contract, the practitioner is not bound to be an insurer
   of adequate results, nor is he required to exercise extraordinary skill and care, nor even the highest degree
   of skill and care possible. (Not all persons can be extraordinary in their ability to perform their profession.
   The law requires only what is reasonable under the
   circumstances.)

4. Disclosure of communications. There exists an implied duty on the part of a physician to refrain from disclosing communications made by the patient within the context of the physician-patient relationship. Disclosure by the physician is justified, however, and may be required, if there is a higher duty involved. For the protection and safety of a third person, disclosure of confidential communication is often required. The nature and extent of such disclosure, however, depends on the immediacy and on the severity of the danger as well as on the availability of other measures for protection of the third parties. Disclosure is permitted, if relevant, in defense of a malpractice suit. Disclosure to the government is permitted as required by statutes, for example, reporting battered child syndrome in many states.

5. Licensing. A state legislature has the power to control the licensing or certification requirements for the practice of the healing arts. It is, thus, within the power of states to provide exceptions from licensing requirements for military health personnel, action in emergencies, and purely spiritual or religious healing.
   a. A state board of examiners, complying with statutory and constitutional due process requirements, may grant or revoke a healing arts license. Revocation may occur for a variety of reasons, including these:
      1) Immoral, dishonorable, or unprofessional conduct.
      2) Malpractice.
      3) Fraud, deceit, or misrepresentation.
      4) Commission of a crime involving moral turpitude.
      5) Drug abuse.
   b. Branches of the healing arts for which licensing is oridinarly required:
      1) Physicians and surgeons.
      2) Dentists.
      3) Osteopathic physicians. (Under most statutes which permit the practice of osteopathy, an osteopath may diagnose and treat disease according to generally accepted osteopathic procedures, although usually he may not be allowed to practice

medicine or surgery. Many states, however, do permit osteopaths to prescribe certain drugs, perform surgery, and practice obstetrics and radiology.)

4) Nurses and nurse-practitioners.
5) Psychologists.
6) Occupational, physical, or respiratory therapists.
7) Social workers.
8) Pharmacists.
9) Optometrists.
10) Chiropractic practitioners. The scope of chiropractic practice authorized varies in accordance with state statutes. These standards include:
   a) The practice of all treatment methods which are normally taught in chiropractic school.
   b) The practice of mechanical, hygienic measures, incident to the care of the body, which do not invade the fields of medicine or surgery.
   c) Chiropractors are generally not allowed to penetrate tissues nor prescribe drugs.

(Case 3; *Joyner v. State,* 181 Miss. 245,
179 So. 573)

A chiropractor was found guilty of the unlawful practice of medicine for administering an anesthetic.

B. Injury, damages, and causation.
1. Injury and damages. Even though a practitioner commits an act of malpractice, no recovery is allowed and no damages awarded if that act does not result in an injury. For example, a nurse who negligently fails to insure that instruments under her responsibility are properly sterilized for use in an operation commits malpractice. If no infection develops as a result, however, she is not liable for damages, since her action has not resulted in injury.
The theoretical basis for awarding damages is to compensate the injured party for the harm inflicted by the defendant.
The expressed goal of the legal system in awarding

damages is to place the injured party in as good as, but no better, position than he was prior to suffering and injury. In the absence of gross negligence, intentional tort, or fraud, punitive damages (damages intended as punishment to the defendant rather than as compensation to the plaintiff), are not allowed in malpractice cases. The determination of damages is often more difficult than deciding whether liability exists.

Damages are awarded for two types of injury. The first is for concrete physical disability; the second is for pain and suffering. Compensation for physical disability may include payment of medical bills, convalescent care, and other reasonable expenses made necessary by the injury. Damages may also include compensation for loss of income during recovery and expected loss of income resulting from a permanent disability. Although it is relatively easy to determine past medical expenses, forecasting future expenses and loss of income is a difficult and uncertain matter.

The second basic type of compensable injury is pain and suffering. Placing a price on pain and suffering is based on the legal fiction that money can serve as compensation. No method exists to validate a judgment that a given amount of money compensates for a given amount of pain and suffering. The fact finder's decision on the matter is the ruling principle.

2. Proximate cause. Proximate cause is a legal term used to describe the causal link between an act and its effect.

The question of causality is often a major issue in malpractice cases. It is not sufficient for a plaintiff to prove that the doctor's actions "might have," or "could have," or "possibly did" cause the injury. The law has required that causation be established to a "medical certainty." It is important to note that this is medical, not legal, certainty, and it is based on medical, not legal, criteria. For this reason, the determination of causation must be established, with rare exceptions, by medical expert testimony.

The "medical certainty" standard, although governing

in a great majority of cases, has occasionally been replaced by a less severe "medical probability" standard in some instances. An example would be misdiagnosis, where the negligent failure to diagnose a problem lessened the chance for successful treatment and recovery.

(Case 4; *Grady v. Turlin,* 170 Conn. 443,
365 A.2d 1076)

The legal application of proximate cause and the medical certainty standard was the main issue in a case of malpractice by physicians who failed to diagnose a highly malignant spinal cancer. Despite the failure of diagnosis, the court directed a verdict in favor of the physicians. The court found that proximate cause was not established, because of absence of sufficient evidence that if the correct diagnosis had been made, surgery would have prolonged the patient's life.

(Case 5; *Lockhart v. Besel,* 71 Wash.2d 112,
426 P.2d 605)

After a tonsillectomy performed by the defendant, the patient began to hemorrhage and lost a great deal of blood. The physician-defendant did nothing to control the condition. Although there was no medical testimony concerning the cause of death, the testimony by lay witnesses as to the excessive amount of blood which the child lost was held to be sufficient to justify the verdict that the child had bled to death.

(Case 6; *Stejskal v. Darrow,* 55 N.D. 606,
215 N.W. 83)

After going to a physician for treatment, a woman was brought by the physician to a hospital, where she was refused admittance. Although the physician was directed to take her to another hospital, he returned her to his office, where he put her on a couch and gave her no treatment. Her death was later determined to have been caused by peritonitis, hemorrhage, and shock, brought about by a rupture of her uterus following instrumental interference with pregnancy. The evidence established the physician's negligence with sufficient certainty.

3. Res ipsa loquitur. In rare instances, the plaintiff asserting a malpractice claim does not have the burden of proving how his injury was caused; for example, the plaintiff can make his case without presenting expert medical testimony. The following conditions must be present to invoke res ipsa loquitur in a case:
   a. An injury resulted.
   b. The situation was one in which such an injury would not usually occur unless there was negligence.
   c. The defendant was in control of the situation.
   d. The defendant is more likely than the plaintiff to know what happened.

(Case 7; *Brown v. Shortlidge,* 98 Cal.App. 352, 277 P. 134)

Res ipsa loquitur was applied to a case where a patient's tooth was knocked out while the patient was under anesthetic during an operation for removal of his tonsils. Normally, a patient's tooth would not be knocked out during such an operation. Since the surgeon and other doctors, along with the nurses present, were in control of the situation, and because they would be expected to know what happened to cause the injury while the patient would not, the doctrine was applicable.

4. Contributory negligence. If the patient's own negligence is a contributing cause of his injury, the doctrine of contributory negligence bars the patient from recovering damages from the practitioner even though the injury was also proximately caused by the practitioner's negligence. The doctrine of contributory negligence applies even in those cases where the negligence of the patient is relatively small in comparison to the negligence of the practitioner. As long as the patient's negligence constitutes any part of the proximate causation of the injury, recovery is barred. The development of the doctrine of contributory neg-

ligence lies deeply rooted in the English Common Law. It is based on the reasonable premise that a person owes a duty of due care to himself as well as to others. As applied to the medical malpractice area the doctrine has been applied to such situations as these:

a. An injury resulting directly from the patient's own action.
b. Interference by the patient.
c. Failure to follow instructions given by the physician for care of an injury.
d. Refusal to submit to proper treatment.
e. Failure to return for further treatment.

(Case 8; *Rochester v. Katalan,*
320 A.2d 704)

After a patient died of multiple drug intoxication, an action was brought against the patient's physician for wrongful death. Although the physician had administered a large dose of methadone, the action was barred by the decedent's contributory negligence, where the decedent had falsely told the physician that he was a heroin addict. He had also deliberately manifested physical symptoms of heroin withdrawal after soliciting the medication, without informing the physician that he had consumed alcoholic beverages and librium pills earlier that day.

5. Comparative negligence. The doctrine of comparative negligence has been adopted in some states. This doctrine provides that if the plaintiff's negligence is less than that of the defendant, the plaintiff may recover. The plaintiff's award, however, is reduced by the percentage of his own fault.

C. Skill and care.

1. The general standard. A practitioner is required to possess ordinary skill and exercise ordinary care. More completely stated, he is expected to possess and exercise the degree of skill and learning ordinarily possessed and exercised by practitioners of the same

school of medicine in the same or in similar communities, and to use ordinary and reasonable care and diligence in the application of his skill and learning to the case. In the absence of a special contract, a practitioner is not bound to be an insurer of adequate results, nor is he required to exercise extraordinary skill and care, nor must he perform with the highest degree of skill and care.
The ordinary standard of skill and care is applied to both diagnosis and treatment. The determination of whether the practitioner's actions have met this standard is a question of fact to be made by the fact finder.

(Case 9; *Cobbs v. Grant,* 8 Cal.3d 229,
104 Cal.Rptr. 505, 502 P.2d 1)

The application of the ordinary standard of skill relieved a surgeon from liability in a case where the surgeon severed an artery at the hilum of the spleen during an operation for a duodenal ulcer. Expert testimony established that even with due care, the spleen may be injured in approximately five percent of such cases.

2. The specialist. A physician who holds himself out as a specialist must exercise that degree of skill and knowledge possessed by other specialists in the field. A specialist, like a general practitioner, is only required to exercise "ordinary" skill and care, but the standard by which his performance is measured is that of the "ordinary" specialist. It is not sufficient that his actions are reasonable by comparison with nonspecialists.

(Case 10; *McPhee v. Reichel,* No. 4 CIR,
461 F.2d 947)

The plaintiff charged her ophthalmologist with malpractice for failing to diagnose an eye condition soon enough and for allowing iris matter to remain incarcerated in her eye following an operation, thus, leading to infection and sympathetic ophthalmia. After a jury rendered a verdict for the physician, the court of appeals remanded the case for a new trial, finding that the trial court had not properly instructed the jury on the correct standard to be applied. The court of appeals held that the jury must be instructed that an ophthalmologist acting within his specialty owes to his patient a higher standard of skill, learning, and care then does a general practitioner.

D. Standard practices and experimental procedures:

1. Compliance with established practice. Physicians and surgeons are generally expected to follow standard practices and procedures in the diagnosis and treatment of their patients. If the established practices of the medical profession allow only one procedure or method of treatment, the practitioner is expected to follow that procedure or method. Where there are generally recognized and accepted alternative treatment methods, however, the determination of which method to use is left to the discretion of the practitioner. In order for a treatment method to be acceptable to the legal system, it must be acceptable to a respected minority of the medical profession. The essential criteria by which the reasonableness of the procedure is judged are medical, not legal.

2. Compliance with the practitioner's school of practice. The law recognizes that there are various schools of medicine and that it would be unjust to test the practices and procedures of one school of medicine by the standards of another. For this reason, the courts generally require that evidence relating to the standard of skill and care be presented through the testimony of an expert witness who belongs to the same school of medicine as the practitioner charged with malpractice. The judicial system recognizes that there are different schools of medical practice and does not give preference to any particular school over another. In order for a school of medicine to be accepted, however, it must have some significant and responsible following. A practitioner who follows such a school, even though it may not be the most advocated school, is protected

from malpractice liability if his actions conform to that school's standards of skill and care. Additionally, a patient selecting a practitioner of a particular school is assumed to accept the general tenets of that school, as well as its usual methods and procedures of treatment. Despite the general rule that experts testifying concerning the standard of skill and care in a medical malpractice case must be of the same school as the practitioner accused of malpractice, there are these exceptions:

a. The witness has extensive knowledge of the defendant's school of medicine.
b. The defendant actually used the methods and procedures of the witness' school of medicine.
c. The method or procedure in question is common to the school of medicine of both the defendant and the witness.
d. The practice involved is within the general knowledge and experience of practitioners from both schools.

The specific allowability and application of these exceptions varies from state to state and may also depend on the availability of expert witnesses from the defendant's school of medicine.

(Case 11; *Bivins v. Detroit Osteopathic Hospital,*
77 Mich. App. 478,
258 N.W.2d 527, reversed on other grounds
403 Mich. 820, 282 N.W.2d 926)

A thoracic surgeon with an M.D. degree was allowed to testify in a case against an osteopathic thoracic surgeon because the medical doctor was familiar with the surgical procedures and standards of the osteopathic school. The medical doctor testified that there would be no difference between his school and that of the defendant in the performance of a bronchoscopy.

(Case 12; *Pearce v. Linde,* 113 Cal.App.2d 627,
248 P.2d 506)

A physician who specialized in internal medicine and who had no experience in orthopedics or surgery was

not allowed to testify as an expert in a case alleging that
the defendant had not used proper care in operating on
the plaintiff's head.

3. Experimental procedures. In order to be liable for
   malpractice based on the use of an incorrect procedure, it must be proved that the physician abandoned
   accepted medical practice and knowledge. Despite
   good intentions, a departure from accepted methods
   renders the physician vulnerable.

   In cases where a physician wishes to use an experimental or unusual method, it is critical that the patient be
   fully informed of all relevant facts and of the risks.
   Only with well-documented, fully informed consent of
   the patient will the physician be protected against malpractice allegations.

   Even if a procedure has not been established as a common practice and even if it is very difficult, however,
   use of the procedure does not necessarily mean malpractice.

(Case 13; *Karp v. Cooley,* 492 F.2d 408,
cert. denied 419 U.S. 845)

A patient died following a heart transplant. The surgical procedure consisted of three stages; a wedge exci-
sion (ventriculoplasty), implantation of a mechanical
heart, and heart transplant.

It was without serious dispute that the surgical procedure was performed with requisite skill and care by the
surgeons. The plaintiff, the patient's widow, alleged
that the defendants should be held liable, however, because there was a lack of informed consent and because
the procedure was experimental and should not have
been used. The court rejected both arguments and upheld a directed verdict for the defendants. In speaking
of the informed consent question, the court stated that
the standard for judging the degree of disclosure required is a medical one; in this case the doctors were
not required to inform the patient of the results of ani-
mal experiments which indicated that the mechanical

heart could cause permanent injury in some cases. Turning to the issue of whether the procedure itself was experimental, the court observed that there was no evidence that the treatment was other than therapeutic.

(Case 14; *Hood v. Phillips*, 537 S.W.2d 29a)

After performing carotid surgery on a patient suffering from an advanced case of emphysema, a physician was sued for malpractice. The suit alleged that removal of the carotid glands from the neck was not an accepted medical practice in such cases. The evidence at the trial established that although it was a highly controversial procedure, at least two other physicians in the U.S., as well as several doctors in other countries, performed the surgery in such cases. The court determined that the evidence was sufficient to establish that the procedure was accepted by a "respectable minority" of physicians.

E. The local community standard.
   1. The traditional rule. Accepted methods of medical practice may vary with geographic location. What is accepted as standard practice in a sparsely populated rural setting may not be reasonable in a large city. Moveover, the standard methods in one large city may be significantly different from those in another. The courts have determined that it would be unjust to use the practice of one local community as the standard for evaluating the action of a practitioner in another community.
   Under this common law rule, the standard of skill and care in a medical malpractice case must be established through the expert testimony of a practitioner from the same community as the practitioner accused of malpractice. This is referred to as the "strict locality rule." Under the rule, expert witnesses from outside the local community in which the defendant practices are not allowed to testify concerning the adequacy of the methods or procedures used:

(Case 15; *Thompson v. Lockert,* 34 N.C.App. 1,
237 S.E.2d 259)

An appeals court determined that the trial court had
properly excluded the testimony of a diplomate of the
American Board of Surgeons from the state of New
York in a case concerning the standard of care exercised by the defendant physician, a diplomate of the
American Board of Orthopedic Surgeons, in Salisbury,
North Carolina. The court stated that there was no evidence showing that the medical practices in the two
communities are similar or that the witness was familiar
with the standard of professional care and competency
customary for the defendant's situation.

2. Nationalization of the community standard. The local
   community standard rule was developed during a period of slow communications that prevented adequate
   dissemination of medical information. With modern
   improvements in communications and transportation,
   new medical procedures are now quickly disseminated.
   Because of these advances, at least some of the supporting reasons for the strict application of the local
   community rule have diminished or have disappeared
   altogether.
   Some courts have rejected a strict application of the
   locality rule and have held that determining whether a
   physician has exercised the required degree of skill
   and care must take into account the advances of the
   profession. Although consideration should be given to
   the community standard and local medical resources
   available, according to these courts the local standard
   is not the sole criterion. Indeed, a doctor may have a
   duty to transfer a patient out of his own locality to a
   hospital with more sophisticated facilities, if those facilities are reasonably necessary and are unavailable in
   the local community.

3. The specialist. Recognizing that the expertise of a specialist is of a national rather than a regional character,
   some courts have been more willing to abandon the

locality rule in cases involving specialists. These courts believe that a practitioner who holds himself out as a specialist in a field should be responsible for having the knowledge of professional advances equal to that possessed by the average member of that specialty on a national basis.

F. Case responsibility.
  1. Attending a case.
    a. A physician has no obligation to take an individual as a patient. Once a patient is accepted, however, the physician has a duty to continue treatment as long as the patient requires attention, unless the relationship is properly terminated. The failure of a physician to continue necessary care in light of this obligation constitutes abandonment and renders the physician liable for any resulting injury.
    b. A physician who is called into a case for a specific and limited purpose has no continuing duty to the patient. For example, a specialist who is called in for a consultation by the patient's physician has no continuing duty to care for the patient. The specialist's only duty in this context is to exercise ordinary skill and care in the consultation process.
    c. A physician is not responsible for the refusal of a competent patient to submit to necessary procedures, nor is the physician responsible for injury caused by a patient's refusal to follow instructions.
    d. A physician may advise hospitalization or treatment procedures to a patient, but the doctor has no authority to order hospitalization or treatment against the wishes of a competent patient. (See Chapter 13, Special Legal Problems in Mental Health.)
  2. Termination of the professional relationship. There are three ways in which the physician-patient relationship can be properly terminated.
    a. By mutual consent of the physician and patient.
    b. By discharge of the physician by the patient.

c. By the physician's withdrawing from the case with sufficient notice to the patient. Withdrawal from the case is appropriate under these situations:
1) The patient treats the professional abusively.
2) The patient continually and repetitively refuses to pay even when he has the means to do so.
3) A disease foreign to the practitioner's expertise is present.
4) The patient repeatedly fails to follow the practitioner's advice.
5) The practitioner decides to limit his practice generally, or retires from practice.
6) The patient repeatedly consults with other practitioners without telling the practitioner about the relationships with the others.

d. A patient should not be summarily abandoned. Formal notice should be given, and the terminating practitioner should continue to care for the patient until the patient has had a reasonable opportunity to obtain another practitioner.

e. Although a physician can neither abandon his patient nor fail to provide necessary attention and treatment, he is not liable for malpractice if he temporarily leaves and provides for necessary care by another physician.

f. When the relationship is properly terminated, the physician is no longer responsible for caring for the patient and is, therefore, not liable for subsequent injury. A physician who abandons a case improperly, however, is liable for injury to the patient caused by that abandonment.

(Case 16; *Lee v. Dewbre*, Tex. Civ. App., 362 S.W.2d 900)

After being treated for several months during her pregnancy, the patient was admitted to the hospital by her physician. After giving birth, she went into shock, due to extensive internal bleeding, and another physician was called in to assist. After visiting the hospital the next day, her original physician left town. After being treated by the assisting physician that same day, the patient was transferred to another hospital and underwent a hysterectomy, performed by two other physicians. She was released from that hospital 10 days later. The court found that the original physician had not abandoned his patient, because she had continued to receive competent medical care after he had left.

(Case 17; *Bruni v. Tatsumi*, 46 OhioSt.2d 127, 75 OhioOps.2d 184, 346 N.E.2d 673)

Upon completion of treatment, the defendant physicians sent the patient back to the original physicians who had referred the case. The patient, herself, then chose to seek another physician. The court held that there was no abandonment.

(Case 18; *Casey v. Penn*, 45 Ill.App.3rd 573, 4 Ill. Dec. 346, 360 N.E.2d 93, supp.op. 45 Ill.App.3rd 1068, 6 Ill. Dec. 453, 362 N.E.2d 1373)

After performing an open reduction on a broken forearm, the orthopedic surgeon failed to inspect the wound for 72 hours, despite indications of lack of circulation. No tests were conducted until three days after this inspection, and the surgeon did not inspect the test results for another two days, although the test results were available in an hour and would have shown that the penicillin used to treat the patient was ineffective. Based on this evidence, the court overturned the jury's verdict in favor of the defendant.

3. Referring a patient to a specialist. A practitioner has a duty to refer a patient to a specialist when the physician knows or should know that the diagnosis or treatment of the patient's illness is beyond his area of expertise. This rule has also been applied to the duty of a practitioner of one school of medicine to refer a patient to a practitioner from another school of medicine when reasonably necessary. Under such situations, a practitioner who determines that specialized treatment or treatment by a practitioner of another school is required and accordingly makes the referral,

is under no continuing obligation to continue treating the patient.

(Case 19; *Fairchild v. Brian,* La. App.,
354 So.2d 675)

An optometrist and the HMO he worked for were held liable for delay in the discovery of a patient's detached retina, which resulted in the loss of the eye. The optometrist had diagnosed the patient's condition as a cataract without dilating the eye, and did not refer the patient to the staff opthalmologist. It was determined that early referral to the ophthalmologist would have resulted in a correct diagnosis, and the eye could have been saved.

(Case 20; *Richardson v. Holmes,* Tex. Civ. App.,
525 S.W.2d 293)

After undergoing a hysterectomy the patient developed complications, including vomiting blood and dark liquid. The condition was diagnosed as paralytic ileus, and the patient was intubated. Eight days later, she was transferred to the care of a specialist, who diagnosed mesenteric thrombosis. Surgery performed the same day confirmed the condition, but it was too late, and she died. Expert testimony established that the patient should have been referred earlier to the specialist and that the delay in instituting appropriate treatment caused her death. The court found that the evidence established malpractice for failure to refer her to a specialist in accordance with ordinary medical procedure.

G. Informed Consent:

1. The basic premise. Every competent person is entitled to exercise control over his body and to decide what medical treatment will be performed. The key concept is that the patient, not the practitioner, is entitled to make the final decision regarding whether to undergo diagnostic procedures or treatment. Although the decision of a competent patient to forego a procedure may be medically inadvisable, nevertheless, it is the

patient's decision. The physician who attempts to substitute his judgment for that of an unconvinced patient leaves himself vulnerable. Application of this basic premise has resulted in several rules, which are generally applicable, but which may vary somewhat in different jurisdictions.

a. A competent person who signs a written consent form is considered to have read the contents of that form.

b. The relationship of husband and wife does not, by itself, allow one spouse to authorize an operation on the other spouse, when the spouse who is the patient is competent to give or to withhold consent.

c. A temporary custodian of a child, such as a babysitter, does not have the authority to give consent for the treatment of the child.

d. Consent need not be written. Verbal consent is binding. (There are often difficulties with proving verbal consent, however.)

e. Consent may be by actions of the patient. A patient who submits to a procedure voluntarily, with full knowledge of what is going to happen, may be held to have voluntarily consented. (Whether the patient has full knowledge may be another issue, however.)

f. Consent may be given to a hospital for the benefit of one or more physicians, surgeons, or staff members.

g. Consent for treatment of an incompetent person may be given by that person's legal guardian. (See Chapter 13, Special Legal Problems in Mental Health.) Consent for a child must be given by the child's parent or legal guardian. (There is a newly developing minority of decisions giving minors some rights to give or withhold consent. Also, see the emergency exception below.)

   An exception to the usual parental consent rule, however, is that a state cannot prevent the performance of an abortion on a minor simply because of parental objection.

h. A physician who performs a procedure on a patient without proper consent can be held liable for any resulting injury, even if the procedure is performed with the highest degree of skill and care. The physician also commits a battery against the patient and may be held liable on that account.*

(Case 21; *Offutt v. Sheehan*, 168 Ind.App. 491, 344 N.E.2d 92)

After a cesarean birth, the physician discovered that the patient had a large, scarred uterus. Because the patient was obese, with high blood pressure and a tendency to diabetes, and because cancer smears were atypical, the physician performed a complete hysterectomy. The patient had not specifically consented to a hysterectomy but had signed consent forms requesting tubal ligation, cesarean section, and tubal resection. The patient also authorized the physician "to do whatever he deems advisable." The court determined that the physician was not liable for failure to obtain consent prior to the hysterectomy.

(Case 22; *Kennedy v. Parrott*, 243 N.C. 355, 90 S.E.2d 754)

In this case, the court clearly stated the rule that where a patient is incapable of giving his consent and where no one with authority to consent for him is immediately available, the surgeon may extend an operation to remedy an abnormal or diseased condition in the area of the original incision, if necessary in his sound professional judgment.

2. Disclosure of information. The "informed" element of the informed consent rule requires that the physician provide the patient with sufficient information concerning the proposed operation or treatment process to allow the patient to make a reasonably informed and intelligent decision. Without having a basic understanding of the operation or process, or without information concerning the basic risks involved, the patient

---

*If sued on a theory of battery, that is, an intentional tort, the physician is subject to punitive damages.

is unable to make a reasonable decision. Because the patient does not possess the requisite knowledge, the law imposes a duty on the physician to provide the necessary information to the patient.

a. Under the traditional rule, the standard for determining how much information is necessary was judged by the customary, or standard, practice of other physicians in the community.

b. The newly developing standard for determining the information that must be disclosed is based on the reasonable needs of a patient. This new standard is objective rather than subjective and is governed by the needs of a reasonable patient rather than by the desires of any one individual.

c. A physician is not obligated to disclose obvious risks that are extremely unlikely. (Disputes may occur regarding how unlikely must a risk be before it should be regarded as extremely unlikely.)

d. If the physician knows of an alternate treatment method which would probably be successful, he is obligated to disclose this to the patient. He should also disclose the likely consequences of failing to undergo a diagnostic or treatment procedure.

e. A physician may not withold material information from a patient simply because the physician believes that knowledge of the information would cause the patient to reject the treatment procedure or operation.

f. A physician is not responsible for disclosing information which the patient already knows.

g. Some courts have held that full disclosure to a patient is not required where a more limited disclosure is in the best interests of the patient. Usually, however, it is inadvisable for a physician to rely on such a rule. Full disclosure is the best policy unless the patient is incompetent, in which case the patient's guardian, or under necessary circumstances (For example, there is no legal guardian and there is not sufficient time for one to be obtained.), next of kin, should be given the information and should give the consent.

(Case 23; *Longmire v. Hoey,* Tenn. App.,
512 S.W.2d 307)

It was determined that a surgeon was not liable for failing to inform his patient of the risk of developing a ure-
terovaginal fistula after a hysterectomy. The court
found that the development of a fistula in an area not
associated with the surgery was not of such a material
nature as to invalidate the consent.

(Case 24; *Hamilton v. Hardy,* 37 Colo.App. 375,
549 P.2d 1099)

A plaintiff alleged that her physician failed to inform
her of the risk of abnormal blood clotting or other side
effects before prescribing contraceptive pills. After suffering a stroke, she sued for malpractice. The court
held that her allegation established a prima facie cause
of action against the physician. (That is, she had a legally sufficient case so that the jury could hear it and make
a decision. In this situation, the defendant had moved
for dismissal. The court merely said that there was
enough of a case to be heard. Note, though, that there
are many steps between presenting a case to a jury and
actually having the defendant found liable.)

(Case 25; *Belcher v. Carter,*
13 OhioApp. 42,
OhioOps.2d 218,
234 N.E.2d 311)

A physician was determined to have had an obligation
to inform a patient of potential risks of bodily lesion
due to hypersensitivity in connection with radiation
treatment.

(Case 26; *Walker v. North Dakota Eye Clinic, Ltd.,* DCND,
415 F.Supp. 891)

An ophthalmologist had no duty to disclose to the patient that she ran less than a one percent risk of long
term or permanent diplopia as the result of strabismus
surgery. (The plaintiff did not present any expert testimony establishing such a duty.)

3. The emergency exceptions. When an emergency exists which threatens the life or severely threatens the continued health of a person, a physician may take whatever medical action is reasonably necessary even though consent has not been given. If practical, the physician should obtain consent from the person's spouse, parent or other relative, but where obtaining this consent is impractical in light of the emergency, no consent is necessary. Ordinarily, however, this does not imply that treatment can be forced onto a competent patient over his objections. Even in an emergency, one must respect such a patient's refusal of treatment. (Cases involving the emergency exception usually arise when the patient is in surgery or is in coma, or confused, etc., from acute illness or a traumatic accident.)

(Case 27; *Kennedy v. Parrott*, 243 N.C. 355,
90 S.E.2d 754)

It was determined that a surgeon who discovered enlarged cysts on the patient's ovary was not liable for an assault or trespass in puncturing the cysts, because the evidence showed that the cysts were a potential danger to the patient. Therefore, the procedure was allowed under the emergency exception, although the patient had not specifically consented to the puncturing of the cysts.

(Case 28; *Wheeler v. Barker*, 92 Cal.App.2d 776,
208 P.2d 68)

While performing surgery for vaginal bleeding, the doctor discovered the existence of a large fibroid tumor of the uterus with multiple tumors and nodules on its inner walls. It was held that removal of two-thirds of the uterus was justified by the emergency nature of the patient's condition.

H. Vicarious and joint liability.
1. Vicarious liability (respondeat superior). The doctrine of vicarious liability has its foundation in common law.

It was believed that a master should be liable for paying damages for injury caused by the negligent act of his servant, if the act occurred while the servant was performing duties for the master. The rationale behind the doctrine is simply one of economics. In most cases, the servant would not have enough money to compensate the injured party. Since the servant was performing duties for the master, it was considered fair for the master to be responsible for injury caused by the servant, provided he was acting within the scope of his employment.

In its modern context, this doctrine is referred to as vicarious liability; the economic rationale remains the impetus for its continued viability. The doctrine states that an employer (master) is liable in damages for the negligent acts of the employee (servant) performed within the scope of employment.

a. In the medical context the master-servant relationship may be between a hospital and its doctor, nurse, or technical employees, or between a doctor (employer) and an employee, who might be a nurse, a technician, or, depending on how much direction is given, another doctor.

b. In most instances, surgeons are not employed by a hospital. In such situations, the hospital is not vicariously liable for the negligence or malpractice of the doctor.

c. Hospital nurses are usually not employed by a surgeon, and the surgeon would not be vicariously liable for a nurse's negligence. The hospital employing the nurse, however, would be liable for the nurse's negligence.

d. The essential test for determining whether a master-servant relationship exists is control or the right to control. In order to be vicariously liable, the employer must have the right to control the actions of the employee. The right of control is evidenced by such factors as the ability to tell the employee when to work, where to work, and how to work. If there is no right to control, there is no vicarious liability.

e. A physician is not liable for injury resulting from the

negligent administration of a drug to his patient by a nurse employed by the hospital. If the nurse negligently administers the drug under the doctor's supervision, however, the doctor may be held liable.

f. In any case of vicarious liability, the servant remains liable, although the master is also liable.

(Case 29; *McKinney v. Tromly,* Tex. Civ. App.,
386 S.W.2d 564, disapproved on other grounds,
547 S.W.2d 582)

A physician was held vicariously liable for the negligence of a nurse working under his supervision. The anesthetic she was administering exploded during the operation.

(Case 30; *Bernardi v. Community Hospital Assoc.,*
166 Colo. 280, 443 P.2d 708)

When leaving written postoperative instructions regarding an injection that a patient was to receive, the physician did not know which nurse would administer the injection. It was held that the physician could not be found liable under the doctrine of respondeat superior for the negligence of the nurse in administering the injection, when the nurse had been employed by the hospital and was not under the control and direction of the doctor.

(Case 31; *Stovall v. Harms,* 214 Kan. 835,
522 P.2d 353)

The court held that a physician is not vicariously liable for the malpractice of another physician he calls in or recommends, if there is no concert of action and no negligence in the selection of the other physician.

2. Joint liability. Practitioners who work together on a case may be held jointly liable in some situations.

a. If two physicians working on a case are independently employed, each is liable for his own negligent actions. In addition, each is liable for negligent actions of the other physician if he knows or should know of the negligent acts and if he does not take reasonable steps to stop or to prevent negligence.

b. An operating surgeon is generally not liable for the malpractice of an anesthesiologist who is not in his employ.

c. Perhaps the most frequent occasions of joint medical liability occur in cases where res ipsa loquitur is applied. Because in such cases no evidence is available to the patient concerning the cause of the injury, all the doctors and nurses who participated in the operation may be held jointly liable.

I. The liability of hospitals. A hospital, which is usually, although not always, a corporation, acts through its agents and employees. As such, it is responsible for the actions, and in some cases the inactions, of these agents and employees.

Under the law, a hospital owes a duty to its patients to exercise due care. The standard for this duty is determined by the level of skill and care normally exercised by other hospitals in the community. As with the standard of care required of practitioners, a hospital is not obligated to provide the best or finest care available but is only required to provide reasonable care.

1. In some states a hospital can be held liable for injuries resulting from a failure to meet accreditation or licensing standards.

2. The general position adopted by the courts is that a hospital is not liable for failing to monitor and supervise the care given to its patients by physicians whom it does not employ. There is a small but growing trend of cases, however, holding that a hospital does have such a duty and that the hospital can be held responsible for injuries caused by the malpractice of a physician, where the hospital knew, or should have known, of the physician's general inability or incompetence. (That implies that hospitals should verify credentials and check references of physicians who apply for staff privileges. There should also be procedures for deal-

ing with physicians on the hospital staff who become, or appear to become, handicapped in their practices.)

3. A hospital is vicariously liable for the negligent acts of nurses, technicians, and doctors it employs when such acts occur within the scope of their employment.

4. A hospital is not liable for the acts of physicians or of others who use the hospital facilities when the hospital does not have a right to control their activities.

5. A hospital has an obligation to provide facilities and equipment which meet the ordinary standard of hospitals in the community, considering the purpose of the hospital.

(Case 32; *Cramer v. Hoffman,* 390 F.2d 19)

After being released from the hospital, the plaintiff suffered cervical injuries and was paralyzed during a football practice. He contended that his doctor had discharged him from the hospital in an ill and physically weakened condition and that this caused his injuries. The plaintiff sought to hold the hospital responsible for the doctor's alleged negligence. The court ruled as a matter of law that the hospital could not be held responsible for the actions of the physician, who was an independent contractor exercising his own discretion.

(Case 33; *Shields v. King,* 40 OhioApp.2d. 77, 317 N.E.2d 922)

A hospital could be held liable* for the death of a patient who suffered chronic kidney disease. The evidence showed that he had died as a result of a bacterial infection which could have been caused by contamination of the kidney dialysis machine or by improper storage of blood used to prime the pumps of the machine.

---

*There are many cases in which the issue is the legal one as to whether the defendant could be held liable, given the facts of the case. For example, in a trial an award may be given against a defendant, and the defendant might appeal on the basis that with the facts of the case he could not legally be held liable. The appeals court might well decide that he could legally be held liable and would not otherwise comment on the case. Many appellate decisions relate to such issues.

(Case 34; *Hord v. National Homeopathic Hospital,*
102 F.Supp 792, affd. 204 F.2d 397)

After a child was born, he fell through an opening
meant for drainage in the middle of the delivery table,
and he hit his head on a pan standing on the floor. He
died three days later. The jury determined that the hospital was liable. The hole should have been small
enough so that a baby could not fall through.

II. Special Problem Considerations.

A. Negligence which is almost completely preventable, that
is, situations which can either be all but completely
planned for in advance or which require virtually no on-
the-spot exercise of judgment;

1. Surgical, obstetrical, and anesthesia.
   a. Operating on the wrong patient.
   b. Failing to count instruments and sponges before and
      after a procedure. (Leaving items inside the patient is
      probably the most frequent aspect of malpractice. It in-
      cludes items left by anesthesiologists, also.)
   c. Failing to insure that proper equipment, in properly
      functioning order, is available for use when it might be
      needed.
   d. Performance of a nonemergency procedure when prior
      consent has not been obtained.
   e. Failing to be available or to have proper coverage for
      potential post-surgical emergencies.
   f. Failing to ensure that the patient's position during sur-
      gery will not lead to damage from stretched nerves,
      blocked blood vessels, etc., or allowing the patient to
      become hypothermic during surgery.
   g. Beginning nonemergency surgery with an intoxicated
      or incapacitated staff person involved.
   h. Failing to inform and obtain permission from a preg-
      nant patient regarding the possibility that the obstetri-
      cian may not personally be able to perform the actual
      delivery.

i. Failing to have a protocol for pre-anesthesia workup of a patient and for monitoring the patient during anesthesia.

j. Undertaking a procedure for the first time or after a long time without reviewing the procedure itself, including potential anatomical and other complications.

2. Medical or surgical.

a. Not ascertaining to which medications the patient is allergic.

b. Failing to supervise and monitor subordinates to whom one has designated authority.

c. Administering, or even prescribing, a different drug from the one intended, or giving a drug to the wrong patient.

d. Prescribing a new drug without knowing in advance what the side effects might be.

e. Failing to deal with the family when a patient is incompetent.

f. Failing to have a set of written procedures to verify periodically that one's diagnostic and therapeutic systems are functioning and in place.

g. Releasing information without consent to an unauthorized party.

h. Prescribing drugs indefinitely to a patient without reviewing the case periodically in person.

i. Refusing to have a consultant called when it is requested by the patient.

j. Using unusual or experimental procedures without appropriate prior consent.

k. Failing to inform the patient when something important has gone wrong (for example, a sponge left in a body cavity).

l. Failing to keep a note of telephone contacts with patients, including advice given, drugs prescribed, etc.

m. Allowing one's practice to get out of control, so that one is always rushed, tired, overworked, and under pressure.

n. Failing to inquire of colleagues, professors, or the literature when one is puzzled about a case.

o. Becoming involved with a patient other than in a strict doctor-patient relationship, for example, sexually, in business dealings, as a recipient of other than token gifts from the patient, or as a beneficiary of the patient's will.

p. Failing to inform the patient if an important diagnostic finding is discovered after the patient has left contact with the doctor. (For example, an important abnormal x ray report is received after the patient has left the hospital.)

q. Writing a prescription or a hospital order illegibly.

3. Nursing.

a. Failing to inform the practitioner managing the case when potentially serious developments in a patient's condition are occurring. Properly informing the practitioner may require efforts to leave messages at various places and to contact the practitioner directly. In severe emergencies, it may mean finding another practitioner on an ad hoc basis.

b. Failing to inform appropriate parties on discovering that important equipment is not functioning.

c. Verifying every order that seems inappropriate to the case. Making such inquiry to a practitioner is appropriate if the verified order seems unusual for the type of case. (One should obviously be polite in inquiring; one's role does not call for challenging the practitioner's judgment except in an extreme situation. In such a case, it is important to discuss the situation with one's nursing service supervisor.)

d. Failure to request assistance when patient needs become too great to be accomplished by available staff.

e. Giving the wrong medication, wrong dose, wrong form (liquid or tablet), by wrong route of administration, to the wrong patient, or even at the wrong time.

f. Failure to protect a helpless patient, for example, by keeping side-rails up when necessary, as in the very old, the very young, or those not completely conscious.

4. Hospital technicians and therapists.

a. Failing to ensure that every tissue, blood sample, or x ray, etc. is properly labeled as to date, patient, hospital

number, and part of the body (including right-left, superior-inferior, etc.).
  b. Failing to match blood for transfusion properly.
  c. Failing to inform the practitioner in charge when a problem concerning the patient arises.

5. General:
  a. Failing to have a protocol to monitor the environment to which patients and others are exposed so as to ensure patient safety.
  b. Failing to rectify potentially dangerous situations when they are found, for example, a chair with a loose leg, a rug that slides, etc.

B. Common malpractice problems which are somewhat preventable, but not completely so: (insurance companies' categories)

1. "Failure to diagnose."
  a. Examples.
    1) Many failures to diagnose occur when the patient asks for a diagnostic procedure and the physician refuses, for example, a mammogram.
    2) It is worse to fail to consider a common disorder for which a simple diagnostic procedure is available, (for example, failing to take a cardiogram when there is chest pain) than it is to miss an uncommon disorder which requires elaborate studies.
    3) It is probably worse yet to fail to diagnose a condition which occurs because of a procedure one has performed oneself (for example, a cast which is too tight and leads to insufficient blood supply or a side effect of a drug one has given).
    4) It is worst of all when the patient actively complains about a symptom that occurs after treatment, the symptom represents a common complication of treatment, and the practitioner fails to order the test that would diagnose the problem. (For example, failing to take an x ray when the patient complains of back pain after having had electric shock treatment, so that a fractured vertebra is not detected.)
  b. "Positive defensive medicine," the ordering of tests in

order to rule out every possible cause of a patient's symptoms. Often tests are "unnecessary" in terms of the practitioner's working diagnostic hypotheses, but are ordered to protect the practitioner against the slim possibility of a malpractice suit.

1) The ordering of unnecessary tests does not shield the physician from malpractice suits. The physician should use care in ordering those tests that are necessary in accordance with accepted medical standards.

2) It is easier to order diagnostic tests when third parties, rather than the patient directly, pay for them.

c. "Negative defensive medicine," the avoidance of high-risk procedures which might be helpful to the patient. Positive defensive medicine is more common than negative.

d. The most common diagnostic failures ending in malpractice claims involve fractures and cancer.

2. "Technical surgical errors," including overly tight casts and tooth damage caused by anesthesiologists. Such errors can have effects ranging from mild discomfort to death.

3. Adverse drug reactions to penicillin and to tetanus antitoxin;

4. "Improper treatment," which includes these. Too much of the right treatment, not enough of the right treatment, or use of the wrong treatment. It also includes consequences of treatment, such as drug side effects, burns from x ray therapy, or excessively long contact with pooled antiseptic solutions used in surgery. Failure to care properly for cardiac arrest is also similar, though few medical situations are of such an order of severity as cardiac arrest with so little time to think about and maneuver with respect to the problem.

5. Lack of proper informed consent.

6. "Improper supervision," which probably relates to situations in which the practitioner fails to alert the patient to some potential complication or side effect

from treatment, and the patient, ignorant of the significance of it, does not report to the doctor as the harm increases.

C. Preventing malpractice claims on an individual basis.
1. Competence and maintaining proficiency. Although it may not be possible for a physician to avoid all malpractice claims, a competent and aware physician can do much to avoid malpractice pitfalls. Continuing to maintain one's own proficiency through educational efforts is highly important.
2. Rational disposition of time. Time is one of the difficult problems a physician faces. It is essential that a physician devote the necessary time to each patient. Undue haste prompts malpractice suits.
3. Considerations about informed consent. The subject is a difficult area. Questions to balance are these.
   a. Problems.
      1) How much should one tell an easily frightened patient, who, out of fear, might refuse a relatively benign and beneficial treatment?
      2) How relatively rare must serious side effects be before they are too inconsequential to have to mention? A difficulty even in considering that problem is that frequency tables of the relative risks and benefits of procedures are generally not available. Some estimates can be made but often require a thorough literature search.
      3) Sometimes, patients sign a consent form and then ask further questions, the input of which is not reflected in the form.
      4) It can be a very time-consuming process to discuss all the risks and benefits of any procedure.
      5) Sometimes, patients are not able to comprehend the issues and cannot make a rational treatment decision.
   b. Possible ways of dealing with informed consent.
      1) Merely keeping the possibility in mind will help.
      2) It is advisable to discuss a procedure with a family

member of anyone who has difficulty in understanding. It is also a good idea to have the family member sign the consent form.

3) Some day a standard set of forms explaining different procedures and their complications may be available. Until that day, it is advisable for the physician to make notes of his conversations with patients regarding disclosure of risks, procedures, and alternatives.

That is quite different from having a ward secretary, a nurse, or even another physician present a consent form to a patient, especially at the last moment before a procedure, saying "Here, sign this." The latter approach is an invitation to problems. Indeed, even if one is a surgical specialist whose only contact with the patient is performing the surgery itself, it is advised that he personally discuss the procedure with the patient in advance.

If an elective procedure is contemplated during the course of surgery for some other purpose, for example, performing an elective appendectomy while doing a hysterectomy, informed permission for the elective procedure must be obtained separately.

Similar considerations are involved in prescribing drugs. The patient's concern in taking a drug involves risk in relation to benefit. The risks that must be mentioned depend on their seriousness and on their frequency of occurrence. If any of the following side effects occurs with any appreciable frequency, it must be mentioned:

a) Death.

b) Drowsiness, fainting (including postural hypotension), seizures, bleeding, vomiting, etc.

c) Temporary or permanent cosmetic effects, for example, loss of hair, skin darkening, tremors, etc.

d) Allergic reactions.

e) Irreversible health effects.

f) Severe interactions with other drugs or foods, etc.

g) Potentiality for drug dependency.

4) The best protection for a physician is to have the pa-

tient sign a consent statement that discloses the risks and alternatives. Second best is a note in the patient's record concerning the discussions.

5) Note also that informed consent includes presenting the patient with information regarding alternative forms of treatment for the problem he has. Indeed, at times the prudent approach is to offer the patient the opportunity for consultation with another physician who uses alternative approaches to the problem. Offering such a consultation also tends to increase a patient's confidence that his doctor is conscientiously acting in the patient's best interests.

D. The medical record.

1. Purposes.

a. A systematic aid to memory in managing a patient's case over a time period.

b. An aid to others who may subsequently manage a case. Information as to what has happened before is important in making decisions.

c. Knowledge of what occurred between a patient and professional is often important for legal or insurance purposes.

d. Hospitals and clinics, etc., demand that a record be kept, and kept up to date, as a condition of being on their staffs.

2. Basic information on the record.

a. What one did to or for the patient.

b. Why one did it.

c. What the patient regarded as his problems.

d. What the practitioner regards as the patient's problem, including diagnosis.

e. What the prognosis is.

f. Why the prognosis is that.

g. Information that may be relevant to any of the above, including phenomena which are seen for the first time, represent changes from previous observations, or are unusual.

h. In short, the problems, the diagnosis, the treatment, the prognosis, the course of the illness, unusual incidents, and the reasons for any medical conclusions and decisions.

3. Requirements of the record.
   a. That it be legible.
   b. That entries be made at the time of interaction with the patient or reasonably immediately thereafter.
      1) If a change or crossout is made, the change should be dated.
      2) Marginal entries should be avoided.
      3) Making any entry significantly after the fact is prejudicial to the maker at a trial. It might even be regarded as fraud.
   c. That entries be in ink, signed, and dated. It is preferable to include the time on a record entry as a matter of routine.

4. General consideration. It is time-consuming to create a legible, accurate, informative record. No way of avoiding investing the time, however, has yet been devised.

5. "Objective" notes are preferable to "subjective." For example, "Patient reports that he ate boiled ham without suffering," is preferable to "fewer GI sx."

6. Opinions on questions not immediately related to patient care, or derogatory statements, have no valid place on the medical record.

7. Patient accessibility to the record. The patient who is curious about his treatment (and every intelligent person should be curious about his own health and what is done to him) can, and will, read the record. His attorney will, too. It is only prudent to bear in mind when making an entry that various others may read it some day.

(Case 35; *Miles v. Brainin*, 224 Md. 156, 167 A.2d 117)

The court ruled that the hospital record, made in the normal course of hospital procedure, could be introduced as evidence in a case of malpractice. The court also noted that relevant entries made by persons other than the defendant could be introduced if the entries were part of the hospital record. In addition the court held that the third party entries could be considered as adoptive admissions by the defendant, because he had made an endorsement on the record, stating that he had examined and approved those entries.

III. Special malpractice consideration in mental health.

(See Chapter 13, Special Legal Problems in Mental Health.) The requirement that others may have to protect the patient or be protected from him.

A. In contrast to other fields of medicine, in which a patient either can protect himself or needs only to be protected from his physical environment, in mental health the patient must also be protected, at times, from his tendency to harm himself. Others, including other patients, must also be reasonably protected from him, especially when he is in a psychiatric ward in a hospital.

B. Theories of treatment. The history of litigated mental health cases indicates that there is no single "best" theory of mental illness or of treatment, accepted by all authorities. It is the responsibility of the law to consider the reasonableness of methods and theories from this perspective.

C. Affirmative harm. The courts have demonstrated that they will not tolerate behavior which is clearly abusive and which results in harm to patients, whether performed by psychiatrists or by other mental health workers. Difficulty arises in those instances where abusive treatment is not frankly apparent. In cases which involve psychiatric judgment, the courts have attempted to allow the practitioner sufficient latitude, while protecting patients from extreme misjudgments and lack of care.

(Case 36; *Bellandi v. Park Sanitarium Assoc.*, 6 P.2d 508)

An extreme case of affirmative harm was demonstrated in a situation in which the decedent-patient, a shy man, broke out of a confinement room in an attempt to find clothing. He was pursued up and down the hall by the institution's medical doctor, who was holding an upraised chair. After being tripped by a male nurse and falling to the floor, the patient was set upon by the doctor and several nurses. They placed a tourniquet around his neck and tightened it, causing a stoppage of the flow of blood to the brain. A nurse was sent to a nearby drugstore to obtain a can of ether, which was then applied to the patient. Although the doctor's attention was called to the patient's cyanotic condition, the doctor continued to deny the patient air, thereby causing his death.

D. Inadequate treatment. The area of inadequate treatment is one of the most difficult in which to define the standard of care. Since the treatment of mental health disorders is often not governed by criteria as objective as those available in some areas of physical medicine, the courts have been reluctant to establish specific rules to govern liability. The law merely asks whether the treatment method used is reasonable under the circumstances. In order to arrive at this determination, the courts consider the factual basis from the perspective of the mental health sciences.

Courts have been reluctant to impose liability for inadequate treatment, and in order for the plaintiff to recover, there must be proof of negligence in the diagnostic or treatment procedures.

E. Unjustifiable confinement. The determination of whether or not to confine an individual involves many factors, such as the danger to the patient or to others, the theory or methods of treatments, available support for the individual in society, the severity of his condition, and, of course, due process consideration in terms of objective, verifiable standards which can be adequately tested in a court of law. (See Chapter 13, Special Legal Problems in Mental Health.)

Although these are judgments which cannot be made with total accuracy, the fact that precision cannot be achieved does not diminish the responsibility of practitioners to use all means at their disposal to protect an individual against unjustifiable confinement. The difficulty is in defining the standard which can be used to judge adequately whether the behavior of the practitioner meets the due diligence and skill requirements. How a psychiatrist or psychologist may best discharge his obligation to his patient is primarily a question of professional or medical judgment.

A psychiatrist is not always protected from liability for unjustifiable confinement by virtue of acting under the authority of a state statute. Even if he confines a patient to a mental hospital based upon a statutory certification process, it is possible that he may be found to have failed to utilize the minimum standard of skill required, for example, if he were to commit a person only on the basis of an anonymous phone call. Such a determination can hold true even if the mechanical requirements of the statute are met.

F. Duty to third parties. In addition to possible liability to the patient, a practitioner owes a duty to third parties. Because mentally ill persons may pose a risk to others, the practitioners must exercise reasonable care to prevent such harm; however, such a duty does not make the doctor an insurer of the patient's harmlessness.

The courts have, traditionally, been reluctant to find negligence on the part of a psychiatrist for the release of a patient who later inflicts harm on another. Although a patient may be known to have a mental disorder, there is no negligence on the part of a practitioner for reasonably releasing a patient where there is nothing to indicate that the patient is potentially dangerous. (Since future human behavior is so unpredictable, it would place an unreasonable burden to hold either the practitioner or the hospital liable for all of the acts of a patient after release, unless the plaintiff can show more than an honest error in professional judgment. The courts generally recognize that the decision to release a patient is subject to the risk of error in the prognosis and that the elimination of this risk would require the virtual elimination of all releases.)

IV. Some malpractice cases in different health professions and specialties.

A. Surgery and anesthesia.

(Case 37; *Bradshaw v. Blaine*, 1 Mich.App. 50,
134 N.W.2d 386)

Three hours after suffering a five-hour asthmatic attack, a patient underwent elective abdominal surgery performed by a surgeon who was aware of the attack. The appellate court sustained the trial court finding that expert testimony at trial was sufficient to prove that the surgeon had been negligent in conducting the operation, which resulted in the patient's death.

(Case 38; *Smedra v. Stanek*, 187 F.2d 892)

After suffering a serious injury to his spine, a patient underwent a two-phased operation in Denver to immobilize one of his vertebrae. One surgeon made an incision and removed a ruptured disk. Two other surgeons then made an incision in the ilium, removed a portion of bone, prepared it, and inserted it between the two vertebrae where the disk had been removed.

After being discharged from the hospital, the patient developed an irritated area in the area of the ilium incision. The patient consulted another physician, in Nebraska, and that doctor discovered an abscessed area which he treated for some weeks without success. The patient then returned to one of the two Denver surgeons who had made the initial ilium incision. The surgeon performed another operation and removed a piece of surgical gauze from the wound. The patient was sent home and was not informed of the removal of the gauze. Later, while changing the dressing, the patient discovered a string and a piece of gauze extending from the incision. The patient returned to the Nebraska physician, who removed a piece of surgical dressing 10 inches long from the incision. Both surgeons who had performed the original ilium incision were found liable for malpractice.

(See also Cases 5, 9, 11, 13, 14, 15, 18, 20, 21, 22, 23, 27, 28, 29.)

B. Orthopedics.

(Case 39; *Bowles v. Bourdon,* 219 S.W.2d 779)

An hour after the patient fractured his left elbow, a physician x rayed the fracture, set the arm, taped and bandaged the arm, and took another x ray. Approximately four hours later, the boy's parents called the physician, telling him that the hand was blue and cold. The physician responded that the hand was all right and asked that the boy be brought in the next day for an examination. The physician examined the boy every day for the next week, at which time he referred the case to a specialist, who diagnosed a Volkmann's contracture of the arm. The court found no negligence on the part of the physician, stating that there was no proof of proximate cause.

(Case 40; *Kingston v. McGrath,* 232 F.2d 495.)

The court held that a prima facie case of malpractice was established where a patient charged her physician with negligence in diagnosis of her neck and upper back fracture. Although the original x rays did not reveal the fracture, she continued to complain of severe pain and instability of her head for five weeks. The testimony of other physicians established that those were the usual symptoms of a neck fracture and that where such symptoms persist despite the original negative x rays, common medical standards call for further x rays.

(See also Cases 12, 16, 18, 58.)

C. Obstetrics and gynecology.

(Case 41; *Dazet v. Bass,* 254 So.2d 183.)

Following an operation to remove a cyst from the patient's ovary, a vesicovaginal fistual developed. The trial court directed the jury to find that there was no malpractice on the part of the physician because as a matter of law there was insufficient evidence to prove that the fistula had been caused by the operation or that the physician had not used ordinary care.

(Case 42; *Johns v. Gauthier*, 266 So.2d 504,
cert. denied 263 La. 376, 268 So.2d 260)

It was determined that a physician was guilty of malpractice for failing to remove the retained placenta following a spontaneous abortion, thus, necessitating a subsequent hysterectomy.

(See also Cases 2, 6,16, 20, 21, 27, 28.)

D. General practice, family practice, pediatrics, and internal medicine specialties.

(Case 43; *Caron v. U.S.*, 410 F.Supp. 378,
aff'd. 548 F.2d 366.)

A physician was held liable for malpractice because he injected an infant with a combination of typhoid, diphtheria, pertussis, and tetanus vaccines without conducting a physical examination of the infant or ascertaining the family's medical history. As a result the infant suffered seizures and brain damage.

(Case 44; *Smith v. West Calcasien-Cameron Hospital*,
25 So.2d 810.)

The extent of a physician's duty to instruct hospital personnel in the care of a patient was explored in this case. It was decided that the physician was not liable for malpractice because he did not specifically order the side rails on the patient's bed to be raised when he ordered medication for the patient. The evidence at trial established that raising the side rails was a matter normally and routinely performed by hospital personnel.

(Case 45; *Winchester v. Meads*, 372 Mich. 593,
127 N.W.2d 337.)

A physician was held liable for malpractice as a matter of law when a patient recovering from an ulcer operation was given an intravenous feeding of 1,000 cc. of distilled water without glucose because the physician had neglected to enter an instruction to add glucose.

(See also Cases 4, 8, 17, 24, 25, 30, 31)

E. Mental health practice.

> (Case 46; *Seavy v. State,* 21 App.Div.2d 445,
> 250 N.Y.S.2d 877, aff'd. 17 N.Y.2d 675,
> 216 N.E.2d 613, 269 N.Y.S.2d 455.)

The balance between the conflicting rights of a party seeking compensation for injury resulting from the acts of a released patient and the rights of the patient to receive rehabilitative treatment was noted by the court in a case brought by an injured third party. The patient was an educable mentally retarded young man who burned a barn on a dairy farm where he had been sent to work on a convalescent leave. There was no indication of a propensity toward pyromania in his history, and he had been responding favorably to treatment. The court found that the open door policy of the hospital had been widely accepted as a method of helping patients to return to participation in society and acknowledged the policy of favoring rehabilitation methods that were in accordance with sound medical knowledge.

> (Case 47; *Tarasoff v. Regents of the University of California,*
> 17 Cal.3rd 425, 551 P.2d 334, 131 Cal.Rptr. 14.)

In 1969, Prosenjit Poddar killed Tatiana Tarasoff. Two months earlier, Poddar, a psychiatric patient, had confided his intention to kill Tatiana to a psychologist at Cowell Memorial Hospital at the University of California, Berkeley. At the doctor's request, the campus police briefly detained Poddar but released him when he appeared to be rational. No one warned Tatiana that Poddar had threatened to take her life.

Following the death of their daughter, Tatiana's mother and father filed separate suits in state courts against the psychotherapists and the hospital. The trial court sustained a demurrer* by the defendants, thus dismissing the suits, and the plaintiffs appealed. The appellate court held that the plaintiffs could amend their complaints to allege that the failure of the psychotherapists to warn Tatiana constituted a breach of their duty to exercise reasonable care to protect her.

(See also Case 36)

F. Dentists.

(Case 48; *Simpson v. Davis*, 219 Kan 584,
549 P.2d 950)

A dentist was found liable for malpractice due to injuries suffered by a patient who swallowed a dental reamer. The evidence demonstrated that the dentist could have used a rubber dam to prevent the patient from swallowing the reamer. In addition, although the dentist was not a specialist in endodontic procedures, he undertook to perform endodontic procedures and was therefore held to the standard of a specialist.

(Case 49; *Negaard v. Estate of Feda*, 152 Mont. 47,
446 P.2d 436)

The court held that a dentist could not be presumed negligent when the plaintiff's mandible broke during extraction of a wisdom tooth. The evidence demonstrated that he could not have known before or during the extraction that there was insufficient buccal plate left to withstand the pressure or that the patient's mandible was so brittle.

(See also Case 1)

---

*A demurrer is a statement by the defendant to the effect that even if plaintiff's allegations are true, there is no legal basis of action, that is, a motion to dismiss. The demurrer was based on the notion that the doctor-patient relationship was only between the defendant and Poddar and that Tatiana, as an outside third party, had no legal right to sue. The demurrer was granted by the trial court, and the suit was dismissed. Plaintiff appealed. The case went to the California Supreme Court twice. Both times the ruling overturned the trial court's decision and stated that the defendant did have a duty to Tatiana, including a requirement, if necessary, of warning her of the danger. The duty to protect third parties overrode the duty and the right of patient-doctor confidentiality.

G. Nurses.

A nurse is obligated to possess reasonable skill and to apply that skill with care. The standard for judging the skill and care in this area is less well defined than for physician malpractice. In most cases, it appears that the courts require that a nurse exercise the skill and care ordinarily utilized by others in similar positions. Because the specific function involved may vary considerably depending on local custom and practice, a nurse should be responsible for complying with the standards of the local community.

(Case 50; *Medical & Surgical Memorial Hospital v. Cauthorn,* 229 S.W.2d 932)

It was determined that a nurse was negligent for burning a patient's foot with a heat cradle. The cradle was supposed to be used every other hour for an hour at a time. While it was in use during one of these periods, a nurse threw a blanket over it. It was apparently forgotten about and remained turned on for several hours.

(See also Cases 30, 45)

H. Hospital technicians.

(Case 51; *Mazer v. Lipschutz,* 327 F.2d 42)

That two patients with the same name were in the hospital at the same time resulted in the death of one of them when the wrong type of blood was used in a transfusion during a gall bladder operation. Although aware that there were two patients with the same name, the technician in charge of the blood bank confused the two, and as a result the wrong blood type was used. The court held that the blood bank technician could be found negligent, and that, in addition, the physician in charge of the case could possibly be found vicariously liable.

(Case 52; *Gilles v. Rehabilitation Institute of Oregon,* 262 Or. 422, 498 P.2d 777)

A physical therapist was held liable for negligence where a patient was injured when she slid down a tilt-table as its position was being changed from vertical to horizontal.

I. Ophthalmologists and optometrists. Courts generally require that a plaintiff establish the standard of skill and care for an optometrist through the testimony of other optometrists. On occasion, however, the courts have allowed ophthalmologists to testify in this regard. As with other specialties, the standard is increasingly one of national, rather than local, scope for both ophthalmologists and optometrists.

(Case 53; *Hoton v. Pfingst*, 534 S.W.2d 786)

In performing a detached retina operation, an ophthalmologist placed a hollow polyethylene ring of tubing around the eye as part of the procedure. It was later discovered that it was a type of tubing which could result in erosion through the sclera. Accordingly, a softer type of plastic was substituted. After losing the use of the eye the patient sued the ophthalmologist. The decision was in favor of the doctor, the court finding that there was insufficient evidence that the defendant had not used acceptable medical practice.

(Case 54; *Maedgen v. Kolodny*, 384 S.W.2d 410)

In order to correct a ptosis of the eyelid, the physician performed a fascia lata sling-type operation, by which support is given to the upper eyelid by attaching it to the occipito-frontalis muscles of the forehead by means of a strip of fascia lata tissue from the patient's thigh. After the operation the patient experienced complications, including a corneal ulcer caused by constant exposure of the cornea to the air. Based on the testimony of an ophthalmologist it was determined that the defendant could be held liable for the injury to the patient.

(Case 55; *Barbee v. Rogers*, 425 S.W.2d 342)

A patient who suffered eye damage after wearing improperly fitted contact lenses brought an action against the optometrist and the manufacturer of the lenses. Relying on the factual conclusions of the jury, the appel-

late court held that there was no proof that improper fit
of the lenses had caused the corneal damage and that,
therefore, the optometrists could not be held liable. Regarding the cause of action against the manufacturer,
the court held that there was no application of the doctrine of strict liability (liability for injury without negligence) to contact lenses.

(See also Cases 10, 26)

General References

1. *American Jurisprudence* (2nd ed.). Physicians and Surgeons. Ban-
   croft-Whitney, San Francisco, to date
2. *American Law Reports* (3rd ed.). Sections on Malpractice. Bancroft-
   Whitney, San Francisco, to date
3. Shea, T.E. Legal Standard of Care for Psychiatrists and Psychologists. *Western State Univ. Law Rev.* 6; 71–99, 1978

Questions on Chapter 8, Malpractice

1. Is the basis of a malpractice case contract or tort law?
2. Is a general practitioner held to the same standard as a specialist?
3. Can a physician be held liable for the actions of someone else?
4. Does a physician always need the consent of the patient before operating?
5. Can a physician in Boston be judged by the standards of physicians in California?
6. What should a physician do if he is going on vacation?
7. Is verbal consent from a patient sufficient?
8. Is a physician obliged to reveal to a patient methods of treatment which are alternatives to those the physician recommends?
9. Is a hospital liable for the negligence of physicians who use the hospital facilities?
10. When is a physician required to consult with a specialist?

CHAPTER 9

Coping With the Medical Malpractice Problem
Thomas E. Shea and Nathan T. Sidley

Coping With the Medical Malpractice Problem

Thomas E. Shea and Nathan T. Sidley

I. Background of the malpractice problem.

A. Introduction.

From the perspective of the patient the goal in seeing a physician is to be assured of competent and conscientious medical treatment; the practitioner's desire is to practice effectively free from legal harassment and interference. In a theoretical sense there is no conflict, but a practical reconciliation of these two valid perspectives has not yet been achieved. The present system for handling allegations of medical malpractice is slow, often inefficient, costly, and capricious.

B. General facts about malpractice claims.
1. It is estimated that five percent (approximately 16,000) of practicing physicians are "incompetent."[1] A total of five percent of practicing physicians are considered to be impaired because of alcoholism or drug use.[2]
   a. It is thought that approximately 1 in 100,000 physician-patient encounters leads to a malpractice claim.[3]
   b. Only 1 in 10 malpractice incidents which could give rise to a claim actually results in one.[4]
   c. It is estimated that approximately one-third of malpractice claims have "merit."[5] The proportion is greater with respect to malpractice suits filed in court, because of the weeding out or settling of frivolous, nuisance, or trivial cases.

233

2. Approximately five percent of practicing attorneys handle medical malpractice cases (over a three year period).[6]

   a. Attorneys who are plaintiffs' specialists handle an average of 6 such cases a year; defendants' specialists handle an average of 30 cases annually.[7]

   b. Plaintiffs' attorneys accept approximately 10 percent of the potential cases they evaluate. A total of 40 percent are rejected because of no perceived liability; 5 percent are rejected because potential awards are not high enough.[8]

      1) Attorneys almost never accept malpractice cases without consulting a practitioner first.[9]

   c. Interestingly, the incidence of medical malpractice cases has risen coincident with a decline in auto injury cases, after passage of no-fault auto insurance laws.[10]

3. In perhaps one-half of the cases that become claims, some payment is made.[11]

   a. Specialists' clients receive some payment approximately 80 percent of the time.[12]

   b. The average gross malpractice recovery for all attorneys prosecuting such claims in the early 1970's was $22,000; the median payment was $3,500.[13]

      1) 3 percent of claims resulted in payments of more than $100,000.[14]

      2) The average amount awarded is less than 2 percent of the amount demanded.[15]

   c. The average gross recovery to clients of plaintiffs' specialist attorneys was $81,000; the median payment was $25,000.[16] (Case selection factors as well as skills are involved in the differences of specialists' recoveries from those of nonspecialists.)

   d. Human factors in determining the sizes of awards.[17]

      1) Juries and judges tend to evaluate awards relatively similarly, although some judges tend not to be as liberal as juries.

      2) Ethnicity and economic background are more important factors determining the size of jury awards than are age, sex, marital status, religion, or political party.

    a) Unskilled laborers award the most, then skilled laborers, then clerical workers. Proprietors award the least.

    b) Blacks award the most, then Mid-southeastern European descendants, then Yankees. Scandinavians and British award the least.

  e. Lawyers' fees (usually on a contingency basis) most commonly are one-third of the amount received (with expenses deducted),[18] depending on the stage of the case at the time of recovery.

    1) In some states, an attorney referring a case to another attorney may receive a percentage of the other attorney's fee.[19]

    2) Specialists estimate that they spend 100 hours in a case for each $25,000 recovered.[20]

4. The incidence of claims has been increasing.

  a. In 1970 the industry had 2,434 outstanding claims; in 1973 there were 4,348.[21]

  b. In 1970, 1 in 20 doctors was sued; in 1973, 1 in 13 faced a suit.[22]

5. The amount of payment per claim has also increased.

6. Disposition of claims in psychiatric malpractice cases. (Other professionals' malpractice cases may be different.)

  a. Approximately one-half are settled or are abandoned without the filing of a court suit.[23]

  b. A total of 90 percent of those in which a suit is filed are either settled with payments or are abandoned before trial. (Approximately one-half go each way.)[24]

  c. Many suits that go to trial are settled during the course of the trial. The great cost of trying a case is a strong incentive to both parties to resolve the issue by settlement. Fairly objective considerations determining the value of the case lead to reasonable settlement appraisals by plaintiff and defendant, although intangible considerations reward the better poker players.

  d. A total of 1 in 5 verdicts is in favor of the plaintiff.[25]

    1) Only small numbers of cases are appealed, partly because of the great costs.

C. Physician's malpractice parameters.

1. A disproportionately large number of malpractice cases involve a relatively small group of physicians, some of whom are the targets of multiple suits.

2. Practitioners in urban areas (for example, New York, Florida, or California) are more likely to be sued than those in rural areas or in other states.[26]

3. A total of 4 of 5 malpractice claims involves hospital practice; only 1 in 5 is related to office visits.[27]

4. Three of four malpractice claims are against physicians. The rest involve hospitals, clinics, and other health-care professionals.[28]

   a. A total of 1 in 3 claims against physicians were for "high-risk" surgeons (who perform complicated major surgery); 1 in 5 were against "medium-risk" surgeons; 1 in 10 were against "low-risk" surgeons, and 1 in 10 were against those who perform only minor surgery or assist in operations on their own general practice patients. Approximately 1 in 4 claims against doctors are against physicians who do not perform surgery.[29]

   b. Surgery and its consequences also account for a disproportionate share of costs of malpractice awards.

      1) More things ordinarily can go wrong in surgery than in medical cases; therefore, more things do go wrong, given the same degree of skill and attentiveness on the part of practitioners.

      2) There is ordinarily a shorter space of time available to evaluate situations and to correct errors than there is in medical cases.

      3) The above two factors tend to put more psychic tension on practitioners, which also tends to decrease effectiveness.

D. Malpractice insurance:

1. General principle. Groups of people at risk pay premiums. Claims and jury awards are paid from the premium pool.

   a. Insurance financing.

      1) Insurance company expenses.

         a) Administration and sales costs.

    b) Defending against suits. (Between 1970 and 1972, the average legal cost for defending against a suit was approximately $5,000,[30] money which had to be paid whether the case was won or lost.)

    c) Claims paid.

  2) Insurance company income.

    a) Premiums.

    b) Income from investments.

  3) A private company must also generate profit from its activities.

  4) Premiums go down in good years, for example, years with low claim payments or with high investment returns; premiums go up under the opposite conditions.

b. Types of policies.

  1) Occurrence. If a practitioner is sued for an incident which occurred when he was insured with the company, the company defends him and pays to the limits of the policy.

  2) Claims made. The company defends and pays, based on the making of a claim during the time period when the individual is insured. The time of occurrence of the incident is not important.

c. Timing.

  1) Approximately one-half of malpractice claims are resolved and paid within two years of the incident. Almost all are paid within six years.[31] As a general rule, cases disposed of later tend to result in higher insurance company payments than those closed earlier.[32]

  2) Problem—the "long tail." Because of inflationary factors, cases that last a long time are often resolved at high costs because of financial standards in effect at the time of settlement rather than at the time of occurrence. An insurance company has a difficult time anticipating future losses[33] because of this inflationary factor.

d. Premium classes. For purposes of assessing premiums for medical malpractice insurance, the major insurance companies in the field have developed a system of five classifications based upon expected claims:

1) Class I. This classification includes physicians who perform no surgery. They pay the base rate for malpractice insurance.

2) Class II. Physicians in this category perform minor surgery or only assist in major surgery on their own patients. (This category includes radiologists.) These physicians pay 1.75 times the base rate.

3) Class III. Physicians who perform surgery and are not included in another category pay three times the base rate.

4) Class IV. Specialists, including anesthesiologists, cardiac surgeons, general surgeons, gynecologists, plastic surgeons, thoracic surgeons, urologists, and vascular surgeons, pay four times the base rate.

5) Class V. Orthopedists and neurosurgeons pay five times the base rate.

2. The "malpractice insurance crisis." Due to unpredictable losses and because of poor investment performance, companies writing medical malpractice insurance have either tried to abandon the field or have raised their premiums precipitously. Many strong feelings were engendered among practitioners, institutions, and consumers.

II. Specific proposals suggested for coping with the malpractice problem.

A. Streamlining, cost-cutting, and practice-improving measures.

1. Screening panels.

a. Concept. The idea behind a screening panel is to have the merits of a medical malpractice claim evaluated by a group of experts prior to litigation, so unmeritorious cases can be weeded out. The composition of the panel may include attorneys and laypersons in addition to physicians. Under some systems, the panel may base its decision only on a written record, consisting of statements from the patient and other witnesses, reports from medical experts, and briefs from counsel. Under more formal systems, the panel may actually conduct a hearing, with sworn testimony by witnesses and arguments by counsel, in effect a "mini-trial."

Submission of a case to a screening panel may be made voluntary or compulsory. A voluntary system can provide the plaintiff with the benefit of an impartial evaluation of the case or help protect the practitioner from unjustified litigation. A voluntary system may also encourage submission of cases to the panel by supplying medical witnesses at trial for cases which the panel judges to be meritorious. Because of the difficulty plaintiffs often have in finding physicians who are willing to testify against other physicians accused of malpractice, this can be a significant incentive. Under a compulsory plan, submission of a medical malpractice claim to the screening panel is a requisite to litigation. Sanction for failure to abide by the decision of the screening panel can take various forms:

1) At one extreme is the possibilty of legally disabling the plaintiff or defendant from contesting the panel's decision or from litigating further matters decided by the panel. This alternative is clearly unconstitutional, however, because it bars a person's right of access to the courts.

2) Less drastic, but highly effective, is permitting the screening panel's findings to be introduced at a later trial. This procedure has been challenged on constitutional grounds with mixed results.

3) The plaintiff may be required to post a bond to cover court costs, if the screening panel determines the case to be without merit.

Even without formal sanctions, screening panels can prove effective by providing independent evaluation of a claim.

b. Evaluation.

1) A screening panel may provide several benefits as a mechanism for relieving some of the defects of the medical malpractice system by:

a) Encouraging settlement of claims based upon independent evaluation of the facts by experts.

  b) Discouraging frivolous suits.

  c) Clarifying the issues if the case does go to trial.

  d) Providing expert witnesses for plaintiffs with legitimate claims.

 2) Screening panels have received criticism as well as praise, with critics presenting several arguments, such as:

  a) Compulsory screening panels infringe on the constitutional rights of due process and free access to the courts.

  b) Admission of a panel's findings at a trial is improper because of inadequate assurances that a panel's procedures will be fair and will comply with minimum due process requirements.

  c) The introduction of such evidence usurps the function of the courts and the jury system.

  d) Voluntary screening panels have generally proved to be ineffective.

  e) Many panels are biased against patients and in favor of practioners.

  f) The panel only duplicates the function of the court and adds to the costs of administering the malpractice system and to the time required to process a case.

2. Arbitration.

 a. Concept. Arbitration is a non judicial method of dispute settlement, which has been widely advocated as a mechanism for resolving a variety of disputes. Under arbitration, the parties agree to submit the case to an arbitrator, who is usually an attorney, rather than to a court, for resolution. This decision to arbitrate may be made prior to the time the dispute arises, or it may be made after the problem has been manifested. Because of the constitutional right to have legal disputes settled by a court, both parties must freely agree on who the arbitrator shall be and on what procedures he will use. The courts will often look closely at an arbitration agreement, and the agreement will be narrowly construed.

The mechanics of arbitration are less formal than judicial proceedings. Rules of evidence are more liberal, and the arbitrator's role differs from that of the judge in that the arbitrator generally plays a more active role in the hearing. An arbitration agreement generally provides that the decision of the arbitrator is final and binding on the parties, although provisions may be made for exceptions to finality. The binding effect of arbitration, when agreed to by the parties, has been recognized by most states.

Several states have adopted voluntary arbitration statutes which detail the rights and obligations of parties agreeing to arbitrate their disputes. In most states, the decision of the arbitrator is subject to judicial review, on such grounds as fraud, a clear misinterpretation of the law, or a factual determination that is unsupported by any substantial evidence.

As applied to medical malpractice claims, arbitration could be brought about through an agreement signed by the practitioner and the patient prior to treatment, or it could be the result of an agreement between the parties after a dispute has arisen. Selection of an arbitrator could be made by naming potential individuals in the agreement, or as is more usual, by providing a method for mutual selection of an arbitrator at the time the dispute occurs.

b. Evaluation.
1) As compared with a judicial proceeding, arbitration provides several advantages to one or both parties:
   a) It is less costly than a trial.
   b) It is less time consuming.
   c) The procedure is less formal.
   d) The absence of a jury results in a less emotional, more direct presentation of the evidence.
   e) The expanded role of the arbitrator allows him more flexibility in getting at the truth.
   f) The arbitrator has greater discretion than a judge concerning focusing of issues and admissibility of evidence.

g) Settlement of a case on a realistic basis may be enhanced by the role of the arbitrator.

2) Despite these several advantages, arbitration has not had the widespread use its proponents advocate, and in the medical malpractice area, it has played a minor role. Some of the advantages of arbitration for one party correlate to disadvantages from the perspective of the other party.

a) The faster resolution of a case by arbitration can be seen as a disadvantage to plaintiffs, because delay sometimes works to a defendant's advantage but seldom to a plaintiff's advantage.

b) Selection of an arbitrator satisfactory to both parties is difficult, especially in malpractice cases.

c) An unsophisticated patient may sign a pre-treatment arbitration agreement, with provisions favoring the practitioner, without understanding its consequences.

d) Some arbitration decisions are later appealed to the courts, thus eliminating a substantial part of the time-cost advantages.

3. No-fault compensation (analogous to Workers' Compensation).

a. Concept. One possibility for resolving aspects of the present situation is through the use of a no-fault compensation system. Under a no-fault system, a patient who is injured during medical treatment would be compensated, whether or not the injury was caused by malpractice. Payment would be made through a comprehensive insurance program. Because the patient is compensated for his injuries, there would be few instances in which the patient could sue his doctor. Since fault would not be an issue, there would be no litigation on the question of whether the actions of the physician constituted malpractice.

The effect of a no-fault system would be to broaden greatly the number of patients receiving some type of compensation for injuries. Patients who are injured in the course of treatment would be compensated even though the physician exercised requisite skill and care. Patients would be compensated for unavoidable injuries as well as injuries resulting from malpractice.

b. Evaluation. The principal advantage of a no-fault system would be to reduce the amount of litigation. The reduction would chiefly occur in the area of determining whether the actions of a practitioner constituted malpractice. Nevertheless there may still be substantial litigation concerning whether an injury occurred during treatment and concerning the amount of compensation to be paid.

A no-fault system would probably be more expensive than the present system. Its detractors also argue that a no-fault system would be very difficult to administer effectively. Proponents have asserted that although such a system would be expensive, it would be more equitable, providing compensation more effectively and spreading the cost more evenly.

4. Professional self-regulation and awareness.

a. Concept. One partial solution to the medical malpractice crisis is to increase self-regulation by the medical profession in order to reduce the number of malpractice incidents. Such a proposal does not address the question of unwarranted malpractice claims but is aimed only at preventing malpractice on a recurring basis by those few doctors who continually do not comply with professional standards.

The medical profession, as a whole, has traditionally been reluctant to discipline its members formally, and physicians, individually, have been reluctant to criticize others publicly. As a result, there have been instances where an incompetent or impaired physician has been allowed to continue practicing unimpeded, even though other physicians were aware of the situation. It has been suggested, therefore, that commitment by the medical profession to regulate itself more effectively could significantly reduce the incidence of malpractice. The mechanisms for a system of increased self-regulation are generally already in operation. The problem is not that the procedures do not exist, but rather, that they are not used as effectively as they might be. Hospitals, as well as state medical boards, have usually provided methods for disciplining physicians who do not live up to the standards of the medical profession. These regulatory systems should, and usually do, provide necessary due process requirements in order to protect the rights of the physician as well as the public.

b. There are several factors that seem related to the low level of disciplinary actions against physicians by their fellow doctors.

1) Physicians tend to recognize that no one is perfect and that in some instances, a bad result which leads to a lawsuit is a matter of chance. There is a need to stick together for self-protection, and there is also a sense among doctors that a physician who testifies against another is a turncoat.

2) Physicians, especially certain specialists, have practices built on referrals from other physicians. To discipline other physicians runs the risk of alienating referral sources and prejudicing oneself professionally.

3) Finally, physicians tend to practice in the same locations and in the same hospitals over long periods of time. Friendships and patterns of social camaraderie develop. It is very difficult for a practitioner to discipline a friend, which almost invariably terminates the friendship and invites enmity. The situation is further complicated because physicians' spouses are often involved in the social relationships.

   To some extent, an emphasis on helping the individual to correct his deficiency, either by further education or by treatment, might make it easier for other physicians to deal with the doctor who performs in a substandard manner. The substandard practitioner, however, is likely to have denied to himself the implications of his defects and is likely to resist and resent efforts to change his behavior.

c. A corollary approach, based on the assumption that losing a malpractice case means that the practitioner's capabilities are inadequate, would be for the medical licensing board to place such a practitioner on a kind of probation and appoint a supervisor of his practice. There might also be requirements of further training imposed. If the level of practice did not improve, the practitioner's license might be suspended.

d. Peer review audits of physicians' practices and professional standards review organizations are another mechanism to monitor physician performance. The same limitations exist as in other modes of physician discipline. Sometimes, outsiders are involved in peer review, but they are usually regarded as interfering and unsympathetic "hatchet" men. The situation is even worse when nonphysician reviewers, usually nurses with some additional training, are employed as reviewers. The medical profession, insofar as it is organized, has resisted any type of mandated review procedure. At present, there is no clearly effective method of disciplining, or of even helping, substandard physicians effectively.

e. Continuing medical education (CME) programs represent another effort to maintain proficiency of practice among physicians. Such programs are time-consuming, costly, not of uniform quality, and often inconvenient, especially for solo practitioners located at a distance from urban centers. There is opposition to mandatory continuing education as a requirement for continued licensure. There is no satisfactory method of determining whether such education programs have resulted in significantly improving practice. In view of government and consumer efforts to upgrade physician performance, however, the profession prefers the imposition of continuing education requirements to the imposition of an even more disliked and burdensome system of periodic recertification by examination.

f. Evaluation. The main benefit from increased self-regulation would be to prevent continued malpractice by those few physicians who are responsible for a disproportionately large share of malpractice claims and recoveries. A determined effort by the medical profession to discipline its incompetent and impaired members would probably result in a decrease in the incidence of malpractice.

Awareness by physicians of fundamental legal principles and an understanding of their general application could also avert some malpractice claims. Since the standard for determining whether an action constitutes malpractice, however, is essentially a medical one, an awareness of the legal principles would not alter the basic medical judgments or practices of most physicians.

B. Insurance company-sponsored proposals to reduce claim payments.
   1. Change from occurrence coverage to claims-made coverage.
      a. Concept. This enables more predictability of loss by reducing the uncertainty of payout to the period following filing of a claim, as opposed to the present system in which the insurer may not learn of a claim until years after the incident occurs. (A long statute of limitations, the "discovery rule" (which means that the statute of limitations does not begin to run until the malpractice was, or should reasonably have been, discovered), and the fact that for a minor the statute of limitations does not begin to run until he comes of age, all result in some long, unpredictable delays between the occurrence of the incident and the ultimate disposition of the case. Those delays increase unforeseen costs to the insurance companies.)
      b. A practitioner retiring from practice would have to pay premiums even though he wasn't seeing patients, in order to provide for delayed claims against him. Usually after paying such premiums for three years, the retired practitioner would be regarded as permanently insured, however.

   2. Modify the Statute of Limitations.
      a. Concept. The statute of limitations in the area of medical malpractice protects practitioners. There are three principal justifications for imposing a statue of limitations in medical malpractice cases.

1) The evidentiary advantage to the parties and court of trying a case while the witnesses can still recall the facts and before relevant records are destroyed or lost.
2) The general principle is that a practitioner should not have to continuously look over his shoulder into the distant past, wondering if he is going to be sued.
3) The most general principle is that at some time the open book must be shut; past actions must be set aside as no longer being legally relevant.

b. Based upon these concepts, the law has insisted that an injured party has a duty to file a suit within a statutorily defined period of time. The time period allowed varies from state to state, with the most common limitation being three years from the date of the injury. Legislatures have usually carved out several exceptions to a strict application of the limitations period, however.

1) In many states, the clock does not begin to tick until the patient discovers (or reasonably should have discovered) the injury. The reason for this exception is that there are some instances in which an injury will not be manifested until a later date.
2) Many statutes also exempt cases of fraud from a strict application of the limitations period. When a practitioner purposefully conceals information of a negligent act from a patient, the limitations period does not begin to run until the fraud is, or should have been, discovered.
3) Most states provide that the statute of limitations does not run against a minor or a person with a mental incapacity. Once the child reaches the age of majority (now, usually 18) or the mentally incapacitated person is cured, the time period begins to run. Some states have tightened up on the exceptions, with Texas leading the way by eliminating all exceptions.

c. Evaluation. At best, a statute of limitations modification can play only a small part in the solution to the malpractice problem; a statute of limitations does not alter the basic process of dispute settlement or affect the basic inequities.

Eliminating or narrowing the exceptions to a statute of limitations also provides greater predictability to the practitioner and to the insurance company. The effect of restrictions necessary to achieve this certainty may be to deny access to the courts for deserving individuals, though. The argument is made that a strict statute of limitations will prevent at least some unmeritorious claims, but it will also prevent some meritorious ones as well, without distinguishing between the two.

3. Limit recovery amounts.
   a. Concept. One of the important facets of the medical malpractice system is the amount of recovery awarded. Large awards, especially those more than $1 million, often receive extensive publicity, while awards of lesser sums, as well as judgments of no liability, seldom receive attention. The fact is that the large awards are newsworthy and glamorous; they are attention-getters. Unfortunately, this phenomenon leads to a common misconception that judgments against doctors in malpractice cases are the rule and that the damages awarded are often huge. Laymen may assume that the cases they read about or see on television are representative, while, in fact, they are the extreme exceptions.

   Despite their infrequency, however, there have been many judgments in excess of $1 million, and the question has been raised as to whether such awards can ever be justified. Some physicians, insurance companies, and attorneys have answered by urging the establishment of some type of ceiling on damage awards.

   The concept is not without precedent. Workers' Compensation laws have been accepted throughout the United States. Their main functions have been to compensate persons who are injured on the job and, at the same time, establish definite ceilings on the amounts such persons are able to recover from their employers. Several states have already mandated comparable satutory limitations on the amount of recovery allowed in malpractice cases.

   As opposed to providing a single dollar amount ceiling

for all medical malpractice claims, it would also be possible to establish a series of ceilings for different types of injuries. The legislature of a state could determine the maximum recovery that would be allowed for specified particular injuries or categories of injuries, especially for the intangible and unmeasurable, "pain and suffering."

A corollary to the limitation of damages is abolishing punitive damages in malpractice cases, partly on the grounds that the offender doesn't get punished; rather, his colleagues and the public pay.

b. Evaluation. The goal of the legal system in awarding damages in medical malpractice actions is to place the injured party in as good a position as he was prior to the injury. The aim is to compensate the plaintiff but not to provide a windfall. Because of the nature of the compensation process, a jury finds itself with little in the way of firm guidance concerning the award of damages. Some aspects of the plaintiff's injuries can be measured accurately, for example, medical bills and the loss of past earnings. Other aspects, such as the values of sight or of pain and suffering are virtually impossible to quantify in terms of dollars.

It is no surprise that the damages awards of juries vary greatly, even when plaintiffs' situations and injuries are similar. The decision of the jury results from an interplay of the background, ideas, and emotions of each member, and of the strategies and techniques of the attorneys, in their arguments and presentations of the evidence. As a result, the amount of damages awarded is often influenced as much by the personal conceptions and emotions of the jury and by the skill of the attorneys as it is by the actual facts of the case.

Because of these factors, it has been argued that the damages awarded in medical malpractice cases are often excessive. The excessive awards drive up the cost of medical malpractice insurance, and ultimately the cost of medical treatment. By placing limitations on recovery in such cases, the system could still provide adequate compensation for injured plaintiffs, while preventing windfalls. As a result, insurance companies could more accurately predict and limit costs, thereby holding the line on premiums.

The counterargument to such a system of limitations on recovery is that such a concept is unfair and usurps the function of the jury system. The jury, rather than the legislature, is in the best position to tailor an award of damages to a particular case. Moreover, a limitation on recovery might leave a particular plaintiff without adequate compensation.

The constitutional argument has also been successfully raised that this unreasonably discriminates against those who have been injured because of medical negligence as compared with those injured because of other kinds of negligence.

The reconciliation of these opposing sets of arguments is difficult, and any conclusion must be based on a balancing rather than an absolute process. Necessarily, any limitation on recovery infringes on the rights of an injured party, but if the ceiling is placed at a reasonably high level and recognized to be only part of the solution, the benefits may be significant enough to justify implementation.

4. Limit attorneys' fees.
  a. Concept. Attorneys generally charge their clients in one of two ways, on an hourly basis or by a contingency fee. For most matters, including commercial law and the defense of personal injury suits, attorneys usually charge by the hour. A problem arises, however, in medical malpractice and other personal injury cases, where the injured party may not have enough money to pay for the services of an attorney. In such cases, attorneys generally work on a contingency fee, receiving an agreed-upon percentage of any recovery. The percentage may vary in accordance with the stage of the proceedings at which a settlement or judgment is obtained. For example, an attorney may receive 30 percent if a settlement is reached before trial, 35 percent if the case is tried and 40 percent if the case is appealed.

Contingency fees of more than 40 percent are rare except where small amounts of money are involved.

As a result of the contingency fee system, an attorney who represents a plaintiff in a case where a large recovery is involved may receive a very substantial fee. On the other hand, an attorney makes nothing on those cases where recovery is denied. In theory, the earnings of an attorney will balance out to a reasonable level of compensation over a period of time. On an average, this theory seems to hold true. Attorneys specializing in personal injury and medical malpractice cases have earnings approximately equal to the average of the profession as a whole. The parity holds true for both plaintiffs' and defendants' attorneys.

Despite the general level of earnings, it makes one pause to think of an attorney's receiving a $350,000 fee for winning a $1 million case or even receiving $50,000 for handling a $150,000 case that is settled prior to trial.

In fact, attorneys receive a greater percentage of the malpractice insurance premium dollar than the injured parties. This means that the sum, of the money paid to defense attorneys by insurance companies and the money paid by plaintiffs to their attorneys, is greater than the net payments received by the plaintiffs themselves. The inefficiency of such a system cannot be denied.

As a partial remedy for this imbalance, several states have imposed limitations on the contingency fees that attorneys may charge. An attorney may not charge a greater percentage than provided in the statute. For example, the attorney's fee might be limited to a schedule like this:

> 40 percent of the first $50,000 recovered;
> 33⅓ percent of $50,000–$100,000;
> 25 percent of $100,000–$200,000;
> 10 percent or the amount over $200,000.

b. Evaluation. Reasonable contingency fee limitations serve no injustice to the legal profession. A good system can provide sufficient compensation to attorneys while, at the same time, preventing undeserved fees. The rights of injured parties unable to pay for legal services are protected because such systems retain adequate incentive to attract qualified attorneys.

5. Change the informed consent rule.
   Formerly, the standard required the physician to provide as much information as was customary in the locality. Now, the tendency is to demand that enough information be given so that a reasonable person could make an informed decision.
   a. Concept. Treating a patient without his permission is a battery and subjects a practitioner to liability. The patient must be given adequate and accurate information in order to give his permission reasonably.
      1) Under most circumstances deliberately misinforming the patient is fraud and invites liability. This is uncommon.
      2) The real question of importance is how much information to give. Saying too much about side effects may frighten the patient into avoiding an important treatment. Not mentioning the side effects may give rise to litigation for not providing adequate information.
      3) A further complication is that patients often forget what they have been told. They may even forget that they have signed consent forms. Sometimes the patient is told to sign a printed form and the terms are later verbally modified, or one of the parties thinks they are verbally modified.
   b. Recommendation. Provide a criterion for informed consent by statute in order to remove some of the ambiguity for the practitioner.
   c. Evaluation.
      1) Such a statute might help, particularly if evidence of oral qualification of a signed permission is not allowed.
      2) Though informed consent is an area of concern, less than 3 percent of malpractice claims allege lack of informed consent.[33]

6. Require that the plaintiff submit an itemized list of damages claimed and require the jury to make awards on an item-by-item basis.
   a. Usual damages categories:
      1) Medical expenses—past and future.
      2) Loss of earnings—past and future.
      3) Loss of "consortium," that is, what a family member loses when another family member is disabled.
      4) Pain and suffering.
      5) Usually an effort is made to figure in expected effects of inflation.
   b. Concept. Forcing the jury to think in terms of specific items may lower the overall award.
   c. This proposal is usually linked with the idea that specific item awards could be appealed.
   d. It is also usually linked with a proposal to prevent the plaintiff from expressing an overall damages amount (the ad damnum statement).
   e. Evaluation. The amount finally paid in a malpractice claim usually amounts to less than 5 pecent of the ad damnum. Eliminating it would probably not radically alter costs.

7. Some miscellaneous recommendations.
   a. Allow the award to be paid in installments. This would compensate for lost earnings and other costs but would often cost less in the long run to the insurance company, and it would render experience more predictable.
   b. Allow introduction of evidence concerning other moneys the plaintiff may have received, from health insurance, sick leave, or disability insurance, in connection with the effects of the malpractice episode. (Forbidding mention of those moneys is called the "collateral source rule.")
      The purpose is to prevent the plaintiff from collecting twice for the same injury. Generally, though, if the plaintiff has collected from one insurance company and then collects from another for the same loss, the first insurance company can be paid back by the "right of subrogation." (See Chapter 7, Torts).

    c. Allow abuse-of-process counterclaims by the defendant against the plaintiff even before the initial action is terminated; require the plaintiff to pay costs if he loses the case; require the plaintiff's attorney to file an affidavit that he regards the case as meritorious before he files suit. These measures are designed to make a plaintiff think twice before bringing a suit.

    d. Eliminate res ipsa loquitur. The doctrine of res ipsa loquitur is infrequently used, however. Attorneys generally believe it is ineffective compared to live expert testimony. Adopting the recommendation would not save much money.

    e. As a combination method of driving home to practitioners the necessity to practice up to standard and also as a money saver on small claim payments, it has been also suggested that there be a deductible amount on insurance company payments such that the practitioner would pay the first $1,000 (or similar amount) on each claim that has successfully been made against him.

8. The general concept of the foregoing proposals is that of reducing the numbers of claims and the amount paid on each claim. None of these suggestions relates to the actual occurrence of incidents of malpractice but, rather, all involve the subsequent legal handling. The major legal problem in these approaches involves ensuring that malpractice cases are treated equitably in relation to the entire tort system.

The fundamental problem is to reduce malpractice. The major issue here is not to compromise the practitioner's right to practice conscientiously.

The total cost to society of human error in the practice of health care is beginning to be appreciated. The field of error control has been less explored than monetary loss. More work in these areas must be done. It is hoped that such health care errors will be at their irreducible minimum soon.

References

1. Medical malpractice Part II: What to do now. *Consumer Reports* 42;598–601, 1977 (p. 598)

2. Gitlow, S.E. The impaired physician: New York State's approach. *Alcoholism Update* 4;2, 1981 (Ayerst Laboratories)

3. Butterfield, A. The malpractice jungle. *Psychiatric News*, May 19, 1975

4. Medical liability insurance market shows improvement. *Malpractice Digest* Jan./Feb., 1979, p. 4. (St. Paul Fire and Marine Insurance)

5. Chayet, N. The physician and the jury. *NEJM* 275; 1242–1243, 1966

6. Curran, W.J. *How Lawyers Handle Medical Malpractrice Cases: An Analysis of an Important Medicolegal Study.* US Gov't DHEW Publication No. (HRA) 76-3152, 1976, p. 7

7. *Ibid.,*

8. *Ibid.,* p. 9

9. *Ibid.,* p. 11

10. *Court Docket Survey.* Physicians Crisis Committee, 1930 Buhl Building, Detroit, MI 48226, 1975, p. 9

11. Curran, W.J. (1976), p. 32

12. *Ibid.,* p. 19

13. *Ibid.*

14. Curran, W.J. The Malpractice Commission Report: Controversy unabated: The findings. *NEJM* 288; 1222–1223, 1973

15. *Malpractice in Focus.* American Medical Association, Chicago, 1975, p. 14

16. Curran, W.J. (1976), p. 19.

17. Kalven, H. & Zeisel, H. *The American Jury.* Little Brown, Boston, 1966, quoted in Chayet, N. supra

18. Curran, W.J. (1976), p. 15
19. *Ibid.*, p. 10
20. *Ibid.*, p. 19
21. *Ibid.*, p. 32
22. *Ibid.*
23. Dissatisfaction said to cause most lawsuits. *Psychiatric News,* Nov. 12, 1979, p. 17
24. *Ibid.*
25. Study shows malpractice claim delays both common and costly. *Malpractice Digest,* Jan./Feb., 1977, p. 6.
26. *Malpractice in Focus* p. 13
27. *Malpractice Digest,* Jan./Feb., 1979, p. 6
28. *Ibid.*
29. *Ibid.*
30. Curran, W.J. (1976), p. 29
31. *Ibid.*, p. 36
32. *Ibid.*, p. 32
33. *Malpractice Digest,* Sept./Oct., 1978, p. 5

Questions on Chapter 9,
Coping With the Medical Malpractice
Problem

1. What fraction of alleged malpractice cases presented to them are accepted by attorneys? What are the two most common reasons for attorneys to reject such cases?
2. What characteristics would a malpractice plaintiff most like to see in a jury?
3. Most malpractice trials result in high awards by sympathetic juries. True or False?
4. One would expect that in times of recession, malpractice insurance would go down along with costs of consumer items. True or False?
5. Cardiac, thoracic, and vascular surgeons pay malpractice premiums as high as any other specialists. True or False?
6. What is the major advantage of a malpractice screening panel?
7. Give three possible advantages of arbitration in alleged malpractice.
8. When does the statute of limitations begin to run in a case where a practitioner fails to mention to the patient that a sponge was left in a body cavity after surgery?
9. a. What is a contingency fee? b. What is the ordinary range of contingency fees in malpractice cases? c. In the early 70's, approximately how much hourly pay did attorneys receive in successful cases?
10. Give three factors which mitigate against vigorous self-policing within a profession.

CHAPTER 10

Contracts

Nathan T. Sidley with John M. Reed

Contracts
Nathan T. Sidley with John M. Reed

I. Introduction and overview.

Besides being involved in actions involving crimes and torts, courts are occupied with matters in which individuals are dissatisfied with the conduct of other individuals, because the others have failed to live up to their manifestations of intention to act (or to refrain from acting) in some specified way, that is, their promises. Should courts intervene and force an individual to do what another wants, merely because the second individual has broken a promise? The answer is that courts must intervene in promise situations, because keeping commitments, which contributes so importantly to predictability of behavior and reliable expectations of conduct, is so necessary a part of our social, professional, and commercial lives.

The two important issues about promises are these: What kind of promises or manifestations of intention will courts enforce, and how will they enforce them? Or to put it another way, if a person is going to commit himself to another and have another be committed to him, what must he do in order to make it likely that a court will come to his aid if problems arise? The answer to this question is the law of contracts.

A. Definition.

A contract can be defined as a promise or a set of promises or other manifestations, which are enforceable at law. Of course, like everything else that is covered in the

law, definitions, qualifications, and conditions constitute
the essence of the law of contracts.

B. Constituent elements.

1. The first aspect of contracts is that they represent
   promises,* that is, declarations or manifestations by a
   party that he will behave in a predictable way in the future. Courts cannot be concerned with any set of mutual promises, however. Usually, they only are
   involved with promises which involve the idea of a bargain, and the court requires something of substance to
   be bound in the mutual undertakings.

2. That important substance on both parties' parts is
   called "consideration."

3. If the subject matter is of certain historically important
   types, the agreement must be in writing or reflected in
   a memorandum signed by the party to be charged (the
   "statute of frauds").

4. A contract is generally initiated by one party's making
   an "offer" of a promise or undertaking and the other
   party's giving a promise as an "acceptance" of the offer.

5. Both parties must understand that they are agreeing
   on the subject matter. Of course, the parties have to be
   capable of understanding the promises.

6. They must make their promises voluntarily as well.

7. In addition, courts will not be put in the situation
   where they would encourage breaking the law or doing other harmful things by enforcing promises.

8. Also, courts will not enforce contracts in which it is impossible for a party to keep a promise. (Because courts
   look at things broadly, however, many things that a lay
   person would regard as impossible would not be seen
   that way by a court.)

9. Finally, there is the question of what the courts will do

---

*An important qualification is the situation in which one party doesn't
promise but performs something. The fundamentals are similar, however.

when there is a broken or unfulfilled promise or undertaking (a "breach of contract"). That involves the
question of damages or other remedies, including
"specific performance."

C. Thus, to review our thinking about contracts and to give
the organization of the chapter, we give an expanded,
itemized definition of contract. A contract is* (with few
exceptions):

1. Mutual promises or manifestations of intended future
conduct.
a. By two or more parties.
b. Mutually understood.
c. Voluntarily arrived at.
d. Supported by consideration.
e. Involving an offer and an acceptance.
f. In some cases requiring a writing.
g. Not illegal or contrary to public policy, and
h. Possible of performance.

2. Enforceable by courts.
a. Toward those with "privity,"**including, sometimes,
third party beneficiaries or those to whom the contract
rights have been assigned.
b. With certain remedies available when the contract is
breached.

D. Recognize that this classical conceptualization is general. At first, many contractual arrangements, like that of
the relationship between a professional person and his
patient or client, may not appear to fit the concepts. But
these arrangements can almost always be put in a per-

---

*Note that there are two main headings regarding promises and their en-
forcement. There are eight sub-heads under promises and two under en-
forceability. It is recommended that the reader take the time at this point to
commit those headings to memory, for they constitute the key to understanding the law of contracts. Problems of contracts will follow the chapter,
and an outline of approach to problems will also be based on this basic outline.
**See infra. Words in quotation marks are words usually used by lawyers in
relation to these kinds of cases.

spective in which the conceptualization applies and can yield valid legal predictions.

The basic outline presented in this chapter is that typified by the American Law Institute's *Restatement of Contracts*, originally issued in 1931 and revised in 1979. The philosophy of the *Restatement* was to present a state-of-the-art view of the general law of contracts, with the hope that the law might be influenced in areas which had remained unsettled. Opinions of prominent judges, law professors, and lawyers were obtained in the work.

A cautionary note, however, is in order. In the last 30 years, there has been some decline in the acceptance by scholars of the philosophical system of contract law, part of which is a reaction against logical deduction as a dominant mode of contract reasoning. In its extreme forms, the criticisms have been that contract law is being absorbed into tort law,[1] that there is no institution of contract as such but, rather, only particular types of transactions, and finally, that fundamental concepts of contract law are too abstract to regulate current and socially significant business problems.[2]

II. Mutual promises or undertakings (expanded).

A. Parties. The range is wide. Parties can be individuals, partnerships, corporations, estates, trusts, governments, or any combination of those.

B. Understanding or interpretation. The test of understanding is objective. In the absence of fraud or misrepresentation, a party usually will not be permitted to argue in a contract case that he did not intend what he in fact communicated.

　　1. Occasions for disputes.
　　　　a. Circumstances, not foreseen at the time of forming the contract, arise.
　　　　b. One or more parties have inaccurately represented material facts.

    c. An important term of the contract is omitted (for example, price or description of goods).

    d. The language is ambiguous.

    e. A party to the agreement lacked the capacity to understand and, therefore, to contract.

2. Courts try to determine what the parties' intentions were when they contracted. Ambiguity in a writing does not invalidate a contract, at least when there is reasonable certainty of subject matter, especially if subsequent actions demonstrated the parties' intentions.

3. Effects of erroneous representation (that is, giving inaccurate information).

    a. Fraudulent misrepresentation.

       1) Consists of knowingly misrepresenting, concealing, or not disclosing an important material fact that could not readily be ascertained on reasonable inspection.

       2) If a party was injured as a result of relying on the misrepresentation, he may:

          a) Void the contract.

          b) Seek to have a new and appropriate contract decreed by the court ("reformation").

    b. Other mistakes.

       1) Mutual mistakes of material facts (but not of law) pertinent to the contract may void it. For example, if both parties thought a painting was a clever forgery and it was later found to be a Rembrandt, the party who sold at an excessively low price could have the sale voided.

       2) Unilateral mistakes do not void it.

       3) Mutual mistakes that are only incidental to the essence of the contract do not void it.

4. Decisions take into account the usual practices of the contractors as well as of others in the same businesses.

5. Capacity.

    a. Legal capacity is presumed of anyone making an agreement. Lack of capacity must be shown. Examples of those who lack capacity:

1) Persons declared legally insane. Their agreements are void on the basis that the individual did not understand what he was doing.
2) Persons grossly observable not to understand what they are doing.
    a) Some mental defectives.
    b) Some psychotics.
    c) Some intoxicated persons.
3) Infants, that is, persons under 21 or 18, etc., depending on the jurisdiction.
4) Usually, parties of the second and third types may seek to "disaffirm" their agreements, but they must return to the other parties any benefits they have received.
    a) If after becoming of age, sober, or non psychotic such a party ratifies (that is, indicates his intention to make binding) an agreement by word or deed, it is binding.
    b) An "infant" who misrepresents his age may be liable for the tort of "deceit," even though he does not make a valid contract. The infant cannot exploit his infancy to the detriment of others.
    c) There are some transactions (for example, opening and controlling a bank account) that an infant can accomplish validly in his own name.
    d) The trend in the law is increasingly to hold minors responsible if they try to void contracts to their own advantage.
5) Agreements made in good faith to incapacitated persons for necessities of life are binding on a theory of "quasi-contract." (That is, no one should be unjustly enriched at the expense of another.)

C. Voluntary, that is, no duress nor coercion.
  1. A contract made under duress is voidable but may be ratified if the coerced individual later voluntarily performs according to the terms of the agreement.
  2. "Undue influence" is equivalent to coercion. If a trusted authority, such as an attorney, a physician, a guard-

ian, etc., engages in a business relationship with, or is named as a beneficiary of a will or gift, etc., from the person in the trusting position, and the authority benefits from his interaction with the party relying on him, the presumption will be made that the authority exerted excessive influence and took advantage. The transaction can be set aside.

D. Consideration.
  1. A benefit to the promisor, or a detriment suffered by the promisee. (In effect, the person making a promise has to get something in return for it in order that a contract be valid.)
     a. An act (for example, paying money or handing something over).
     b. A forbearance (for example, not competing in a certain way).
     c. The creation, modification, or destruction of a legal relation (for example, marriage).
     d. A return promise.
  2. Consideration must be intended as part of the arrangement.
  3. It need not be adequate or fair in relation to what is promised, although gross inadequacy of consideration may affect the willingness of the court to enforce the contract.
  4. An act that a person is legally obliged to do is not consideration (for example, pay a valid debt).
  5. Previous consideration is not valid for forming a contract in the present. For example, if *A* gave *B* an option in the past, he cannot use that same option as consideration for a present contract.
  6. "Promissory estoppel" is a special case. Ordinarily, a person promising to give a gift to another party is not contractually bound, because he receives no consideration in return. But if he promises a benefit, (for example, a gift to a college) and the other party changes position, expecting to receive the benefit (for example,

builds a library), the person promising the benefit cannot claim, as a defense to a contract lawsuit, that no consideration was given. He is "estopped" (that is, not allowed in a legal proceeding) from doing so.

E. Offer.

1. A declaration, by a party, of willingness to form a contract, stating the proposed terms. An "acceptance" is a corresponding declaration by the other party. If a party makes an offer to another, and if it is accepted by the other, both are bound (provided the agreement fulfills the other requirements of a contract as of the time the offerer accepts). An offer must be reasonably definite and must be communicated to the offeree.

2. An offer remains in effect until one of the following happens:

   a. The offeror revokes the offer and communicates the revocation to the offeree. (That means that the offeree must actually receive the communication.)

   b. The offeror dies.

   c. The offeror becomes (or is declared) insane.

   d. A law is passed making that kind of contract illegal.

   e. The subject matter of the contract is destroyed. (For example, the horse dies before the offer is accepted.)

   f. The offeree rejects it (where the offer is made to a specific offeree).

      1) A counteroffer made by the initial offeree is a rejection. (For example, if the initial offer is to sell the horse for $200, and the offeree says, "I will give you $100 for it," he has rejected the initial offer, and it is no longer in effect. "Would you sell it for $100?" is not a counteroffer, but merely an inquiry.)

      2) Acceptance with a condition is a counteroffer and, therefore, a rejection. (For example, "I'll take the car, but I must pay with my personal check.")

   g. A certain time has elapsed, as in either of the following:

      1) The offeror has specified the offer will remain in effect for a certain period. But note: In such a case

the offeror can still revoke it before expiration if there has been no consideration given by the offeree for leaving the offer open the full time. (For example, *A* says, "For a month you can buy my house for $50,000." The next day he can say, "The deal is off." (If he sells an option to *B* to keep the offer open for a month, he cannot retract before the time elapses, however.) If *B* accepts before *A* revokes the offer, *A* is, of course, bound.)

2) A reasonable time has elapsed. In case of sales offers, that depends on the rapidity of price fluctuations of the subject matter of the offer. (For example, with stock certificates or commodities, a reasonable time may be less than a day.)

F. Acceptance: Basic elements.

1. The offer must be in effect.

2. The acceptance must be definite and meet the conditions of the offer.

3. The offeree must communicate his acceptance to the offeror, or he must perform his part of the contract ("acceptance by performance").

4. The offeree must intend to accept the offer. That kind of disputed point may occur at times (such as offers of rewards) when the person does the act, finds out about the reward, and then claims it. His claim is valid only if he knew about the reward in advance.

5. No party, other than a specific offeree or his agent, may accept. The offeree cannot turn over the offer to a third party and create an agreement binding on the offeror. (For example, if *A* offers to buy goods from *B*, he need not take them from *C*.)

6. If silence is the usual pattern of acceptance of offers by a party, silence will be treated as an acceptance, otherwise not.

7. Timing of acceptance. There may be a communication time difference between offeror and offeree. For an offer to be in effect, the offeree must receive the commu-

nication. For an acceptance to be valid, the communication must be sent. (For example, it is enough to drop a letter into a mailbox in order that an offer be accepted; the offeror doesn't have to receive it. The question of timing may be important if the offeror wishes to revoke and the offeree wishes to accept. Then, the question is, which occurred first, the revocation or the acceptance?)

8. In practice, offers and acceptances may lead to confusing situations. (For example, a wholesaler may "offer" to buy machines from a manufacturer, sending a purchase order form with printed terms and conditions. The manufacturer may then "accept," but by sending its own sales order form, containing different terms and conditions (for example, limiting warranties). Neither party signs the other's form, but the manufacturer sends the machines, and the purchaser pays for them. Whose terms, if anyone's, govern a subsequent lawsuit for breach of warranty? (Cases like that are sometimes called "a battle of the forms.")

G. Statute of frauds.

1. Background. Unlike most other features of contract law, the provisions to follow below did not evolve directly out of common law, that is, case decisions by the judges. Rather they were engrafted onto contract law in one stroke by a statute passed by Parliament. (The American states have generally passed their own statutes of frauds.) The purpose was to prevent frauds in important matters by requiring a signed writing instead of mere verbal testimony as evidence of a contract.

The statutes have been modified at times and they have been interpreted by judges too. There has been considerable controversy about them, and some jurists have even wondered whether such statutes have enabled more fraud to occur because of their own provisions than would otherwise been the case.

2. Contracts covered by the statute of frauds.

a. For the sale of land or any interest in land.

b. For a sale of personal property of value of $500 or more.
c. Any contract which cannot be fulfilled within a year. (If there is a possibility that it could be fulfilled within a year, it is not covered by the statute of frauds. A somewhat paradoxical case is that an oral contract to employ another for life is enforceable, but an oral contract to employ another for 13 months is not.)
d. An agreement to be responsible for the debts of another party.
e. A promise of an executor or an administrator of a deceased's estate to pay the obligations of the estate with his own personal funds.
f. Promises made in reference to settlements (for example, of money or of property) to be made in a marriage (but not for a promise of marriage itself).

3. Other contracts may be, but do not have to be, in writing. Moreover, if a contract has been fully executed on one side (for example, a sale with goods delivered), performance takes it "out of the statute" even if a writing is, otherwise, required.

4. If a contract is in writing, the writing may be such as to summarize the entire contract agreement. If so, evidence of prior written and prior or contemporaneous non written agreements cannot modify the contract and usually is not admissible in a dispute. (The so-called, "parol evidence rule")
(Parties can orally modify terms of a contract after it is made, however.)

5. Note that a contract entered into orally is a valid contract. The statute of frauds relates to evidence presented in court regarding the existence and terms of the contract. It is a defense to a suit for breach of a contract, but it is not automatically involved by the court even when a contract concerns a subject area contained within the statute. (If, for example, the defendant doesn't claim the statute, or if the defendant acknowledges the existence and terms of the contract, the statute does not interfere with the progress of the contract suit.)

H. Legality. Agreements for the following are not valid contracts.

1. An agreement to commit a crime.
2. An agreement to commit a tort.
3. An agreement which is contrary to public policy, including the following.
   a. Gambling ("aleatory") agreements (except for legitimate casinos, lotteries, etc.).
   b. Bargains in restraint of trade (for example, an agreement never to open a medical office in a given city).
   c. Bargains in which a party gains a greater profit than permitted by law, including these:
      1) Usurious interest.
      2) Excessive contingency fees in tort suits (where such are regulated).
   d. An agreement made on Sunday or a holiday (in some states).
   e. "Unconscionable" contracts, a rare situation in which a court declares a contract void because one party has excessively and detrimentally exploited another party's weakness or ignorance, even though the other party is not legally incapacitated from contracting. (In effect, the court declares a contract void because of grossly inadequate consideration.)

I. Possibility. This is an uncommon problem in assigning responsibility for contractual obligations. It is assumed that people who contract can foresee the possibility of natural disasters, wars, strikes, etc., and can make provisions for them in their contracts. Certain impossibilities do vitiate contracts, however.

1. Where a change in the law makes performance impossible. (For example, where the district later votes for prohibition, a lease for the exclusive purpose of running a saloon is void.).
2. Where the specific subject matter is destroyed so that performance cannot be accomplished. (For example, a contract to sell Hogarth's "The Milkmaid" is impossible to perform if the painting is destroyed by fire

(which does not occur because of the negligence of the seller). A contract to sell 1000 barrels of oil is still valid, however, even if the tanker sinks, because oil is "fungible," that is, can be substituted for without significant difference, and can be replaced.)

3. In personal service contracts, by the sickness or the death of the person who agreed to perform the service.

4. When one of the contracting parties does not permit the other to perform his contractual obligation. (This may have other consequences as well. The person who is barred from performance may be able to recover for breach.)

III. Enforcement.

A. Privity.
Only the parties to a contract can sue to have it enforced, with the following exceptions:

1. "Third party beneficiaries," that is, parties to whom the rights of performance are intended to accrue according to the terms of the contract or to whom the law, for reasons of policy, accords a right of direct action.

    a. "Donee beneficiaries," parties who are not owed a legal duty but are still given contract rights (for example, a wife as a beneficiary of an insurance policy for which she has not paid the premium).

    b. "Creditor beneficiaries," parties who are owed a legal duty by the party to which contract rights are promised. (For example, B owes C money. He makes a contract with A, and A is to make payment to C. C is the creditor beneficiary.)

2. Assignees. A party to a contract can transfer some rights and duties to others. (For example, an individual may sell to a third person the right to be paid by someone who owes him money. This is like a creditor beneficiary, but differs in that it is not part of the original contract.)

a. The person obtaining the assignment, the assignee, can sue on the contract. Any defenses the person owing the duty (the obligor) has against the party assigning the contract (the assignor), however, are valid against the assignee. (For example, if *A* buys a car from *B* and *B* assigns the right to payment to *C*, *C* can sue *A*, but *A* may claim against *C* the defense that the car doesn't run, just as he could have against *B*.)

Exception. There is a large class of paper transactions, promissory notes, checks, mortgages, etc. which are freely transferred among individuals and financial institutions. As a means of facilitating such commerce, somewhat different rules have developed. These began as the "Law Merchant" (that is, the law of merchants), and are now established as the "Uniform Commercial Code." Promissory notes, drafts, and checks are called "negotiable instruments." Transfers of such commercial paper are called "negotiation" rather than assignment. Such negotiation usually involves "indorsement" (that is, signature of the negotiator) on the "instrument" (that is, the paper) and delivery of the instrument. The party who receives the instrument through a proper indorsement and delivery is a "holder in due course." If he sues on the instrument, as such, many of the ordinary defenses against a contract claim are not valid against him (although some ordinary ones remain).

b. The right to be paid money can generally be assigned. (The older common law was to the contrary. That principle has largely disappeared, but remains applicable to personal injury claims and some claims against the government.) The right to performance may ordinarily be assigned unless it would materially alter the obligation of the other party (for example, to deliver coal to Boston rather than New York or to work for a year for *B* instead of *A*).

c. Duties might be assigned. (For example, the duty to deliver 1,000 gallons of No. 6 bunker fuel might be assigned from *A* to *B*, and *C* may not be able to refuse to accept and pay for oil delivered by *B* under terms of a contract between *A* and *C*.)

1) Personal duties (for example, painting a portrait) might not be assignable.

2) It is prudent to have the permission of the obligee before making a delegation of a duty.

B. Breach. A failure to perform, including failure to perform at a proper time.

1. Breach is usually less than a complete breach of the entire contract taken as a whole.

   a. If a contract is intended to be an indivisible entity, a breach of a major term is a breach of the whole contract.

   b. A "divisible contract" is one with several, more-or-less independent, provisions. A breach of one term does not breach the whole contract.

   c. A breach might be only of a minor term of the contract. The obligor may have accomplished "substantial performance." The situation may arise, for example, when a building firm has contracted to erect a building and has done so; the owner is dissatisfied with some parts of it and refuses to pay. The contractor has some rights of recovery. If he has not willfully deviated from the contract, he can sue for the value of the contract, less the cost to bring the minor deviations from the specifications into conformity with them.

2. If the breach is major but not willful, and there has been "part performance," the performer may sue, not on the contract but on a "quasi-contract" theory for the amount that the other has benefitted from the performer's work. The amount he may receive is often determined on a "quantum meruit" (what it is worth) basis, because there is no contract price fixed for the part performance. ("Fixed-term employment contracts," where the employee leaves before the end of the time, often are covered by this mechanism.)

3. Breach of a condition precedent. Sometimes, a duty

undertaken by one party must be completed before the other party has any obligation to perform. (For example, *A* must build the house before *B* must pay.) That is a "condition precedent." A more general definition is that a condition precedent is an event which must occur (unless it is excused) before performance under a contract becomes due.

    a. Failure of a nonexcused condition precedent to an obligation discharges the obligation.

    b. Performance under a contract must occur within a reasonable time or the time specifically stated in the contract, or the contract is considered to be breached.

4. "Anticipatory breach," "renunciation," or "repudiation" (They all mean the same thing.) occurs when, in advance of the time when performance is due, a party declares that he will not perform his contractual duties. There are two consequences.

    a. The other party may sue for damages immediately, without having to wait for a literal breach to occur. Exception—anticipatory breach does not apply to promises to pay money by a certain time. The other party must wait until the breach actually occurs.

    b. The other party has the obligation to mitigate damages. After an anticipatory breach, he may not continue his performance so as to increase damages. (For example, if the buyer says he will not take the 500 pair of shoes he ordered, and if the manufacturer has only completed 200 pair, the manufacturer cannot subsequently complete the other 300 pair and charge the buyer for them.)

5. Nonperformance is not always a breach of contract. The contract may be discharged, which eliminates the obligation. Ways of discharging a contract are the following:

    a. "Rescission" (That is, both parties agree to rescind, or to call off the contract.).

    b. "Substitution," the making of a completely new contract in place of an original one.

c. "Novation," a creation of a new agreement, identical with the original, except that one or more of the original parties is replaced. (For example, *A, B,* and *C* agree that *B* will no longer supply the bandages for *A,* rather that *C* will do so under the same terms that *B* did.)

d. "Accord and satisfaction," an agreement in which the original parties agree (the "accord") to fulfill different performances, and the newly agreed upon performances actually occur (the "satisfaction").

e. "Waiver," a situation in which one party fails to demand proper performance from the other party.

f. Other discharges.

1) "Merger," that is, one agreement is merged into a second agreement. (For example, a verbal agreement to pay some money is subsequently incorporated or merged into a written agreement, so that a suit on the previous agreement is not valid.)

2) "Alteration," in which a party to a written contract unilaterally alters the written part of a material term. (That discharges the entire agreement.)

3) Bankruptcy. Contractual obligations are discharged after the bankrupt's assets are divided among the creditors.

C. Remedies and damages.

1. A suit for contract damages is a demand that a sum of money be granted as compensation for injury caused by breach of contract.

a. The amount of damages is that which would place the injured party in the position he would be in had the contract been fulfilled. Thus, one remedy is based on the injured party's "expectation interest." (For example, if the breached agreement were to sell 100 cases of penicillin at $30 a case, delivered on July 1st, and on July 1st it would cost the purchaser $32 a case for similar penicillin, damages would be the $2 additional price the purchaser would have to pay to get the equivalent of the agreed value.)

b. The injured party may alternatively sue for his "reliance interest," generally the expenditures he made on the contract up to the time of the breach.

c. If the party breached against suffers no monetary loss, he may sue for nominal damages, such as $1 and costs.

d. A party may not recover for punitive or exemplary damages on a contract. Damages are restricted to those noted above.

e. "Liquidated damages," a specific sum fixed by the contract, to be paid in case of a breach (such as $100 for each day of delay of performance). The sum must bear some reasonable relationship to the amount of loss, however, in order to avoid unjust enrichment or a penalty.

2. Alternatively, one may seek "restitution," the return of the performance of the party breached against or of the value of that performance. (For example, the drug wholesaler sells the druggist some penicillin, but the druggist doesn't pay because of bankruptcy. The wholesaler may sue for the return of the penicillin.)

3. "Specific performance" (that is, the enforcement by court order of the actual promised performance). Because of the historical development of civil law, this is called a remedy in "Equity" (that is, equity jurisdiction) rather than in "Law" jurisdiction. (Both Equity Courts and Law Courts, historically, were branches of the administration of the King of England, but they handled different kinds of cases. Now, a court of general jurisdiction in the United States handles both kinds of cases.) Specific performance is usually involved when there is an agreement to sell something unique, such as a specific piece of land, and the seller changes his mind. The court can order the sale to take place as per the agreement.

D. Procedures.

One must initiate suits for breach of contract according to the usual court procedures. Failure to adhere to them, particularly in the case of statute of limitations, can be fatal to the prosecution of a case. The period of limitations is often longer for contract cases than tort cases.

IV. Approaches to a contract problem.

If one approaches these problems in a systematic manner, one can solve the problems much more expeditiously than without using such an approach. There are four basic questions which must be asked in reference to a contract problem.

1. Was there a valid contract?
2. What were the specific terms of the contract?
3. Is the contract enforceable by a court: Have the proper procedures been followed?
4. What is the appropriate remedy?

Under the first point one must consider the points noted in the foregoing outline: parties; understanding; voluntary; consideration; offer and acceptance; statute of frauds; legality; and possibility.

One must ascertain whether all the points are met in the agreement. Then, one must ascertain what are the specific terms of the contract. (Of course, these must be considered in determining the consideration, statute of frauds, legality, and possibility aspects above.) The specific terms enable one to ascertain whether there has been performance or breach.

If the suit is brought, one must evaluate: privity; breach; and remedy. Finally, one must ascertain whether the type and amount of the remedy sought are appropriate to the situation.

It is suggested that, in approaching a contract question, the reader recognize that a law suit based on contract can take years from the filing of the suit to the ultimate resolution of the issue. The parties and the courts can't rush through things. Thus, we recommend that the reader cogitate about each contract problem or case in terms of analysis, rather than making a snap judgment.

When you approach the problem in terms of the appropriate classical legal terminology, you are very likely to solve it. Judges may disagree with such an analysis, but only by invoking special qualifying principles. In the great bulk of situations, a straightforward analysis will predict the outcome of a case better than any other approach.

Text References

1. Gilmore G. *The Death of Contract.* Ohio State Univ. Press, Columbus, 1974
2. 95 Harv.L.Rev. 741

General References

Restatement of the Law Second: Contracts 2d. American Law Institute, Saint Paul, 1981

Questions on Chapter 10,
Contracts

1. Tom says one morning to Bill, "I will pay you $10 if you deliver two bushels of your best MacIntosh apples to my house today." Bill says nothing but delivers the apples an hour later. What doctrine applies in determining whether there is a valid contract? Is there one?
2. Stan offers to build a five room house of given design for Moe. They agree in writing that the price will be Stan's costs of construction plus an appropriate profit. If Moe changes his mind before construction begins, is he likely to be liable for damages to Stan?
3. George sells Robert a car, telling him that it is in good mechanical condition but knowing that it has a cracked crankshaft. Robert finds out about the fact and the concealment later. What may he do?
4. Phillip, trusted attorney and adviser to Richard, pays $1,000 for Richard's Cadillac, the fair market value of which is $3,000. After discussing the deal with others, Richard feels cheated. Can he do anything to recover the car?
5. In a moment of unguarded enthusiasm, Herman signs a pledge card for $5,000 for the library book fund of his alma mater. He later changes his mind, but after the university has bought the books, relying on his promise to fulfill his pledge. What is the name of the legal doctrine that prevents him from saying there was no contract because there was no consideration on the part of the university?
6. John offers to sell his business to William for $100,000. William says he will pay $92,000 for it. John refuses William's counter-offer. William then says, "OK. I'll take it for the hundred." John says, "Sorry, the price is now $103,000." May he raise the price like that?
7. George and Mary orally agree that he will pay her $100 monthly as long as she lives, if she doesn't object to their moving to California. He pays her for 10 years then stops. She sues. Is the absence of a written contract a good defense for George to use?

8. Walter and Tom agree that Walter will shovel Tom's snow all winter for $25 a storm, payable on May 1. In February, Walter's plow breaks, and there are no spare parts available. Tom refuses to pay anything to Walter, claiming the contract has been breached. What is Walter's approach legally?
9. Give four ways of discharging a contract.
10. Charles promises to sell Arthur his author-autographed copy of *Bleak House* for $20,000 on May 1. Arthur gives a $5,000 earnest money deposit in mid-March. In April, Charles changes his mind, refuses to sell, and sends Arthur a certified check for $5,000. Arthur wants the book. (a) What can he do? (b) What is different about an attempt to get the book from the usual remedy for a breach of contract?

CHAPTER 11

Family and Domestic Law

Ronald A. Pressman

287

Family and Domestic Law

Ronald A. Pressman

I. Marriage.

A. Marriage is a three-party contract among a man, a woman, and the state. All of the incidents of the marriage contract are controlled by the state. Marriage also changes the social and legal statuses of the parties.

B. Contractual requirements.
1. The parties must understand the nature of the promise that they make.
2. They must be of sound mind.
3. There must be a present agreement to marry. (For example, jokingly going through a ceremony does not make a valid marriage.)

C. Differences from an ordinary contract.
1. In the normal contract, the parties may modify the agreement voluntarily. In the marriage contract, the methods of termination or modification are controlled by the state.
2. The parties must observe state regulations.
   a. These regulations are usually mandatory but are sometimes discretionary.
   b. The formality usually takes the form of securing a license. The application may request information on the following:
      1) Health.
      2) Blood types.

      3) Any present relationship of the parties by blood or marriage.

      4) Age.

      5) Status of prior marriages.

  c. In the usual procedure, the parties secure the license, and the marriage is celebrated or solemnized by an official who is empowered by the state to perform the ceremony. Such an official may be a member of the clergy or a civil official, for example, a minister or a justice of the peace.

  d. The procedure may include the following:

      1) Publication of the intention to marry.

      2) A waiting period (usually three days).

  e. Normally, the license is only valid for a limited time, usually sixty days.

D. Restrictions on marriage.

  1. The parties must have attained a minimum age.

    a. Absolute minimums can go as low as 12 years.

    b. The minimum age to marry with no parental permission may be 18, sometimes even lower.

    c. Usually, females are enabled to marry, with or without parental permission, at an age two to three years younger than males. (Undoubtedly, the necessity of dealing with young, pregnant females is an important factor in this difference.)

  2. Blood relationships may prevent a valid marriage.

    a. Those who are permitted by the state to marry are first cousins or those more distantly related.

    b. Persons with closer blood relationships cannot marry (consanguinity).

  3. Legal familial relationships usually prohibiting marriage (affinity).

    a. Stepparent with stepchild.

    b. A person with the spouse of:

      1) A grandparent.

      2) A child.

      3) A grandchild.

c. A person with the same sex parent, grandparent, child, or grandchild of the spouse.

4. Marital status impairments to a valid contract.
   The most common situation is where one or both parties are in the midst of a divorce proceeding, and the divorce has not been finalized.

E. Implications of a marriage entered into under an impediment.

1. A party may annul a marriage, if the party petitions the court prior to ratification (that is, removing the impediment).

2. Certain impediments may be removed by continuing to cohabit over a period of time, but the impediment of consanguinity can never be removed.

3. A child born in a marriage where one of the parties is under an impediment may be legitimated for purposes of taxes, inheritance, or social security benefits, if the marriage is later ratified.

4. Common law marriage. A doctrine allowing parties to develop a legally binding status of marriage without the benefit of civil regulation.
   Usual definition. A mutual present agreement between a man and a woman to enter into a marital relationship with cohabitation and the appearance to the public that the parties are married.

5. Marriage by proxy. The celebration of the solemnization of the marriage by agents of the parties.
   a. It is rare and depends on state statute.
   b. It is useful during times of war to legitimate offspring when the parties are separated by distances.

II. Annulment.

A. Definition. A declaration by a court that a marriage never existed, that is, that it was either void or voidable from the inception.

1. A void marriage is one that is totally invalid.
2. A voidable marriage is valid until it is declared invalid.

B. Grounds for annulment.
  1. Mental capacity of the parties at the time of the marriage.
  2. Physical capacity at the time of marriage.
  3. Consanguinity and affinity.
  4. Examples.
     a. A marriage performed in jest.
     b. A marriage of a person afflicted by venereal disease with another who is not, might be annulled.
     c. Misrepresentations of chastity, non pregnancy, or impotence.
     d. Fraud which goes to the essentials of marriage is the most often mentioned grounds for annulment.
        1) A misrepresentation that a woman is chaste, when, in fact, she is pregnant, goes to the essentials of the marriage.
        2) A misrepresentation of wealth or station does not go to the essentials of marriage.
        3) It is often stated that an unconsummated marriage may be annulled. Evidence of consummation, however, may more properly be thought of as going to the weight of the evidence of whether the parties intended to be married.

C. Defenses to a petition to annul a marriage.
  1. Full knowledge of the moving party, that is, the party requesting that the marriage be annulled, may excuse the spouse from a misrepresentation.
  2. Cohabitation of the spouses after they reach statutory age may prevent a previously voidable marriage from being annulled.
  3. Intercourse with a woman pregnant before marriage may prevent a spouse from annulling a marriage to her even if she had become pregnant by another.

4. Usually, defenses require blamelessness of the party bringing the action.

III. Effects of marriage.

A. Requirements of general support.
   1. Support among family members is not usually litigated unless there is a breakdown of the marriage.
   2. At common law, the husband provided the family with food, clothing, and shelter: the wife provided services as a homemaker and mother. Today, support may be the obligation of either spouse.
   3. The doctrine of necessaries, a logical outgrowth of the agency concept.
      a. An ongoing marriage implies that the husband will supply certain necessities, such as food, clothing, and shelter.
      b. It also implies authority on the wife's part to purchase those necessaries.
      c. It implies that a family of some means may be expected to secure goods and services which exceed bare essentials.
      d. The wife may have apparent, implied, or express authority to purchase these goods.
         Usually, without express or apparent authority, a merchant who sells to a wife who claims that her husband will pay, takes some risk, if:
         1) The husband has already provided the goods and services.
         2) The husband has already given the wife funds.
         3) The wife has independent means.

B. Property Rights.
   1. Under the common law.
      a. Control of the wife's property passed to the husband during the marriage;

   b. The wife could not sue nor be sued during the mar-
      riage.

2. Today, there are married women's property acts which
   allow a woman to make or incur legal obligations as if
   she were sole or independent.
   a. The need for these acts is that common law controls
      unless abrogated by statute.
   b. It has taken a long time historically for women to have
      acquired the rights, comparable to those of men, which
      they now possess. Even now, however, there are vari-
      ous legal impediments suffered by women compared
      to men.

3. Two other marital property concepts are important.
   a. Tenants by the entirety, a concept of marital owner-
      ship.
      1) Both spouses have an undivided interest in the
         property during the marriage. There is a unity of in-
         terest in the sense that both parties are considered
         as one and the same person, usually subject to the
         effects of Equal Rights Amendments and governing
         state legislation. During the marriage, neither
         spouse can transfer an interest in the property with-
         out the consent of the other.
      2) Title to the property vests in the survivor after the
         death of either.
   b. In community property states, the spouses each usually
      acquire a one-half interest in property accumulated
      during marriage. Property brought into the marriage
      separately or property acquired by inheritance, are ex-
      cluded.

C. Criminal non support. Usually, states provide criminal
   remedies against a husband who wilfully fails to support
   his family when he has the ability to do so. Support in
   this context implies the bare necessities of life, food,
   clothing, and shelter. The remedies of this obligation, as
   well as those of divorce or separation, may be enforced
   by an interstate compact known as the Uniform Recipro-
   cal Support Act. By this method, a husband who leaves

the original jurisdiction (state) may be made to answer his support obligations through a court in a new jurisdiction.

IV. Divorce and Legal Separation.

A. Divorce law has evolved within the context of the basic policy of the state, to protect and foster the stability and viability of the ties of marriage.
Divorce, therefore, has only been available on proof of specific statutory grounds, all of which, until quite recently, required fault on the part of the spouse.

1. Requirements of proof of fault have been so strong that divorce could not be granted on the basis of non appearance of the defendant. The moving party still had to prove to the court that the nonappearing defendant had committed the alleged grounds.

2. In some cases, such as where the parties reached an agreement, the court might relax the degree or amount of proof of fault, but the necessity of proof was still present.

3. Modern grounds, such as incompatibility and irreconcilable differences, have abandoned the need for fault, and, instead, recognize the concept of non viability of some marriages.

B. In most jurisdictions, a separate court has jurisdiction over these and related issues, including the handling of wills. They may be called "Probate Courts" or "Family Courts."

C. Fault grounds for divorce.

1. Adultery is probably the best known of the fault grounds for divorce.
Definition. The voluntary sexual intercourse of a spouse with another who is not the spouse.

2. A second traditional ground is desertion.

    a. Definition. The wilful abandonment of one spouse by another without justification and without consent.

    b. A variation of desertion is constructive desertion, which defines, as the guilty party, a spouse who makes conditions so intolerable that the other is forced to leave.

3. Physical cruelty.
Definition. The intentional and repeated use of force by one spouse on the other. Such force could include hitting, slapping, or beating.

4. "Mental cruelty" has expanded this concept to recognize that words or conduct, short of assault, may, nevertheless, have a cruel effect on a spouse. In essence, mental cruelty is the use of words or conduct which cause a deterioration in the health or well-being of the other spouse.

5. Other relatively common grounds for divorce.
    a. Non support.
    b. Imprisonment.
    c. Insanity.
    d. Habitual drunkenness.

D. Defenses to a divorce action (by the person who wishes to remain married).

1. Connivance.
Definition. Secret or indirect consent by one spouse to have the other commit the grounds for divorce.

2. Provocation. Here, one spouse incites the other to commit the grounds for divorce.

3. Condonation.
    a. An effect of state policy to foster the stability of marriage.
    b. Effect. A spouse who, with full knowledge, forgives the other for past marital misconduct is barred from the use of the previous misconduct as grounds for divorce.
    c. Condonation is usually regarded as tentative. A brief reconciliation does not vitiate a spouse's claim for divorce on such grounds as cruelty.

4. Recrimination.
   a. The notion is based on the role of the Probate Court as a court of equity. (In equity, he who seeks relief from the court must, himself, be blameless.)
   b. A party who seeks a divorce, who has, himself, also committed marital misconduct, is, therefore, barred from divorce.
   Perhaps to ameliorate the harshness of keeping two miserable spouses together, some jurisdictions recognize the doctrine of comparative rectitude, which allows the court to quantify the misconduct and to give the divorce to the party who is less blameworthy.

5. Collusion.
   a. A defense which protects the integrity of the court.
   b. It requires that a party who seeks the help of the court to dissolve his marriage, must neither commit perjury nor agree to commit marital misconduct in order to secure a divorce.
   c. Collusion is a defense which the court will recognize on its own initiative.

E. No-fault divorce.
   1. Perhaps in recognition of the harshness of such doctrines as recrimination, or perhaps in recognition of the difficulty of pinpointing the cause why unhappy parties must remain married, new grounds for divorce have been recognized. These grounds abandon the need for proof of fault.
      a. Incompatability.
      b. Irreconcilable breakdown of marriage.

   2. No-fault divorce requires the parties to prove that the marriage is not viable, the parties no longer love one another, or it is not possible for the parties to live together as husband and wife.

F. Separate maintenance, and divorce from bed and board (legal separation).
   1. Somewhat akin to divorce, but preserving the status of

marriage, are divorce from bed and board and separate maintenance.

  a. These decrees provide many of the benefits of divorce.

    1) Freedom of one spouse from interference by the other spouse.

    2) Custody of the children.

    3) Alimony and child support.

  b. The main disadvantage is that they leave the marriage intact and the parties under a disability to remarry.

  c. The usual form of judgment is a decree by the court declaring that a spouse is living apart from the other spouse for justifiable cause.

2. The decrees of divorce from bed and board and of separate maintenance usually share in common the same grounds and the same defenses as divorce.

3. Differences between divorce from bed and board and separate maintenance.

  a. Separate maintenance may be terminated without court action by reconciliation.

  b. Divorce from bed and board may settle the complete property rights of the parties, although separate support usually only provides for support on the basis of need of the parties. For example, a separate support decree would not divide property which the parties own jointly, and the court would not declare which property belongs to which spouse.

4. In some states, either decree may be converted into a divorce by the parties' having lived apart for a stated period of time.

G. Alimony.

1. Alimony usually is considered to be a continuation of one spouse's support duty toward the other, after the marriage.

   In many states, alimony may flow either from husband to wife or from wife to husband.

2. Usually, alimony is only one aspect of the legal product of a divorce or separation.

    a. The decree may also give child custody to either spouse and a corresponding duty of child support to the other.

    b. There also may be a division of the marital property and, in addition, a court order preventing either spouse from interfering with the personal liberty of the other spouse.

3. Usually, the parties decide these issues themselves as part of a separation agreement or a divorce agreement.

4. Alimony may either be temporary (during the pendency of the action) or permanent.

5. Tax consequences.

    a. Usually, alimony is tax deductible to the obligor (the person who has to pay it), and taxable as income to the obligee (the person to whom it must be paid).

    b. Child support is not tax deductible. The party who furnishes more than 50 percent of the support of the child, however, is entitled to the income tax exemption.

    c. A further refinement of these tax consequences is that an order, which contains both alimony and child support, without differentiation, is fully tax deductible to the obligor, and taxable as income to the obligee.

6. The usual standard in awarding alimony is the need of one spouse against the ability to pay by the other.

    a. The court may consider many factors in making its award, including employment skills of the parties, health, ages, contribution of each to the accumulation of assets during the marriage, and the station of the parties.

    b. It is an accepted, if unwritten, maxim in law, that two parties may not live as well separated as they did together.

    c. Despite the fact that the statute may set out factors in making an award of alimony, the usual standard is what is just and equitable, and the trial judge has wide discretion.

    d. Some statutes grant the court the power to divide all assets of the parties upon divorce.

7. Usually, in cases of annulment, there is no duty to support after the judgment is granted. A court, however, may grant support during the pendency of the action.

8. Decrees may be modified due to changes in need or the ability to pay. Usually, the courts have wide discretion to avoid hardship where there is a material change of circumstances.

Common examples of circumstances suitable for modification.

    a. Remarriage by the spouse who receives alimony terminates the responsibility of support.

There is some recognition of a change in ability to pay when the former husband bears the responsibility of a new family.

    b. Substantial inheritance.

    c. Illness.

H. Custody.

1. A usual outcome of a divorce or separation is a decree granting one of the spouses the custody of the children.

2. There are also other proceedings in which custody may be litigated.

    a. Child neglect hearings.

    b. Guardianship hearings.

3. The most often used guideline for custody award is the "best interest of the child." Usually, the trial court's decision will not be overturned except on evidence of clear abuse of discretion.

    a. The mother is usually favored when the child is of "tender years."

    b. The court considers the child's wishes as he or she reaches adolescence.

    c. Other considerations.

      1) "Moral deficiencies" of the spouse as it might affect the children.

      2) The desire not to separate siblings.

      3) The stability of the custodial parent (mental or economic).

      4) The race and religion of the parties.

4. Custody of the child means the right to supervise, care for, and educate the child on a daily basis.

    a. The non custodial parent is usually granted visitation rights in such a manner as to cause the least disruption in the child's normal development.

    b. Custody awards are modifiable with changes of circumstances.

5. "Joint custody" gives both parents an equal opportunity to guide their children.

6. Third parties may be granted custody, but the natural parents are favored unless they are unfit or have abandoned the child.

I. Contempt.

The usual method of enforcing a court order for child support or alimony is by means of contempt of court proceedings.

1. Contempt is a remedy for a wilful breach of the court's order.

2. It is usually directed toward coercing the defendant to make his payments (civil contempt).

3. It may also be directed toward the defendant's flouting of the court's authority (criminal contempt).

4. The end result, civil or criminal, may be a fine or jail. Unfortunately, though, jailing the party in contempt prevents his earning money so as to be able to make up the missed support payments. The courts are often forced to balance punishing the recalcitrant spouse against the loss of any support whatsoever to the other spouse.

5. A defense to contempt is the defendant's good faith inability to pay.

V. Adoption.

A. Adoption is the process whereby a child breaks his legal ties with one or more of his natural parents and establishes new ties with one or more persons who are not his natural parents. The fact of adoption imposes new obligations on the part of the adoptive parent, who is then required to support and care for the child as he or she would support a natural child. In addition, the child acquires the right to inherit from or through his adoptive parents.

B. Adoption is generally a two stage process.
   1. Loss of parental custody and rights.
      a. The parents may voluntarily surrender the child for adoption.
         1) Complete and irrevocable consent for the adoption is given.
         2) Both parents' consent is required.
            The wishes of an illegitimate father, if possible, and if not harmful to the child, are taken into account.
         3) Consent may only be revoked in case of fraud or duress. To prevent this, adoption consent is notarized and witnessed.
      b. Parents may lose custody of a child through abandonment, abuse, or neglect.
         1) Usually, a social agency petitions the court that the child should be adopted despite lack of parental consent.
         2) The court has to determine these issues:
            a) That the parents are unfit.
            b) What are the best interests of the child.
   2. Determining the fitness and suitability of the adoptive parents.
      a. Many factors may be considered, including race, religion, stability, and economic condition of the adoptive parent or parents.
      b. In addition, if the child is of a certain age, usually 12, his consent is required;

    c. Usually, a report of a licensed public agency is required for an adoption.
Where one of the natural parents is the petitioner, the need for a report from a public agency may be waived.

    d. Private placements undertaken without the involvement of an appropriate public agency are banned by statute in many jurisdictions.

    e. In considering the placement of the child, state statutes require placement with parents of the same race and religion as the natural parents, if possible, even though the natural parents are no longer in the picture.

    f. Adoption proceedings are confidential and closed to the public.

VI. Guardians and conservators.

A. Definition.

    1. Guardian. A person upon whom the court has conferred the power to care for another individual, the ward, who is incompetent to act for himself.

        a. The guardian makes decisions about the person and body of the ward.

        b. The guardian also makes decisions about the ward's property.

        c. A guardianship may be time-limited, for example, until a minor attains the age of majority, or it may be indefinite, lasting so long as the ward is incompetent.

        d. Sometimes, the ward reserves certain rights despite the granting of guardianship rights to another.

           1) Recognizing due process rights of the wards, some states have limited the authority of the guardian, requiring the guardian to seek further court approval for admission of the ward to a mental health facility.

           2) Where the court has been asked by a guardian for the authority to authorize or prohibit life-prolonging treatment, courts have required the appointment of a guardian ad litem, in addition to an ordinary guardian, to consider such matters as:

a) The ward's decision, drawn from his views prior to incompetency, that is, "substituted judgment."
b) The state's interest in preserving life or in preventing suicide.

2. Conservator. A person upon whom the court has conferred the power and authority for managing the property of the ward. The legal approach to conservators and guardians is usually the same.

B. Powers and responsibilities.
1. To care for and manage the ward's property (both guardians and conservators) and the ward's person (guardians only).
   a. Either must ordinarily provide a bond for faithful performance.
   b. Authority is exercised subject to supervision by the court. Periodically, usually in one year intervals, the guardian or conservator must file an account showing the disposition he has made of the ward's property.
   c. The guardian or conservator must see that the ward's property and income from his estate are used for the benefit of the ward.
   d. The guardian or conservator does not have legal title to the ward's property. He may not transfer or convey property, therefore, without the court's consent.
   e. He may charge the ward's estate for his services.
2. Usually, courts do not require a guardian to report on the status of the ward's person unless an interested party files a request.
3. Even if a guardian is appointed for a child, residual parental rights are retained. For example, a guardian may not prevent parents from consenting to the adoption of the child by another party.

C. Appointment of guardians or conservators.
1. Generally, by petition of one or more interested parties, usually a relative or friend, but possibly a public agency.

    a. A guardianship may be part of a divorce proceeding when a third party petitions the court that neither parent is fit.

    b. Usually, in the case of a petition by an interested third party, if a child is over a specific age, the child's consent is required.

2. If one parent dies, custody or guardianship devolves upon the other.

3. In many states, a parent may, by will, appoint a guardian for children ("testamentary guardian"). Thus, if parents are divorced and the parent with custody dies, the other spouse receives custody and may appoint a testamentary guardian.

D. Guardian ad litem.

1. A guardian appointed by the court for the limited purpose of representing the ward's interest in litigation is not a guardian in the usual sense, but only is involved in the litigation, to help the court reach a just result. Usually, guardians ad litem are appointed for minors or incompetents with respect to adoptions, divorces, settlement of estates, or resolution of other litigation.

2. A guardian ad litem may be appointed on the court's own motion or on the motion of a party to the litigation.

3. If possible, consent of the family of the ward or the parties to litigation is obtained in order that a guardian ad litem be appointed to help obtain a fair determination.

General References

Clark, H.C., Jr. *Law of Domestic Relations.* West Publishing, St. Paul, 1968

Krause, H.D. *Family Law in a Nutshell.* West Publishing, St. Paul, 1977

Lombard, J.F. *Family Law* (Vols. 1–3 in *Massachusetts Practice*). West Publishing, St. Paul, Latest Supplement, 1981

Mackay, R.C. *The Law of Guardianships* (3rd Ed.) (Sloane, I. Ed.). Oceana, Dobbs Ferry, NY, 1980

Family Law Manual: Guardianship and Conservatorship. Mental Health Legal Advisors Committee, Boston, 1979

Statsky, W.T. *Domestic Relations Law and Skills.* West Publishing, St. Paul, 1978.

Waddington W. and Paulsen, M.G. *Domestic Relations: Cases and Materials*(3rd Ed.). Foundation Press, Mineola, NY, 1978

Questions on Chapter 11,
Family and Domestic Law

1. X and Y enter into an agreement that if Y seeks and secures a job in which Y must travel often, X will secure a divorce from Y and receive alimony of \$100 per week. After several years of marriage, Y secures a job as a long-distance truck driver. X seeks a divorce and alimony on the basis of their agreement. Will X be successful?
2. X and Y live together in state A. They secure a marriage license in state A, but never solemnize the marriage. State A requires licensing and solemnization. Some years later, they move to state B where they hold themselves out as man and wife and live together as such. State B allows common law marriages. After X's death, her son by a previous marriage claims that Y is not entitled to any part of her estate. X died intestate. Will the son prevail?
3. X, a prostitute, has a child by Y, her husband. Y seems very content with X's occupation, but is never at home to take care of the child, since he is a traveling salesman. X, on her part, performs her job as a mother with skill and care. The parties divorce. Will Y be successful in his custody battle?
4. A merchant sells X, the wife of Y, a stylish, but more than adequate coat. The merchant does so on the representation by X that her husband will pay, because he is a wealthy businessman. Y is actually a dishwasher at a local cafeteria. Will the merchant be successful in his claim against Y?
5. Why is it normally more advantageous to secure a divorce rather than a legal separation?
6. If it appears to the court that parties have agreed to get a divorce without having statutory grounds, may the court refuse to grant the divorce?
7. May a husband secure alimony from his wife?
8. Why are courts reluctant to jail spouses who fail to pay support orders?
9. The court awards an order against Husband for Wife in the amount of \$100 per week in alimony. The order is granted at a time when Husband is well and working. Thereafter, Hus-

band suffers a serious physical setback and loses his job. What should Husband do without delay?

10. How does the marriage contract differ from an ordinary contract?

CHAPTER 12

Wills

Ronald A. Pressman

Wills

Ronald A. Pressman

I. Introduction.

As inhabitants of countries whose legal systems descend from English Common Law, we have acquired a set of concepts defining the relationships of persons to objects. We think in terms of such notions as ownership, possession, or property rights. These notions are deeply inbedded in legal structure. They have become fundamental to our thinking about ourselves, so much so that we often take them for granted. Ordinarily, we do not consider how these notions might be different, as, for example, in other countries, where such differences fundamentally affect many aspects of life.

Central notions in our law are those of property, a right of ownership, and a right of possession. We assume that we can exercise exclusive control over objects which we "own." We also assume that an "owner" will be supported by legal mechanisms if others challenge that exclusiveness. We think in terms of transferring that exclusiveness of control over objects to other persons by such mechanisms as "gifts," or "sales," or even by "rentals."

When a person dies, he cannot control or possess anything in a literal sense. What is to happen to those objects he was previously able to control? There are many possibilities. For example, those objects could all be taken over by the State in a gigantic death tax, or could be divided among various people such as family members. They also could be destroyed or declared open for anyone who could take them. Note, however, there is a marked difference between the objects of a live individual and those of someone who is deceased. The live person can personally defend his relationship to objects; the deceased cannot protect them at all. Insofar as the deceased had anything of value, all else equal, other people would covet it, and a struggle would ensue.

Given the principle of individual rights of property, in order to render struggles for the objects of a deceased person to be minimized and to be carried on in an orderly manner, the law has developed procedures. A person can legally dispose of his property when he is alive, and the law also enables him to dispose of his property after death, in a manner of his own choosing. Thus, incredible as it first seems, the deceased is able to direct living people in the disposition of his property and to have a ghostly, but nevertheless profound, impact on the lives of living persons.

The usual legal mechanism by which the dead direct the living is called the "will." It constitutes a voluntary statement by a competent living person regarding the fate his property (that is, estate) should undergo after he dies. Because the maker of a will is dead when the will becomes important, there is a greater than usual possibility that the instructions of the deceased will be misinterpreted, avoided, or otherwise not carried out. In order to prevent this, a fairly elaborate system of safeguards has evolved.

II. Practical problems with wills.

The greatest problem is that the individual must face the unpleasant and frightening prospect of his own death in order to even begin to consider making a will. Many people cannot rise above that barrier. If they do not, however, each one eventually becomes a "deceased intestate," a person whose property must be distributed in a manner prescribed by statute, perhaps incurring taxes which might have been avoided by distributions to a spouse, or having one's property transferred to persons for whom the decedent had absolutely no regard.

Furthermore, difficult as it may be for a person making a will to determine how his property should be posthumously distributed, the result is far more appropriate than arbitrary or inflexible statutory distributions. MORAL: The prudent person makes out a will. (An even more prudent person checks it periodically to determine whether changed conditions, such as changes in family relationships, changes in assets, or loss of loved ones, require modifications in his will.)

III. Requirements for a valid will.

A. It must be in writing and signed by the testator.

1. Only in the rarest cases can an oral (that is, "nuncupative") will be enforced, and then only in a limited fashion.

2. The signing of the will must be witnessed, usually by two or three others, who are, themselves, competent and of the age of majority.

   a. Their signatures indicate that at the very least, the person signing the will is the person who made it out.

   b. If there is a subsequent controversy over whether the person was of "sound mind," or was under duress, the witnesses can be called to testify at the probate court hearing regarding the will.

   c. Witnesses must be disinterested and not be beneficiaries or have an interest in the estate, for example, as a creditor of the testator. If they are beneficiaries, or otherwise have interests in the will, they may forfeit the will's provisions for themselves and may only receive what is prescribed by statute.

B. The document must be intended to be a will and must state that the person definitely intends that his estate be distributed in a given manner (that is, "testamentary intent"). An expression such as that a person "would like" or that he "hopes" that his estate would be disposed of in a given manner is not sufficient to constitute a will.

C. The testator at the time of making the will must appreciate the following to be considered of sound mind:

1. What a will does.
2. What is his property.
3. Who are his family members and who might appropriately benefit from what he bequeaths.
4. There must be some kind of plan for the distribution of the property.

D. The testator must be free from "undue influence" or coercion.

Although each claim which raises the issue of undue influence must be evaluated on its merits, the court may set aside a bequest where circumstances suggest undue influence. Such circumstances assume an even greater persuasiveness where the party exerting the influence is in a close confidential or fiduciary relationship to the decedent, for example, the testator's attorney or his physician. Such circumstances, if they exist, may cause the setting aside of either the whole will or portions which benefit the party who exerted undue influence.

E. Changes or revocations of a will.

A will is an ambulatory (alterable) instrument. It has no effect until the testator dies. Therefore, a will can always be changed, provided that the testator makes the changes with the required state of mind and in the proper manner. Such changes can be made as follows:

1. A "codicil" is an instrument (legal document) which modifies one or more provisions of a will. It must be executed (signed) with all the formalities of the will itself.
2. A new will can be made.
A new will must indicate by its language that the testator intended to revoke the former will. Usually, the

best way is for the testator to declare in the new will that he revoked the former will, but it must be done with a specific intention to revoke it. If two wills have been made, the later one is the governing instrument, provided it has complied with legal requirements.

F. Limitations on a will's provisions.
   1. The will must specify unambiguously what should happen to the property covered.
   2. The will cannot exclude such family members as a spouse. In certain situations, children may be omitted, but only if the specific intention to do so is stated in the will. If a specific family member is unintentionally omitted, he or she may be awarded a statutory share of the decedent's property by the court, (that is, by "operation of law").
   3. The will cannot specify that creditors not be paid. Statutes usually provide these priorities of creditors:
      a. Costs of administration of the estate.
      b. Costs of the last illness.
      c. Funeral expenses.
      d. All others.
   4. Sometimes, an individual makes a will and his circumstances change. For example, John Jones is married to Lucy G. Jones when he makes his will. He divorces Lucy and marries Sandra M. Jones, but neglects to change his will. Sandra, as his wife, has rights to his property by operation of law, and at least part of the original will, which leaves property to Lucy, the first wife, will be set aside in favor of Sandra, the wife at the time of John's death.
      Circumstances that can lead to the setting aside of part or all of an unrevised will are:
      a. Remarriage.
      b. Divorce.
      c. Annulment of marriage.
      d. Birth or adoption of a child. (An adopted child usually inherits in the same way as does a natural child.)

IV. Probate court proceedings.

A. The legal transfer of the property of a deceased person (a decedent) is effected by an order of the probate court. The state has an interest in the orderly and legitimate transfer of assets from the estate of the dead to the custody of the living, and the state usually has a tax interest also. The probate court proceeding is an effort to accomplish both those ends by the court's exercising a supervisory function over decisions which are made concerning the estate's assets.

B. The law usually provides that a person having custody of a will must produce it within a specific time (for example, 30 days) after the death of the testator. (The purpose of the law is to prevent a person from withholding the will because he didn't like what it stated or because he thought he would do better under a distribution by operation of law.)

1. In rare instances, legal inference of existence of a will can be made even if the specific document cannot be produced.

   a. The legal presumption is that absence of a will means that it has been revoked by the testator. The presumption is rebuttable, for example, by evidence that just prior to death, the deceased spoke about his will.

   b. Evidence presented, such as written notes, draft wills, carbon copies, etc. must be quite solid to make inferences on construction of a missing will.

2. In the case of a person who dies intestate (that is, without a valid will), a family member or an interested friend petitions the probate court and opens the administration of the estate. If there are no family members or friends, a creditor (sometimes a town, if taxes have gone unpaid on a piece of property) may petition the probate court for administration of the estate.

C. The court's initial responsibilities are to approve the will and appoint an executor. The will usually specifies who is to be the executor, and the court appoints that party, unless the party refuses or is found by the court to be unsuitable. (In practice, the person named executor would be very unlikely to be found unsuitable unless someone, say a dissatisfied relative, petitioned to block the appointment and showed good reasons. Note that, similarly, the court has the power to remove an executor for unsuitability and to reappoint another in place of the previous one.)

In the case of an estate without a will, a party (usually called an "administrator") is appointed by the court. A creditor, or even a person with no connection with the estate (a public administrator) may be appointed.

D. The executor or administrator has the responsibility for managing and distributing the estate. He can be sued for negligence if he performs irresponsibly and if damages are suffered. He files a bond to assure minimum loss to the estate in case his performance is deficient. His functions include the following:

1. Making a complete inventory of the assets of the estate and of the debts and liabilities of the estate.

2. Preserving the assets of the estate until distribution can be effected.

3. Prosecuting the claims of the estate and paying its debts (in the proper priority, if there is conflict as to which creditors should be satisfied).

4. Notifying all those named in the will as beneficiaries and distributing property to them.

   a. This may require decision-making in order to satisfy the terms of the will. For example, it may be necessary to sell some property of the estate in order to satisfy bequests of specific amounts of money.

   b. The distributions are made according to provisions of statute when there is no will.

   c. If there are no statutorily eligible relatives, the estate is paid over to the state (by "escheat").

5. Completing tax returns for jurisdictions with an interest in the estate, for example, Federal, state, local, and

"foreign state" (where there is property in a state other than the state in which the decedent was domiciled), and paying taxes when due.

6. Periodically filing with the court an account of transactions involving the estate, and a final accounting after it is completely distributed.

E. Statutory provisions for distribution of the estate, in case of intestacy.

1. The spouse generally is given priority after the debts of the estate are paid. Each state has its own formula, but the traditional rule is that the spouse takes one-third of the personal property and is entitled to the benefits of one-third of the real property for life (a "life estate"). On the death of the surviving spouse, the property would revert to the descendants of the initially dying spouse. For example, John, himself, owns an apartment house. He dies. Mary, his wife, is entitled to one-third of the profits from the building as long as she lives, even if she remarries. She cannot, by herself, sell the building or otherwise transfer title, because she does not have the title. On her death, the building goes to John's children (or to his siblings, if there aren't any children). If Mary has remarried and has a new family, after she dies they are not entitled to John's property.

   If a married couple owns real estate as a "tenancy by the entirety," when one spouse dies, the property becomes completely owned by the surviving spouse. The surviving spouse has title to the property and can convey it, sell it, or transfer it by will.

2. Next priority is given to the children of the decedent (or, in an appropriate proportion, to the children's children).

3. If there is no surviving spouse nor children, the parents, siblings, or more distant relatives receive the estate. It is only when no heir can be found that the estate escheats to the state.

F. Advantages of an appropriately drawn will.

1. Financial. The main consideration is taxation. Many legal mechanisms are available by which a testator can provide for certain effects by a will, for example, receiving estate tax deductions for a spouse, making distributions to charitable organizations, or making certain gifts to children. Some lead to more tax savings or costs than do others. It is not considered a dereliction of citizenship to minimize the tax burden on one's estate. Financial prudence dictates competent legal advice in creating and in periodically revising a will.

2. Non Financial. Without a will, there is no way one can control how one's estate is distributed. Given the misfortune that one's estate has to be distributed at all, some distributions are preferable to others. Almost anything chosen by the individual is preferable to that imposed by the state, the situation which could result with an intestate decedent.

General References

Atkinson, T.E. *Handbook of the Law of Wills.* West Publishing, St. Paul, 1953 (19th reprinting, 1975)

Hower, D.R. *Wills, Trusts, and Estate Administration for the Paralegal* (Statsky, W. P., Ed.). West Publishing, St. Paul, 1979

Lombard, J.F. *Probate Law and Practice* (Vols. 20–24 in *Massachusetts Practice*). West Publishing, St. Paul, Latest Supplement, 1983

Mennell, R.L. *Wills and Trusts in a Nutshell.* West Publishing, St. Paul, 1979

Questions on Chapter 12,
Wills

1. What are the general requirements for a valid will?
2. Can a will, when properly drawn, avoid the following:
   a. Payment from the estate of expenses of last illness?
   b. Payment from the estate of estate taxes?
   c. Receipt of any share of the estate by a spouse?
   d. Receipt of any share of the estate by a child?
3. Can a person, of less than normal intelligence but over the age of majority, execute a valid and binding will?
4. What methods, other than will or probate, can provide for the distribution of one's estate?
5. A testator, within hours of his death but still lucid, in looking over his will, discovers that he has forgotten to mention his adopted son. Can he now draft a new will? Does his adopted son have any ability to recover a share of the estate, if the testator is unable to execute a new will?
6. Adam, within hours of his death, informs his family not to worry, for they are all provided for by the terms of his will. After death, they cannot find a will. The attorney who drafted the will has his notes, but he gave the testator the original will. Has Adam died testate or intestate?
7. If a person dies without a will, what happens to his property?
8. What is a "tenancy by the entirety" and how does the concept relate to the distribution of property after a person dies?
9. If a person is a deceased intestate and no relatives are found, what happens to the bulk of the estate?
10. John Doe is the executor of the estate of Mary Doe, his deceased mother. His siblings, the other beneficiaries of the will, believe he is bungling his responsibility and is squandering the assets of the estate. What can they do?

CHAPTER 13

Special Legal Problems in Mental Health

John P. Petrila

Special Legal Problems in Mental Health

John Petrila

I. Competency.

Before an individual may exercise certain rights, for example, to contract, marry, write a will, consent to treatment, etc., or before society may impose certain liabilities, for example, try the individual in a criminal trial, the individual must be "competent." This means, in essence, the individual must have the capacity to understand the nature of the act he is going to perform and its possible consequences.

A. Central Ideas.

1. Different legal criteria of competency may be involved for different acts. For example, legal criteria for competency to consent to complex surgery may be different from those required to dispose of a small amount of property by will. The person asked to evaluate an individual for competency must be certain that he knows the kind of competency for which the evaluation is sought and what the criteria are for that kind of competency.

2. A person is rarely totally incompetent; relatively few persons are so incapacitated that they can exercise no judgment. For those that are, formal guardianship procedures are available. (See Chapter 11, Domestic Law)

3. Admission to a mental health facility does not, in itself, result in a loss of competency. In the past, patients often lost the right to exercise civil rights; that is, they were considered generally incompetent, simply because of admission to a mental health facility. In most states, this is no longer the case. Statutes specifically separate the two issues.

4. Competency is, ultimately, a legal concept. Clinical information can aid a court in deciding whether a person is competent, but the decision is a legal one. There is no clinical category or diagnosis that is equivalent to "competency" or "incompetency."

B. Competency to stand trial.

1. No defendant can be tried in a criminal case unless competent to stand trial.

2. Meaning. The Supreme Court has defined competency in the case of *Dusky v. Missouri*[1] to require that no defendant shall be tried who, because of mental disease or defect, lacks either of the following:
   a. Capacity to understand the proceedings against him.
   b. The ability to assist counsel in preparation of his defense.

3. State statutes define the concept for each state, although these definitions, invariably, track the Dusky case.

4. The emphasis in a competency decision is on the present mental state of the defendant. This is in contrast to mental state at issue in examining responsibility at the time of the offense.

5. Result of an incompetency finding. In most states, a defendant found incompetent to stand trial is committed automatically for mental health treatment. In the past, commitment could be indefinite. Since the Supreme Court's decision in *Jackson v. Indiana*[2], however, a defendant may be committed only for an amount of time reasonably necessary to determine whether his competency will be restored. If it will not, the defen-

dant must be committed through civil process, or he must be released and his charges dismissed.

C. General civil incompetency and guardianship.

1. Meaning. If an individual, because of mental illness or some other mental incapacity, demonstrates an inability to care for himself, manage his property, or both, he may be declared civilly incompetent, and a guardian may be appointed.

2. Procedure. This occurs only after a formal hearing, usually in a probate court. Clinical evidence may be introduced regarding the person's mental state in relation to his ability to handle his affairs.

3. Consequences. The incompetent person usually loses all civil rights. Instead, the guardian exercises those rights (not the right to vote, however).

4. Trends. Some states have adopted "limited guardianship" or "partial incapacity" statutes.
   a. The person is declared incompetent for certain purposes.
   b. Stripping of all rights, which occurs in general incompetency proceedings, is avoided.
   c. Partial guardianship expires when the reason for its creation ends.

D. Competency to contract. (See Chapter 10, Contracts)

1. Situation. A person may wish to avoid a contract either because he was incompetent when making the contract or because the person with whom he was contracting was incompetent.

2. Definition. The contractor will usually be considered competent if he understands the nature of the contract and its consequences. Some degree of "rationality" is also required, although this will usually be determined by the courts on a case by case basis.

3. Consequences. If the contractor is actually incompetent, but has not been declared legally incompetent, the contract is usually considered voidable rather than void.

a. The individual who wishes the contract nullified must seek court action to have the contract declared void.

b. If the contractor was legally incompetent, the contract is usually considered void and, is, therefore, unenforceable.

E. Competency to make a will. (See Chapter 12, Wills)

1. General test. At the time of making the will did the testator have sufficient mental capacity:

a. To know the natural objects of his bounty?

b. To comprehend the kind and character of his property?

c. To dispose of his property according to some plan?

2. Soundness of mind means that a testator:

a. Can understand, in a general way, the nature and extent of his property.

b. Knows his relationship to those who naturally have a claim to benefit from the property.

c. Has a general understanding of the practical effect of his will.

3. Undue influence. The clinician may also be asked to evaluate the susceptibility of the testator, because of mental condition, to the influence of others seeking his property.

F. Competency to consent to medical treatment.

II. **The Criminal Process.** (See Chapter 4, Criminal Law and Procedures.)

A. Competency.

1. A defendant cannot be tried unless he is competent to stand trial.

2. New emphasis on other competencies. Increasingly, attention is focused on the defendant's capacity at other points in the process besides trial. These include:

a. Competency to waive the right to counsel.

b. Competency to make a voluntary and knowing confession. (This can be an issue when an accused has confessed to a crime.)

   c. Competency to plead guilty to charges.

3. The legal standards for these competencies are not fully developed and may vary from state to state.

B. Responsibility at the time of the offense.

1. Issue. Should the defendant be held culpable for conduct which is the subject of the criminal charge? (The insanity defense, that is, a plea of "not guilty by reason of insanity.")

2. The emphasis is on the defendant's mental state at the time of the offense.

3. Tests for responsibility have varied. All, however, require the existence of a mental disease or defect.

   a. Mental disease or defect defined.

      1) The term often is defined broadly to include "congenital and traumatic mental conditions as well as disease."

      2) Usually excluded from the term are:

         a) Alcoholism or drug abuse without psychosis.

         b) Abnormalities manifested only by repeated criminal or otherwise antisocial conduct, even though such abnormality may be included under categories of mental illness, disease, or defect in some classfications of mental disorder.

   b. In addition to mental disease or defect, the insanity defense requires some linkage of disease or defect with the criminal conduct. The disease or defect must be shown to have affected the defendant's conduct so as to render him not responsible as defined by statute.

   c. States use a variety of criteria in defining the impact the disease or defect must have on conduct in order to exculpate (that is, render not guilty) the defendant. Criteria used in different jurisdictions are these:

      1) The M'Naghten* test. This test usually deals with

---

*There are several accepted spellings of the name.

the cognitive functioning of defendant. A traditional phrasing of the test indicates the defendant is not responsible (that is, is legally insane) if at the time of the offense, the party accused was laboring under such a defect of reason, from disease of the mind, as not to know the nature and quality of the act he was doing, or, if he did know it, that he did not know he was doing what was wrong.

2) The "irresistible impulse" test. Many commentators believed the M'Naghten test was too narrow and did not allow consideration of disease or defect affecting volition. As a result, this test was added by many states. The issue is whether, as a result of mental disease or defect, the defendant could not conform his conduct to the requirements of the law.

3) The American Law Institute test (ALI). This test, written by the group that wrote the *Model Penal Code*, combines *elements of M'Naghten and irresistible impulse.* The ALI test maintains that "a person is not responsible for criminal conduct if at the time of such conduct, as a result of mental disease or defect, he lacks substantial capacity either to appreciate the criminality (wrongfulness) of his conduct or to conform his conduct to the requirements of law."[3]

4) The Durham rule was adopted by the United States Court of Appeals for the District of Columbia in 1954.[4] Also known as the "product" rule, it said that "an accused is not criminally responsible if his unlawful act was the product of mental disease or mental defect." The court adopted the rule in order to allow into court a broader range of psychiatric testimony. The rule found little favor elsewhere, however, and was finally abandoned even in the District of Columbia in 1972.

d. A diagnosis of psychosis does not mean automatically that the person is legally not responsible (insane). A number of clinicians and lawyers make this assumption, forgetting that the relationship of the mental disease to the criminal conduct must be explored.

4. Diminished responsibility. Most criminal offenses are defined both by conduct (actus reus) and the actor's state of mind while performing the act (mens rea). The defendant may wish to show by psychiatric evidence that he did not possess the requisite mental state to commit the offense charged.

   a. Result. If the defendent can make this showing, it does not result in complete exculpation for the offense, which is the result when the insanity defense is pled successfully. Rather, the defendant will usually be found guilty of a lesser offense.

   b. Example. A defendant is charged with first degree murder, which requires that the defendant killed the victim "knowingly, deliberately, and with premeditation." The defendant introduces evidence which convinces the jury he could not have acted "knowingly, deliberately, and with premeditation." The defendant is not acquitted; rather, he is likely to be found guilty of second degree murder.

   c. States vary in their use of this doctrine and in the type of condition that may be used in showing that the defendant did not have the requisite mental state. The most frequently allowed evidence is that of mental illness or intoxication.

C. Sentencing.

1. The health care clinician may be asked to evaluate a defendant after conviction, but before the court imposes sentence. The request may come from the court, from a probation officer, or from defense counsel.

2. The scope of the inquiry is often much broader than the inquiry into competency or responsibility. It also falls more comfortably within the traditional health care role, because the referral source is often most interested in whether the defendant would benefit from health treatment. In short, the clinician is often being asked to design a treatment plan.

3. The keys in an evaluation like this are specificity and

feasibility. It does little good to recommend to a court a treatment plan that cannot be implemented, either because it is too vague or because the resources called for do not exist.

4. Special situation—capital cases. Many death penalty statutes allow evidence of the defendant's mental status in mitigation. The psychiatrist may also be asked to evaluate whether the defendant convicted of a capital offense is dangerous. (Documents prepared by the American Psychiatric Association, in the case of *Estelle v. Smith,*[5] state that clinicians cannot make the long-term predictions of dangerousness required by a number of death penalty statutes.)

D. Points for a clinician to remember. The clinician involved in the criminal process should be able to answer the following questions prior to performing the exam. (Note: questions that are not asked him need not generally be answered, and may complicate the case if they are approached.)

1. What is the source of the referral, and in relation to the criminal case, what does the referring source wish to obtain from the evaluation? A private attorney, the court, the prosecution, or the family may have different hopes for the outcome of the evaluation. The needs of the referral source will determine, in large part, what the examiner will emphasize in conducting his examination and in making his report. For example, if defense counsel makes the referral in hopes of making an insanity plea, the examiner will search harder for evidence of insanity than he would if he were conducting an exam at the request of the court for aid in disposition.

2. Who receives the reports? Only the referral source? All parties? That may determine what types of information are placed in the report. One's report to a referring attorney may differ somewhat from a report to the court.

3. What are the confidentiality rules? Is information given to the examiner by the patient confidential? Usually, such information cannot be used in trial at the issue of guilt or innocence, but a clever prosecutor may try to have incriminating evidence admitted under other rubrics.

III. Civil issues.

A. Admissions to mental health facilities. Two general types:

1. Voluntary admissions. The individual signs himself into the hosptial. An emerging issue in this context is whether the individual was competent to make the decision to seek treatment. If the individual is deemed incompetent by the staff of the hospital, some commentators argue that the staff must seek admission by alternative routes, for example, via guardianship or civil commitment. At this time, there are no court decisions on this point.

2. Involuntary admissions. In the past, a person sometimes could only be admitted involuntarily through "medical certification," that is, signature of one or two doctors attesting the individual was in need of treatment. The emphasis was on treatment needs of patient. When court hearings were mandated, they were very informal and often perfunctory.

   a. The due process model now predominates. Since the decision of *Lessard v. Schmidt*,[6] states have required formal court hearings prior to involuntary admissions.

      1) "Due process" in a commitment proceeding means that the patient has a right to an attorney, to present witnesses, to cross-examine opposing witnesses, and to have an impartial fact finder decide the issue.

      2) The case for commitment must be proved at least by clear and convincing evidence.

      In the past, a preponderance of evidence was sufficient. (In quantifying these terms, "preponderance of evidence" is thought to mean that at least slightly more than 50 percent of the evidence supports the position. "Clear and convincing" is equated with 75 percent. "Patients' rights" attorneys have argued that proof beyond reasonable doubt (the standard in criminal cases) should be required, but the U.S. Supreme Court rejected that argument in the Addington[7] case.)

b. The emphasis in commitment statutes today is not solely on treatment needs of patients, as in the past. Now the major concerns are whether the person is mentally ill and whether because of his illness, the person is a danger* to himself or others. The concept of dangerousness has become critical. (There is some debate over whether proving dangerousness requires an overt act or if threats or gestures are sufficient. There is case law on both sides of the dispute.)

c. The role of the clinician is that of an expert witness. Note that whether the individual is to be committed is a legal decision and is made by a court.

1) Because it is an adversary hearing, a clinician involved in a commitment hearing will usually find his opinions questioned during cross-examination.

2) The clinician should also be aware of the potential confusion of roles that may be created by participation in such a hearing. (For example, if the clinician is testifying for commitment, it may be difficult to treat the patient later.)

3. Other types of admissions. Patients may be admitted through other means, falling somewhere between wholly voluntary admissions and court-adjudicated involuntary admissions. Two of the most common are these:

a. Guardian-initiated admissions. In many states, a guardian may sign his ward into a hospital without court authorization, although recent court decisions and

---

*For practical purposes, "dangerousness" means that the individual is likely to harm someone unnecessarily.

statutes tend to require more formality, including prior court approval or even a full-scale court hearing.

b. Admissions of minors. The Supreme Court, in the Parham[8] case, held that the decision to admit a minor is largely one of parental discretion. Although an independent review of the appropriateness of admission is required, the court ruled that a staff member of the admitting facility may provide the necessary review.

B. The right to treatment. Lawsuits arguing that patients had a constitutional "right to treatment" were a primary method challenging institutional conditions in the 1960's and 1970's.

1. The concept of such a right was first articulated in 1961 by Morton Birnbaum, M.D., in an article appearing in the *American Bar Association Journal.*[9]

2. His arguments found no judicial acceptance until the Rouse[10] case, decided by the Federal Court of Appeals for the District of Columbia in 1965. The court ruled that Rouse, acquitted by reason of insanity, then sent to St. Elizabeth's Hospital, had a right to treatment based on a specific statute. The court also held that it was not necessary that the treatment provided would cure or improve the patient's condition, only that there was a bona fide effort being made to do so.

3. In the landmark case of *Wyatt v. Stickney,*[11] a Federal District Court in Alabama held that the Constitution guaranteed a right to treatment for institutionalized patients.

a. The underlying theory was labeled the "quid pro quo" theory. In short, the court said that since liberty is deprived by commitment hearings, and since commitment hearings did not have all procedural protections usually associated with depriving liberty (that is, the criminal process), in exchange, the state had to provide treatment.

b. Content of the right. The court entered very detailed standards by which implementation of the right would

be measured. Such standards fell into three broad areas:
1) A humane physical and psychological environment.
2) Sufficient staff to administer and provide adequate treatment.
3) Individualized treatment plans.
c. The court issued standards for each of those areas, prescribing the numbers and types of staff, and detailing criteria for the physical environment.
d. The Federal Court of Appeals endorsed this reasoning and upheld the District Court's ruling.

4. The impact of Wyatt. Courts in many states held that a right to treatment did, in fact, exist. When facilities for the mentally retarded were involved, courts often labeled the right at stake as the "right to habilitation."
a. Courts have even ordered institutions closed, holding that as a matter of constitutional law, adequate habilitation could not be provided in a large, geographically remote institution.
b. The courts also held that lack of financial resources could not prevent implementation of the right. This raised fundamental issues of Federal-state and judicial-legislative relations, particularly over which body of government should control allocation of state resources. The issue has not been resolved on just how far courts may go in mandating expenditures.

5. Despite widespread acceptance of the right among the lower courts, the Supreme Court does not seem disposed toward a constitutional right to treatment.
a. In the case of *O'Connor v. Donaldson*,[12] the court avoided ruling on right to treatment issues. Instead, the court held only that a non dangerous individual who can live safely in the community by himself or with others cannot be committed to a mental hospital.
b. The quid pro quo argument advanced in the Wyatt case was rejected. It was noted that, traditionally, a state could confine the mentally ill for reasons other than treatment.

c. That reasoning was later adopted by the Court of Appeals which originally upheld the right to treatment. In the case of *Morales v. Turman*,[13] involving a right to treatment for juveniles, the court concluded that the existence of the right was unsettled.

6. The present status of the right must still be described as unsettled. The Supreme Court has yet to rule on the issue, although as noted, indications are that the court is not favorably disposed. The cases already decided, however, have had enormous impact on standards, for example, the JCAH* standards, and on state legislation. In both areas, one finds incorporated, either as law or as an accepted standard, many of the elements handed down by the courts in defining the content of the right to treatment.

C. The right to refuse treatment.

1. Informed consent is the critical concept in every consideration of refusal of treatment. "Informed consent" means consent, which is given voluntarily, knowledgeably, and competently.

   a. Voluntary. The question is whether consent given in an institution (that is, a mental hospital or a jail) can be voluntary.

      1) An important case in development of restrictions was the Kaimowitz[14]** case, where the court ruled that, by definition, a confined person could not consent freely to psychosurgery. The court reasoned that a prison environment was intrinsically so coercive that voluntary consent was impossible.

      2) Other courts seem to disagree, believing that consent given in an institution, at times, may truly be informed consent. It is appropriate for staff and family

---

*Joint Commission on Accreditation of Hospitals, a private body which inspects hospitals and certifies them if they conform to JCAH standards.
**One of the few cases named for the attorney rather than the litigant. (The attempt to keep the prisoner's name confidential led to use of the attorney's name.)

to attempt to persuade the patient to consent, but coercive techniques are prohibited.
b. Knowledgeable. Information must be given to the patient about the proposed treatment, including its risks and benefits, alternative treatments and their risks and benefits, and the consequences if treatment is not administered.
1) Exceptions to the rule of disclosure include emergency situations, for example, when the patient is in a coma and cannot make the decision, and it is a life or death situation.
2) Another exception is the therapeutic privilege. If disclosure would so upset the patient that he cannot make a rational decision about treatment, information may be withheld. (This exception has become less prominent recently.)
c. Competent. Does the patient have the capacity to make the decision?
1) There are several ways of gauging competency.
a) The treater is likely to favor the "reasonable outcome" test, where the pertinent question is whether the decision is reasonable. A refusal decision would be seen as unreasonable and would thereby lead to the conclusion that the patient is incompetent. In effect, the act of refusing would establish incompetence of the refuser. (The courts tend to frown on this kind of Catch-22.)
b) Another test is whether the patient has the ability to understand the choices. This test allows for decisions that others might view as "bad" decisions; the emphasis is on the ability to make the decision, rather than on the decision itself.
2) Competency is obviously an elusive concept. It is prudent for a clinician to familiarize himself with the laws of the jurisdiction in which he practices and to seek peer consultation, as well as consultation with an attorney, when in doubt.

2. Types of treatment refusal.
a. The first restriction on treatment of involuntary pa-

tients occurred with treatment considered either experimental (for example, psychosurgery), or unduly intrusive (for example, electroshock).
  b. The right to refuse medication is a fairly recent development. Early cases involved:
    1) Aversive treatment (see *Knecht v. Gillman*[15]) where medications were given for punishment; the courts said such practices could not be condoned.
    2) Refusal based on other constitutional principles, for example, on freedom of religion (See *Winters v. Miller*[16]); the court held that a competent patient could refuse medication if taking it violated his religious tenets.

3. Who may refuse treatment?
  a. Voluntary patients. There seems to be near unanimity that voluntary patients have an absolute right to refuse treatment. In such a situation, a clinician may do the following:
    1) Explore alternative treatments.
    2) Seek a guardian if the patient is apparently not competent.
    3) Seek hospitalization (if the patient is an outpatient and meets commitment standards).
    4) Terminate the relationship (for example, discharge the patient).
    5) Paying attention to the doctor-patient relationship will often result in the patients' complying with treatment recommendations.
  b. Involuntary patients. Courts disagree in their approach.
    1) Some courts (for example, the Oklahoma Supreme Court in *In re KKB*[17]) have held that involuntary patients may refuse treatment unless they have been declared legally incompetent and a guardian has been appointed. In such a case, the guardian exercises the right to consent or refuse for the patient.
    2) Other courts (for example, the Federal District Court in *Rennie v. Klein*[18]) have said that involuntary patients hold a qualified right to refuse. These

courts seek to resolve patient-staff conflict over the issue through internal mechanisms. Some requirements.

   a) All patients must sign written consent forms prior to administration of treatment. Among other things the forms disclose the potential negative side effects of treatment.

   b) Involuntary patients are able to refuse unless they are functionally incompetent or legally incompetent. The latter means that a guardian has been appointed. Whether a patient is "functionally" incompetent is determined by an independent institutional (not court) review. If the patient is determined to be functionally incompetent, medication may be administered for a limited period of time without his consent. The system also involves creation of Patient Advocate positions to assist the patient and to advocate in his behalf.

3) The law on the issue is still very much in flux.[19] Conflicting decisions are expected in the future, and a resolution satisfactory to all interested parties will probably never be obtained.

D. Release decisions. In many jurisdictions, when staff determine that a patient is not dangerous to himself or others, the facility must release the patient (or at least place him in a less restrictive environment). In cases where the staff determination turns out to be wrong, and where a third party is harmed by the patient, a suit may be brought, seeking to impose liability for that decision.

1. A negligence theory is used in such cases. Plaintiffs utilize a torts analysis, that is, they try to show the breach of the duty to care and that the breach was the foreseeable and proximate cause of the plaintiff's injury. Courts have imposed liability in a number of cases:

   a. Where staff was not aware of information in the medical files.

   b. Where the patient was assaultive (*Williams v. United States*[20]).

    c. Where courts and other parties were not informed of a patient's potential danger (*Hicks v. United States*[21]).

    d. Where the facility failed to provide proper supervision when placing on leave a patient with a prior history of violent behavior.

    e. Note, however, a facility is not an insurer of the public safety; that is, the facility is not liable for all acts subsequently committed by someone who has been under its care. It is only when a patient's likelihood of harming someone is reasonably predictable clinically that the facility is liable.

2. The duty to warn. In the case of *Tarasoff v. Regents of the University of California*[22], the California Supreme Court held that in some circumstances a therapist has a duty to protect third parties from foreseeable harm at the hands of a patient. If necessary, the therapist may have to warn the third party of the danger. This is a departure from traditional tort law, which generally holds that no duty exists to control the conduct of another or to warn third parties of another's conduct. The duty to protect others includes the following criteria and problems:

    a. A special relationship must exist to extablish a duty of care. In this case, it is the therapist-patient relationship.

    b. The prediction of dangerousness involved must be made with the reasonable degree of skill, knowledge, and care ordinarily possessed and exercised (by members of the psychiatric and psychotherapeutic professions) under similar circumstances.

    c. The adequacy of the therapist's conduct will be measured against the standard of what constitutes reasonable care under the circumstances.

    d. The potential victims to be warned are the foreseeable victims of the patient.

    e. Patient confidentiality is an important issue. Disclosure of patient communications must not become routine and must be done discreetly; however, confidentiality must yield to the extent to which disclosure is vitally essential to avert danger to others;

    f. Despite criticism of Tarasoff, a number of other courts have adopted similar holdings.

    g. In a recent case (*Thompson v. County of Alameda*[23]), the California Supreme Court suggested that the duty to warn would only be applied in cases where there is a "known and specifically foreseeable and identifiable victim of the patient's threats." (It is too early to know to what extent this doctrine will be accepted in other jurisdictions.)

Text References

1. *Dusky v. Missouri*, 362 U.S. 402 (1960)
2. *Jackson v. Indiana*, 406 U.S. 715 (1972)
3. Sec. 4.01 *Model Penal Code* (Draft). American Law Institute, St. Paul, 1962
4. *Durham v. United States*, 94 U.S.App.D.C. 228, 214 F.2d 862
5. *Estelle v. Smith*, 451 U.S. 454, 68 L.Ed.2d 359 (1981)
6. *Lessard v. Schmidt*, 349 F.Supp. 1078 (E.D. Wis. 1974), vacated, 414 U.S. 473 (remanded for more specific order), more specific order entered, 379 F.Supp. 1376 (E.D.Wis. 1974), vacated, 421 U.S. 957 (1975) (remanded for reconsideration of the abstention principle), order reinstated, 413 F.Supp. 1318 (E.D. Wis. 1976)
7. *Addington v. Texas*, 441 U.S. 418 (1979)
8. *Parham v. J. L. and J. R.*, 442 U.S. 584 (1979)
9. Birnbaum, "The Right to Treatment", 46 A.B.A.J. 499 (1960)
10. *Rouse v. Cameron*, 373 F.2d 451 (D.C. Cir. 1966)
11. *Wyatt v. Stickney*, 325 F. Supp. 781 (M.D. Ala. 1971), 344 F. Supp. 373 (M.D. Ala. 1972); aff'd. sub nom. *Wyatt v. Aderholdt*, 503 F.2d 1305 (5th Cir. 1974)
12. *O'Connor v. Donaldson*, 422 U.S. 563 (1974)
13. *Morales v. Turman*, 562 F.2d 993 (5th Cir. 1977)
14. *Kaimowitz v. Michigan Dept. of Mental Health*, Unreported, Cir. Ct., Wayne Co., Mich. (1973)
15. *Knecht v. Gillman*, 488 F.2d 1136 (8th Cir. 1973)
16. *Winters v. Miller*, 446 F.2d 65 (2nd Cir. 1971)
17. *In re KKB*, 609 P.2d 747 (Okl. S. Ct. 1980)
18. *Rennie v. Klein*, 653 F.2d 836 (3rd Cir. 1981)
19. Mills, M.J., Yesavage, J.A., and Gutheil, T.G. Continuing case law development in the right to refuse treatment. *Am. J. Psychiat.* 140; 715–719, 1983
20. *Williams v. United States*, 450 F. Supp. 1040 (1978)
21. *Hicks v. United States*, 511 F.2d 407 (D.C. Cir. 1975)

22. *Tarasoff v. Bd. of Regents,* 17 Cal.3d 430, 131 Cal.Rptr. 14 (Cal. Sup. Ct. 1974)

23. *Thompson v. County of Alameda,* 614 P.2d 728 (Cal. Sup. Ct. 1974)

Questions on Chapter 13,
Special Legal Problems in Mental Health

1. The clinical evaluation of competency to stand trial involves an examination of the individual's mental status at what point in time?
2. The clinical evaluation of criminal responsibility involves an examination of the individual's mental status at what point in time?
3. True or False: In most states, admission to a mental health facility results automatically in a finding of incompetence.
4. If an individual is declared incompetent to stand trial, is there any limit on the length of his confinement in that status?
5. What is the legal standard of proof which must be met before an individual can be committed involuntarily by judicial processes?
6. What are the two major issues considered in assessing whether an individual should be committed involuntarily for mental health treatment?
7. What are the three components of the right to treatment, as articulated by the Federal judiciary?
8. Describe two alternative approaches, adopted by courts, in devising procedures for implementing a right to refuse treatment.
9. True or False: A mental health facility is an insurer of the public safety; for example, the facility is liable automatically for the harm caused by a patient in its care.
10. True or False: A psychotherapist has a duty to warn a possible victim whenever he suspects that his patient might harm that victim.

CHAPTER 14

On Being Involved Personally in a Lawsuit, as a Plaintiff, Expert Witness, or Defendant

Nathan T. Sidley and John P. Petrila

On Being Involved Personally in a Lawsuit, as a Plaintiff, Expert Witness, or Defendant

Nathan T. Sidley and John P. Petrila

I. The health professional as a plaintiff.

A. General concerns in plaintiffhood.

It is important in considering plaintiffs to consider two worlds, the world of rational plaintiffs and the world of real plaintiffs. That dichotomy can be supplemented by the worlds of rational competent attorneys and of other attorneys.

A rational plaintiff is one who is knowledgeable about court procedures, and who, after evaluation of the potential gains and losses of a lawsuit, concludes that there is more to gain than to lose by initiating a suit. (Alternatively, he may conclude that there is less to lose by initiating a suit than by not initiating one.) The gains and losses are usually money, but they may include more subjective considerations. In any case, the rational plaintiff acts with *sang froid* in going to court.

The typical real plaintiff, however, acts under the influence of emotion, especially anger. He is almost more interested in revenge than in the financial aspects of the case. He is usually unaware of the costs of a lawsuit, whether financial, time, or mental anguish. Even if he wins his suit, he is likely to emerge with a jaded view of the legal system, a product of frustration engendered by his unrealistic expectations.

355

B. The role of the attorney.

1. Basic considerations.

The rational, competent attorney recognizes that every lawsuit represents the failure of a relationship. The parties involved are not capable of resolving their own disputes satisfactorily, and, in a way-all-too reminiscent of young children, have to call on a father figure (whether male or female) to decide for them. The attorney recognizes that any encounter with a deciding third party is a risky one. All things considered, it is usually more advantageous for two disputing parties to come to their own resolution of disputes than to run the risk of completely losing control of the situation.

Even where the outcome of a law case is highly predictable, such as when a department store goes to small claims court to try to obtain payment of delinquent bills, risks are run, especially if the defendant appears and argues his case. Costs are also incurred.* Rationality in going to court depends on the degree of predictability of the outcome. The greater the gamble associated with a court case, the less rational it is to undertake such a venture.

2. The attorney in relation to the plaintiff's rationality.

a. Emotional considerations.

The ordinary plaintiff doesn't get to an attorney unless he is highly motivated. Court is an unfamiliar place with negative associations. Involvement with attorneys is known to be costly. There is also a sense of struggle and of uncertainty about a court encounter. These inhibiting factors must be overcome motivationally in order for a person to be activated to the point of initiating a suit. The plaintiff is typically in an aroused emotional-motivational state when he consults an at-

---

*From the standpoint of the store, such suits are often seen as necessary, not so much that in the aggregate the value of the money recovered to the store exceeds the costs of the suits. Rather the store uses the possibility of court action as a threat to its debtors so as to motivate the general class of debtors to pay their bills. If a store's debtors generally decide not to pay their bills, the store is in real trouble.

torney, and in such a state, the plaintiff is not capable of operating at his best.

The first task of the attorney is to try to calm the plaintiff to the point where he is relatively capable of making informed and rational decisions. (The situation is actually very similar to that of a first consultation with a physician or a health-care agency.)

b. Informational considerations.

The attorney's next task is to try to ascertain what the client regards as his problem or what is the goal of consulting the attorney. The most common diagnostic problem of the lawyer is to determine to what extent the potential plaintiff is seeking money and to what extent he is seeking revenge.

The attorney then investigates in a preliminary way what are the facts that give rise to the client's grievance. He does that by interrogating the client and reviewing documentation. The attorney's investigation of the case must take place in the context of the following considerations.

1) The relation of the facts of the case to the client's goals.

   a) The likely relationship of the facts as related by the client to the facts as they might ultimately be manifested.

   b) The relationship of the facts alleged to the principles of law that seem to apply; the law may be quite flexible in relation to a case. For example, if the plaintiff alleges that the defendant broke the plaintiff's vase, the following might be defenses:

   1)) The vase was not the plaintiff's in the first place.

   2)) The defendant did not have the vase and, therefore, could not have broken it.

   3)) The vase was intact when the defendant gave it back to the plaintiff.

   4)) The vase was broken before the defendant had it.

   c) The beauty of the law (Some see it as not so beautiful.) is that the defendant can present all four defenses to the case. Presenting one doesn't foreclose him from presenting the others. It keeps the plaintiff on his toes.

2) Aspects of the litigation that can be anticipated, including such issues as conducting an adequate investigation, considering how he might deal with different tactics which might be employed by a scrupulous or by an unscrupulous defendants' attorney, or filing an appeal if the case is lost. He considers all that in relation to the costs that must be borne by the client, including his own fees. (In the case of litigation in which his fee is contingent, he will also have to consider his own fee in relation to the demands of the case.)

After his preliminary investigation, the attorney can present to the client some indication as to what might be in store for him if he decides to pursue the case. If the primary goal of the plaintiff is financial, the attorney can give some indication of the likelihood that the client will come out financially ahead from the suit, at the same time giving the client some idea as to the time, inconvenience, and effort that he will have to expend, especially if there is a possibility that the defense will use every roadblock tactic available in order to increase plaintiff's expense. (Obviously, the case has to be of significant size for there to be any hope that the plaintiff will benefit financially from it.)

If the primary goal of the client is emotional, such as to teach someone a lesson, or to assert some principle, such as fighting for justice, the attorney spells out for the client just what is likely to be involved for him in terms of financial and emotional resource expenditures. Sometimes, nothing the attorney can do will dissuade a client from embarking on a course of action that the attorney regards as irrational, either in the sense that the gains could not possibly exceed the losses or in the sense that the likelihood of winning was too low to make it reasonable to proceed. Sometimes, however, a sober discussion of the overall case by the attorney will lead the client to a more realistic consideration of the pros and cons of litigation than his original view.

3. The attorney's contribution to the case.
It is possible that such a phenomenon as a simple, cut-and-dry case exists. Most often, however, such is a chimera visible only to laymen, not to experienced attorneys. There are always pitfalls; there are always aspects of the case that are ambiguous; there are always aspects of the case that might lead to one conclusion as opposed to another; there are always novel legal theories which can be presented to make the case in hand something special to be considered on its own terms and not according to the usual general principle. And finally, there is the variant of Murphy's law, no matter how thoroughly the attorney prepares a case, the opposition will unerringly find the one weak spot he didn't adequately consider and prepare for.

One of the attorney's basic problems is to avoid being surprised in relation to a case. That means he must be thoroughly prepared, both in the facts of the case and in the law of the case. Moreover, he must know the facts and possible ramifications of these facts, as his client sees them and, maybe even more important, as the opposition sees them. He must sift out what is reality from the self-serving, distorted version of facts his client almost invariably presents. He must try to do the same for the opposition, which frequently, for practical purposes, appears unscrupulous and loose with the truth. If he does not accurately ascertain these things, he is likely to be surprised at trial, and surprise invites disaster.

The legal issues also are never simple. Every pre-trial and trial step occurs in a legal context, and the attorney runs the risk of missing some small, but critical, point, some of which allow for recovery when they are lost but some of which don't. Worse, though, is that every case has many facets, and every facet has differing law which relates to it. Looking up law in a textbook may give general ideas, but the specific approach to a case requires library work and studying case law on the different aspects of the case at hand.

4. Time and costs.
Everything that the attorney does in the case takes time. Whether he is seeing the client, obtaining documents, viewing evidence in the field, talking with experts, becoming familiar with case law, writing briefs, or even discussing the case with colleagues, activity requires time, and the client must pay for the time. Probably the most frustrating situation occurs when the case is scheduled to be heard at 9 a.m. and everyone waits in the courthouse until 3:30 p.m. before the case actually comes before the court, too late to be finished that day and, therefore, requiring another trip to court. A comparable situation is where one party assembles all his witnesses at the time specified for the hearing and the opposition lawyer requests a continuance (that is, that the case be put off to another time) because he hasn't been paid yet. (In such a situation, the initial attorney can protest to the court, but the full facts don't always come out, and courts are usually sympathetic in granting continuances. Attorneys are also usually very courteous to their colleagues, so that there would generally be a pre-decided, mutually agreed-upon rescheduling, that might not be so costly. It has not been unknown, however, that one party will force the other to as much expense as possible without prejudicing his own standing in court.) The attorney will point out these probable costs to the possible plaintiff to help the client know for what he may be financially liable.

C. Types of cases in which the health professional is likely to be a plaintiff.

1. As health professional.
Most common is for a private practitioner to litigate in order to collect a bill for services previously rendered. Usually, practitioners are forgiving of such debts when

patients are insolvent or when they make a sincere effort to pay, even if the rate of payment is turtle-like. Physicians often perform procedures on a charitable basis for patients regarded as deserving.

Suits do occur, though, when practitioners believe a patient is able to pay his bill, but doesn't.

a. In this area as in so many others, anticipation of such problems is the watchword. The most obvious form of prevention is to discuss with the patient, in advance of the procedure, exactly what the fee will be and how the patient wishes to pay the bill. When the fee cannot be determined in advance, if the patient understands why not, and if he understands how the fee will be computed and what the range of fees will be, he is far less likely to be resentful and to withhold payment than if he is surprised at the bill.

   In addition, if the practitioner does not mention a specific fee in advance of performing services, a patient may be able to claim that no specific contract existed. If the patient does not pay and the practitioner must sue, he may only be able to recover a fee based on quantum meruit, rather than his full fee.

   1) It is impossible to express what is a fair or appropriate fee. From the patient's standpoint, fees tend to be too high; from the practitioner's standpoint, fees tend to be too low. But if such a dispute occurs before a procedure, it is far easier to resolve than if it occurs afterward. From a public relations standpoint, some flexibility of fees is also desirable. In fact, a reduction of fees is often an incentive for a more rapid schedule of patient payment.

   2) Why is such an obvious mode of dealing with patients not universally followed by practitioners? A few reasons are suggested.

      a) It appears inconsistent with an individual's image of civic-mindedness to appear to be personally interested in money. People often speak disparagingly of others who emphasize money matters. Practitioners may tend to avoid financial discussions with patients because of their perception of the impact of such discussions on the practitioner's self-image (as well as on his public image).

b) A patient who requires a procedure is a person who is suffering. Paying the bill represents a certain degree of additional suffering. The patient's level of tension also tends to rise when he considers and discusses the costs of a procedure. The patient, too, has a self-image and a public image about his own dealings with money and is likely to have the same inhibitions about such discussions as does the practitioner.

The doctor, whose role is to reduce suffering, is reluctant to increase his patient's embarrassment and suffering by bringing up the subject of fees.

c) Some practitioners feel uneasy about charging fees in particular. They are reluctant to have their fees challenged by patients because they fear they can not defend their fee demands appropriately. Similarly, the doctor may be reluctant to bring up the issue of fees because he expects the patient to become angry, and he wishes to avoid that kind of scene.

d) Seldom is the issue of pricing of services and discussing fees presented as part of a practitioner's training. Thus, at least at first, the situation is awkward for the practitioner because he really does not know how to conduct such a situation effectively. No one likes to expose himself deliberately to an awkward situation.

e) Practitioners wish to exercise their skills in their calling. Spending time discussing fees may be regarded by a practitioner as a time-consuming burden, which is unimportant in comparison to the truly important task of practicing good medicine.

f) The practitioner may also be concerned that the patient would forego an important treatment because of financial considerations.

3) If discussing fees is likely to increase collections and to decrease a necessity for suits and collection agen-

cies, etc., how can a practitioner who wishes to be more effective in negotiating and collecting his fees discuss the situation more adequately with patients?
a) Establish a reasonable fee structure, whether based on time or on procedure performed. Patients understand that health care practitioners work for fees and medical fees are costly. They recognize that any fee hurts and is high from that standpoint, but they also recognize that the costs of training and the expenses of practice for a medical specialist are considerable and must be made up in his practice.

If there is a reasonable fee structure (Usually, the fees prevailing in a community represent a fee structure that has survived over time and can be regarded as reasonable.), and if the patient has, as most do, some awareness of the range of prevailing fees, both the practitioner and the patient can cope more effectively with a discussion of the costs than if the fee is arbitrary. (A complication that pervades fee discussions is inflation. The patient may have an idea of fees based on what a friend or relative paid for a procedure in the past. The patient is unlikely to take the effects of inflation into account when forming his initial pre-discussion expectation of what is an appropriate fee.)
b) Try to appraise, as accurately as possible, what one's practice has been with respect to fee negotiations with patients (To some extent that is possible anyway.), and ask oneself to what extent one's practices enable the patient to know clearly what the fee is for a contemplated procedure (and for likely complications). Enable the patient to ask questions about the fee as well as about the case, so that the patient can be informed and have his uncertainties resolved as far as is reasonable.
c) Try to recognize one's own emotional barriers to discussing fees. Usually, recognizing the barriers is enough to enable one to surmount them. If one can't, it might even be worth while to talk over

those emotional barriers with a psychiatrist for an hour or two for some assistance in surmounting them.

    d) It is a help to know that even with the best techniques some patients are going to be resentful or otherwise upset about fees. But if the negotiations are handled effectively, the likelihood of angry dissatisfaction is minimized.

2. Health professionals are like other citizens and get involved as plaintiffs in ordinary cases. For example, a building contractor does not complete a job properly; someone runs a red light and a collision, with injury resulting, occurs; a divorce is necessary, etc.

The most important approach to plaintiffhood in those cases is to consult an attorney for advice and to try to understand that advice as probingly as possible.

    a. In this kind of situation, the health professional is in a position relative to the attorney similar to the position of a layman relative to the health professional. The client (or patient) hopes to find a practitioner who is both competent and conscientious. But how can the layman evaluate such characteristics in a field about which he is ignorant?

        1) It is apparent that a layman cannot completely evaluate a professional.* But just as a jury of laymen evaluate experts who testify in court cases despite a fundamental ignorance of the field of the expert, some evaluation must take place, and if approached intelligently, such an evaluation can be very useful in decision-making.

The basic logic of such an evaluation is that of ob-

---

*Note that even fellow experts have a difficult time in evaluating their peers. The issue of assessment of professional competence is an unresolved one, despite the necessity for licensing or certifying groups to make such judgments every day. To this time there has not been developed an effective method for assessing professional effectiveness, even when observing a professional in an actual working environment. Different observers tend to make differing judgments of professional performance, particularly when the person observed is of middle caliber and not the very best nor the very worst. In the long run, experts evaluating other experts use the same methods laymen use.

serving samples of professionals' behavior in areas
which are familiar to the layman, and inferring from
those observations that characteristics such as intelligence, knowledge, conscientiousness, compassion,
etc. underlie the observed behaviors. It is further inferred that those underlying characteristics will be
reflected in the same manner in other situations
which cannot be observed or with which the observer is not familiar enough to make competent judgments.

If a layman observes a professional speak of phenomena within the layman's experience in a manner
consonant with the layman's experience, he is likely
to infer that the professional possesses knowledge
when he talks in a similar manner about other areas
not familiar to the layman. If the professional is in
error about subjects known to the layman, the latter
will make the obvious inference. If the professional
listens intently and sympathetically, the layman infers something; if the professional seems to approach the problem superficially or disinterestedly,
the layman infers something else. And so on.

To evaluate an attorney as a layman, one must,
therefore, observe him in as many situations as possible in the course of the contact with him. It is helpful to engage him in conversation about subjects
with which the layman is familiar in order to observe
his command of those subjects. One can observe
how the attorney conducts himself when he isn't familiar with a given subject. How quickly does he
grasp the essence of the problem presented to him?
Do his comments enlarge the client's conception of
the problem?

One can often form a reasonable appraisal of an attorney's competence and conscientiousness in a discussion of the case, and one can often decide
whether to go ahead with that attorney or to seek another one. Note that in dealing with an attorney, as
in dealing with many things in life, the more conversant one is with the subject matter involved, the

more capably one can manage one's own actions in one's own interests. There is no substitute for obtaining knowledge in the area of one's problem. Talking with people and reading are very helpful ways of augmenting one's knowledge about some area, but in the long run there is no substitute for cogitating about the problem to bring to bear on it the resources of one's own faculties, and for conceptualizing the problem in one's own terms. (Health professionals, for all their ignorance of the law, are sophisticated people, and when they bring their own resources effectively to bear on a problem, they can be extremely helpful to themselves. It takes self-discipline to do so, because of a tendency to avoid thinking about hard things.)

3. Just as it is prudent to do what one reasonably can to avoid having to be a plaintiff in one's capacity as a health professional, it is wise to prevent having to become a plaintiff in other capacities.
   a. Taking appropriate precautions as to whom one deals with is the most apparent consideration.
   b. In a contract or sales situation, ensuring in advance that there is a mutual understanding as to what will be done or purchased at what specific price, including how defects will be dealt with, is the obvious method. Yet, just as in the case of discussing professional fees, the subject is often avoided because of embarrassment, anxiety, or other discomfort. Just as one can learn to discuss objectively fees one charges others, so also can one learn to discuss in perspective fees that others charge oneself, either for services or for specific items.

II. **The health professional as a witness** (See Chapter 6, Evidence)

A. The role of the witness.
   1. Any individual, other than those disqualified by age, mental state, or other legally created disability, may serve as an ordinary witness at trial if he or she has

firsthand knowledge of the situation or transaction at issue.

2. Some individuals may serve as "expert" witnesses. The expert has the power to draw inferences from the facts when a jury would not be competent to do so.

3. Two elements must both be present in order to warrant the use of expert testimony.

   a. The subject of the inference to be drawn must be so distinctively related to some science, profession, business or occupation as to be beyond the ken of the average, or "nonexpert" layman.

   b. The witness must have sufficient skill, knowledge, or experience in the field, such that his opinion or inference will probably aid the trier of the case in his search for the truth.

B. Qualifying as an expert.

1. In order for a person to testify as an expert witness, the court must find that the individual is, in fact, qualified as such.

2. This decision is one left to the discretion of the trial judge, and appellate courts rarely disturb the court's decision on that issue.

3. The parties may jointly stipulate to the court that a witness is qualified to serve as an expert. If a stipulation is not entered, counsel will question the witness concerning his qualifications. Cross-examination is permitted. The decision to stipulate qualifications will often be a tactical decision made by counsel. (For example, counsel may be reluctant to stipulate that one of his witnesses holding impressive credentials is qualified, because counsel may wish to have the trier of fact hear those qualifications.)

C. Preparation of the expert witness.

The successful presentation of testimony by the witness depends, to a large degree, on the willingness of the witness and counsel to prepare for trial. There are a number of preparatory steps that the witness can take.

1. Provide counsel with a written list of qualifications, for example, education, years in practice, publications, and other pertinent material demonstrating familiarity with the subject of the lawsuit.

2. If the testimony involves a particular individual, for example, a patient, review and become familiar with the patient's medical records. Be aware of the frequency of times of visits with the patient.

3. Acquire at least a rudimentary understanding of the legal issues at stake in the lawsuit. This information can be obtained from counsel for whom the witness will be testifying.

4. Insist that counsel take the time to prepare and to discuss the questions that he intends to ask on direct examination. Counsel should also assist in anticipating and preparing for questions that are likely to be asked on cross-examination.

5. If about to testify for the first time as an expert witness, visit a trial in advance of the date of testimony and observe the examination and cross-examination of a number of witnesses.

6. Prior to testifying, explore with counsel the issue of what information is protected by privilege or confidentiality.

D. Direct examination.

1. A counsel who calls a witness presents his side of the lawsuit through the direct examination of the witness.

2. The goal of counsel and the expert witness on direct examination is to present the technical aspects of the case in layman's terms so that both judge and jury may understand.

3. In direct examination, counsel cannot "lead" his witness. That is, the witness must testify without the aid of suggestions from the lawyer conducting the examination. Because of this, pre-trial preparation is very important.

4. The expert witness must remember that the judge or jury is the ultimate decider of what is "fact" in a given case. Thus, in presenting testimony to the fact finder, the witness may enhance his effectiveness by carefully tending to his courtroom image. It is desirable, for example, to do the following:

   a. Arrive on time.
   b. Remember courtroom etiquette, especially in addressing the judge as "Your Honor."
   c. Dress conservatively and neatly.
   d. Maintain a generally serious demeanor, and not talk about the case in hallways, restrooms, or other public places. (Chewing gum is unseemly.)
   e. Avoid nervous mannerisms, such as pulling at a part of the face or wringing hands, when in the witness chair.

5. The manner in which the witness listens and responds to counsel's questions is also important. He should:

   a. Listen carefully to each question and be certain that the question is understood. If necessary, ask that the question be repeated.
   b. Directly and simply, in appropriate layman's language, answer only the question asked, then stop. He should not volunteer information.
   c. Address the jury (or if there is no jury, the judge) when responding, rather than the lawyer asking the question. Never forget that it is the jury or judge who weigh the testimony.
   d. Speak clearly, slowly, and sufficiently loudly so that he will be sure to be heard; he should not answer simply by head shaking "yes" or "no."
   e. He should not answer questions in an arrogant or a joking manner.
   f. He should not exaggerate nor misrepresent in his answers.
   g. He should be as assured as possible in his answers.
      1) Language such as "perhaps" or "possibly" presents problems.
         a) Mere speculation or possibility is usually not rele-

vant to a legal decision, which demands at the
least a preponderance of the evidence, that is, that
a proposition presented is more probably true
than not. Thus, in any situation involving less than
certainty in a health expert's testimony, the expert
must be prepared to give a reasonable appraisal of
how probable is the truth or falsity of the proposition. The usual standard sought is "to a medical
certainty," ambiguous as that is. At times, the best
one can say is that a proposition is true "to a reasonable medical probability.

   b) Qualifying words like "possibly" suggest uncertainty and lack of confidence.

 h. On the other hand, if the expert does not know the answer to a question, or can do no more than provide an
estimate, he should say so. (The expert is only human
and fact-finders appreciate an honest recognition of
that.)

 i. Avoid looking at counsel or judge in a manner that suggests seeking assistance from them.

 j. When an objection is made by counsel, stop until the
court or counsel indicates the witness may continue.

E. Cross-examination

 1. After direct examination, in which the witness has usually been questioned in a sympathetic manner, counsel
for the opposing party cross-examines the witness.

 2. During cross-examination, counsel will test the credibility of both the substance of the expert's testimony
and the expert as well.

 3. On cross-examination, counsel may ask "leading questions." Counsel will also attempt to frame questions in
a manner requiring a "yes" or "no" answer.

 4. Common methods of attempting to discredit the expert witness include:

 a. Challenging the thoroughness of an evaluation by asking whether the examiner was aware of certain facts
when performing the evaluation. Sometimes, certain

facts that may bear on the expert's opinion surface only during the trial itself. It is, of course, perfectly reasonable on cross-examination to ask if those facts change the expert's opinion, as indeed they might. Counsel calling the expert must apprise him of those facts, however, otherwise, a surprise for the expert may occur, with potentially disastrous consequences.

b. Challenging the witness by the use of treatises giving an opinion contrary to that given by the witness.

c. Challenging the witness by attempting to demonstrate that his viewpoint, as presented on direct examination, is either internally inconsistent or has changed over time.

d. Challenging the expert by attempting to show that he is not competent because of a lack of necessary training or experience. (Although this will not serve to disqualify the expert, it may reduce the probative value of the testimony in the fact finder's eyes). The cross-examiner may deliberately ask obscure questions from the witness's field expressly for that purpose.

e. Challenging the expert by attempting to show that he has a financial interest in the outcome of the case.

5. The expert who is undergoing cross-examination must remember that his demeanor and style of presentation are, if anything, more important on cross-examination than on direct examination. The witness should do as follows:

a. Above all remain calm, and answer opposing counsel's questions in a courteous manner. Nothing is worse than emotionalism on the witness stand. A cross-examiner who is able to provoke the expert to an emotional display has scored a major triumph.

b. Ask to have a question repeated if it is not understood.

c. Indicate when an answer of "yes" or "no" is insufficient and that an explanation is necessary by answering "yes, but . . . " or "no, but . . . " (Remember that counsel on cross-examination will attempt to restrict the witness to "yes" or "no" answers).

d. Refrain from asking the judge if he must answer a question when he does not wish to answer. If the question is improper, one's own counsel should object to it.

e. Remember, the trial is orchestrated by the attorneys. If the attorney who requests the expert's presence is at all competent, he will know better than the expert whether to object to a question or to allow it to be presented to the expert without challenge. It is, of course, worthwhile for the witness and the attorney to discuss in advance how to deal with such questions on cross-examination.

6. Counsel may also ask one or more "trick" questions in an effort to discredit the expert. Examples are:

a. "Have you talked to anybody about this case?" A response of "no" is easily disproved, because inevitably the witness has discussed the case with others, including counsel for whom he has testified. A response of "yes" may lead counsel to suggest that the witness was told what to say. The best response is to acknowledge that the case was discussed. If the cross-examiner persists, the witness can mention that he was advised only to tell the truth.

b. "Are you being paid to testify in this case?" This question implies that the expert's testimony is "for sale." An appropriate answer to this question would be, "No, I am not being paid to testify. I am being compensated for time I have spent on this case and for my expenses associated with it."

7. Because of cross-examination, health professionals often do not like to participate in medical-legal work. Small wonder. Preparing for testimony is more demanding than preparing for a final examination in school. (There are usually only two "grades," barely passing and zero!) One has to prepare completely; there are not definable limits on what questions might arise, and one faces not a semi-sympathetic objective examiner, but, rather, a diabolical, sadistic critic, whose main object is to discredit the witness's message. The truth, and careful preparation, are one's al-

lies, and comfort can be taken in the knowledge that unlike the school situation, one invariably knows more about the subject than the examiner. Most people, once they testify, come to appreciate the battle-of-wits aspects of the endeavor. The sense of intellectual challenge in evolving and defending an appropriate, accurate, and legally useful opinion can be very rewarding.

F. Re-direct examination.

1. After cross-examination is concluded, counsel who has called the witness originally will have the opportunity to conduct "re-direct" examination.

2. This gives counsel and the witness the opportunity to provide clarification on any points made by opposing counsel during cross-examination.

3. A further round of cross-examination may follow the re-direct examination.

III. Issues involved in being a defendant in a lawsuit.

A. It is important to recognize situations which might lead to a lawsuit.

1. In many cases, investigation, at the time it happens, of an incident which might lead to litigation will forestall serious and costly complication. A prime example is a situation in a hospital in which a patient is injured at the time equipment is being used.
It is important to keep the entire equipment system in place until it can be investigated. At times, equipment failure is the cause of injury. If so, what might at first appear to be professional negligence may result as a manufacturer's liability. It may not make much difference to the patient whether the professional or the manufacturer is liable, but it makes a great deal of difference to the individuals who might be sued.

2. Patient dissatisfaction is an important factor in initiating law suits. The result of treatment is generally less important in engendering dissatisfaction than is a pa-

tient's perception that health professionals did not treat him with due care and respect. Most of that kind of dissatisfaction is preventable if one does one's job conscientiously and with consideration.

3. In cases of doubt as to whether a situation has potential for becoming a suit, it is wise to discuss it with a colleague, or someone from one's insurance company, or if available and an institution is involved, with staff legal counsel.

B. Obtain an attorney. Since there are so many potential complexities in any lawsuit, it is extremely risky to defend against a legal attack without having an attorney as one's champion.

1. One must be absolutely complete in giving the attorney the facts of the case. If anything, one must deliberately try to exaggerate the weak points of one's own side of the dispute.

   a. There is a natural tendency for a litigant to emphasize those aspects of a situation favorable to himself and to turn a blind eye to his weak points. Even when one tries to compensate for that bias, one is still likely to look favorably on one's own viewpoint.

   b. It is critical for the attorney to know exactly and in advance what the weak spots of the case are. Otherwise, he may be surprised at a later stage of the case. The case might, therefore, be unnecessarily harmed.

2. It is wise to learn about the law that applies to one's case. Knowledge of the law often leads the mind in thinking about the case and is helpful in making associations which, otherwise, might not arise. The general rule is: The more one thinks about and understands the case, the better prepared one is.

3. Be prepared for the important fact that as a litigant, especially as a defendant, even if one wins, one loses. The involvement of time, monetary costs, and emotional anguish can be very heavy indeed, no matter what the outcome of the case.

C. Try to resolve the case by negotiation out of court. The plaintiff should recognize that a compromise decided upon by the parties is almost always better than running the risks and costs of a court trial.

1. The case may be settled at any time, even during trial.

2. It is desirable that negotiation lines of communication be kept open. Of course, the value of the case to plaintiff and defendant may change as a trial procedes. Flexibility in arriving at a negotiating position is of critical importance.

D. Prevention is probably even more important with respect to being a defendant than with respect to being a plaintiff.* (See Chapters 8, Malpractice, and 9, Coping with Malpractice.) To a certain extent, prevention involves one's lifestyle and self-discipline. "Honesty is the best policy," is an excellent rule of thumb for most occasions. Thinking through situations in which one contracts for work done and considering how to deal with problems that might occur is helpful and, of course, is appropriate before one commits oneself to a contract. If a problem arises, trying to deal with it rationally and dispassionately is usually better than dealing with the problem in anger.

E. A special concern in being a defendant in a malpractice case when one has malpractice liability insurance: The attorney is engaged, and paid, by the insurance compa-

---

*Editor's note. In many ways, the focus in this chapter has been on thinking through decisions and activities in advance of undertaking them. It has stressed negotiations and coming to agreements. The approach has been pragmatic, emphasizing doing things that might work, as opposed to saying that one should act in a way which is "right" according to some abstract ethical principle.

It is much more difficult to think through things than to act on the basis of some simple principle; in fact it can be downright fatiguing mentally. It is very taxing to be a reasonable person of ordinary prudence. The problem, however, is that there is no other way one can deal effectively with a complex world.

ny. (Insurers are usually very accommodating, however, in trying to engage an attorney desired by the insured.)

1. Defendants often worry that the attorney is going to place the interests of the insurance company above his own interests. The law is otherwise.
   a. In insurance litigation the attorney's client is the insured (that is, the defendant), not the insurance company. The attorney's loyalty must be to the client.
   b. The attorney may not disclose confidential communications from his client, not even to the insurance company.
   c. If the attorney should fail to honor those principles, he is, himself, subject to malpractice action.

2. Of course, there is a possibility of dissatisfaction with the attorney selected by the insurance company.
   If so, one can approach the problem similarly to the way one would approach that of dissatisfaction with any professional—or with almost anyone with whom one enters into a service relationship. Indeed, it is the reverse side of the situation in which a patient who is dissatisfied with his health care professional might deal with the problem.
   If there seems to be any hope of salvaging the situation, discuss the dissatisfaction with the attorney; the insurer may help to resolve the situation; one might even request a second opinion.
   If there seems no hope of salvaging a productive relationship, one might discuss the issue with the insurer, requesting a change of attorneys.

3. Because an insured is not ordinarily familiar with members of the bar who specialize in the different kinds of malpractice cases, it is wise, before working with an attorney selected by an insurance company, to request that the company, if possible, provide the names of three attorneys, so that one might make an informed initial choice after contact with them. It is also prudent, if one deals with a multi-attorney firm, to know specifically which of the firm's attorney's will be dealing with one's case.

References

McGinn, J.C. *Lawyers: A Client's Manual.* Prentice Hall, Englewood Cliffs, 1979

Brown, L.M. and Dauer, E.A. *Planning by Lawyers: Materials on a Non-adversarial Legal Process.* Foundation Press, Mineola, NY, 1978

Questions on Chapter 14,
On Being Personally Involved in a Lawsuit,
as a Plaintiff, Expert Witness, or Defendant

1. It is frequent for litigants to leave the court system disgusted with it. What is probably the most common reason for such disappointment?
2. Give 3 reasons why practitioners might be reluctant to discuss fees with patients.
3. What most important measure can a person take to avert the need to get involved in a lawsuit?
4. What is the basic principle involved in the process by which a person who is a layman in a given field evaluates a professional in that field?
5. a. What is an advantage to attorneys, litigants, and the court in stipulating that an individual is qualified as an expert? b. What might be a disadvantage?
6. If one testifies as an expert witness, what is the best way to ensure that one will not be surprised and embarrassed by cross-examination?
7. A patient goes into a cardiac arrest in the operating room and dies. It is suspected that some problem may have arisen because of the anesthetic. What special action might the anesthesiologist take before leaving the operating room?
8. What is probably the most important factor giving rise to the initiating of malpractice suits?
9. In discussing a case against oneself with one's attorney, for what natural tendency in a litigant should one try to compensate?
10. When a malpractice insurance company appoints an attorney to defend a practitioner sued for malpractice, the attorney's primary responsibility is to the defendant, not the insurance company. True or False?

CHAPTER 15

Medical and Professional Ethics

Nathan T. Sidley

Medical and Professional Ethics

Nathan T. Sidley

I. General considerations.

A. Medical ethics is a field in which medical situations are considered from the standpoint of choices and values. There is no sharp boundary between what is and what is not a medical situation; it is apparent that the word "medical" covers a broad range of activities, many of which present special areas for ethical consideration.

B. Approaching medical ethics involves considering the following different groups of individuals involved in medical situations and evaluating their special interests in those situations.

    1. Patients, are the most important group, for whom, ultimately, the entire medical system is created. Patients are people who perceive themselves, or those about whom they are concerned, as possessed by some undesirable physical or mental state. They usually seek help from a medical practitioner (or institution, etc.), expecting that some kind of operation (surgical, chemical, verbal, etc.) will be performed on them and that as a result, their undesirable state will be alleviated.

        a. The medical interest of a health care recipient is primarily that of receiving individualized attention from health care professionals in such a way that he is protected from harm to a reasonable degree in relation to the benefit that he expects from his interactions with health professionals. For a patient, it is important that medical interactions are carried out in his own benefit and are carried out knowledgeably and conscientiously by medical personnel. Harm and benefit are objective, although not precisely determinable. The concepts relate to a person's overall, long-term adaptation.

1) Determination of harm and benefit is also somewhat subjective, however, and different parties making the same determination may well disagree. In addition, when probability of benefit must be weighed against the risk of harm, the likelihood of disagreement regarding the balance is greater. (As much as anything, it is these kinds of considerations which are so subject to disagreement and give rise to the great burden of "informed consent" placed on health professionals and experimenters.)

2) Patients also generally wish their contacts with health care providers to be at the lowest cost to themselves. There is a conflict between quality of care and economic cost factors in essentially every health care interaction.

b. Patients' relatives and friends are a comparable interest group.

c. The general public is a comparable group of laymen who are involved in medical situations in relation to public health measures carried out in the community, although they are not patients. They are often unwitting, unwilling, or unhappy payers for various aspects of health care. Other nonpatients are involved when they are subjects of research studies.

2. Health professionals are people who individually and collectively must understand the problems that patients present and who must know how to deal with those problems. The degree of knowledge involved is such that any professional can master only a small part of it, thus, the many different health care fields. Practitioners of their art, teachers, and researchers are all health professionals.

Some of the important interests to health professionals are the following:

  a. The opportunity and professional freedom to practice one's art adequately and conscientiously.

  b. The opportunity for study to maintain skills in relation to professional developments.

  c. Adequate remuneration.

  d. "Good" patients. A good patient is a patient who:

   1) Above all, gets better.

   2) Cooperates with his treatment.

   3) Appreciates professionals' skills and efforts and understands their limitations. He does not demand the impossible, for example, to be cured when he is a hopeless case.

  e. The families of health professionals have interests related, in part, to those of the professionals.

  f. Sometimes, there are conflicts of interest among different health professionals. These usually relate to economic issues rather than fundamental health practice areas.

3. Payers for health care.

  a. Government.

   1) Also an employer and direct provider of health care.

   2) Also a health care regulator and licensor.

   3) Also a factor in people's health through public health and research activities.

   4) No government action can ignore political considerations. Therefore, insofar as government is in the medical arena, politics must also be there.

  b. Insurance carriers (including large health care employers).

4. Hospitals.

  a. Including hospital nontechnical employees.

  b. Including administrators and trustees.

  c. Economic factors, ethical values, and politics are interests.

5. Attorneys and law enforcement agencies. Their interests are secondary, but always lurking in the background.

6. Suppliers of medical equipment, supplies and drugs. These are parties with primarily economic interests.

7. Religions and other value-oriented social groups.
   a. Involved indirectly usually.
   b. Ethical, political, and, sometimes, economic interests.

C. Insofar as medical ethics involves choices among goals
   in medical situations, moral considerations that transcend the most primitive and simple-minded deontological precepts must take into account the interests of the
   different populations which might be involved. Every interest group makes, contributes to making, or attempts
   to influence the making of medical decisions. In making
   a medical decision, anyone who neglects to consider the
   interests of every involved person and group is likely to
   encounter undesired problems.

D. When is an issue a medical ethical issue? Technically,
   any medical action is. A health care action is not ordinarily viewed as an ethical issue, however, unless it is
   readily apparent that someone who will potentially react
   adversely has an interest in the particular action and its
   outcomes. The intensity of regard for an ethical issue
   depends on the strength of the interest groups involved
   and the importance of the issue to them.

E. With time and increasing experience, many ethical issues
   have transcended their rather amorphous status as ethical issues and have become institutionalized as defined
   legal issues. That tendency, which has diminished the
   flexibility and range of action of participants (although it
   protects them by giving more predictability to the outcomes of their actions) is only likely to increase further.

F. Given modern techniques of publicity and appeal, medical ethics issues of various kinds have become highly
   partisan, polarizing political issues. Intense political par-
   tisanship usually diminishes the potential for optimal solutions to the health problems involved. Although even
   the optimal solution of a problem is usually far from the
   ideal solution, a feasible political solution may be far
   from a potential optimal solution.

G. Individual versus group ethics.

1. Essentially, everyone wishes to regard himself as an ethical person—one who has good standing in the community and is morally equal to his neighbor. Virtually everyone deviates in some ways from what he regards as an appropriate ethical code, rationalizing his deviations as either beneficial, or at the least, harmless. In effect, he is creating higher-level general ethical principles which transcend ordinary principles.

2. Higher-level general principles alone, however, seem insufficient to guide groups of people. Abuses tend to occur, and specific principles of morality related to specific situations are a result.

   In many ways, almost everyone acts as if he is above some ordinary principles of morality, because the ordinary principles of morality are insufficient to cover certain situations. That is a limitation on any code, which must balance the evils of over-generality against those of over-specificity. The individual faces a similar problem of balancing general principles of conscience against specific rules, which are usually seen as appropriate but which seem inappropriate to a given situation. Expediency and temptation also enter into the individual's picture because of humans' emotional weaknesses. Such situations arise in medical activities just as they do in any other activities.

3. Both an individual conscience and a group code also face two kinds of ethical demands.
   a. How much of a person's own interest should one sacrifice for others?
   b. How much should one avoid doing harm to others in order to advance one's own interests? (In a competitive arena, advancing one's own interests tends to imply at least some decrease in the interests of others.)
   c. The issue as to how one should deal differently with the individuals in a different reference group from one's immediate group, be it at times family, profession, nation, etc. is also interesting. (For example, how much of a society's resources should be devoted to the treatment of prisoners of war?)

H. Time. A fundamental problem of acting ethically. When a decision is guided by a rule which can be directly and immediately applied, making the decision requires minimal expenditure of time. When a decision requires weighing of alternatives, time must be taken. If the facts of a case are ambiguous, if there is also ambiguity as to which ethical principles should govern in the decision, and above all, if there are reasonably high stakes involved in the decision (as is frequently the case in medical decisions), making the decision can take considerable time and can also be accompanied by a good deal of anxiety as well. If one faces many such decisions, significant professional time can be required merely to consider the ethics of medical decisions. The pressures of time costs and anxiety from unresolved issues combine to make the very process of decision-making an ethical issue. It requires effort and self-discipline to resist the temptation to make hasty decisions merely to resolve the problem situation.

I. Ethics and regulations.
  1. Because there are some professionals who do not always act ethically, control-oriented regulations to prevent or minimize abuse have been developed. The regulations are, of course, unnecessary for the conscientious and skilled practitioner, but they may have a useful effect on others. The red tape forced on those who don't need them, however, is a time and financial burden.
    a. The problem is that authorities are unable to discriminate practitioners who are conscientious and who don't need the regulations from those who act unethically and who do need them.
    b. Thus, the conscientious must pay a price for the sins of their deviant colleagues. That price is inevitable.
    c. Sometimes, the price is too high, when well-intentioned regulations turn out to be counterproductive in design or implementation. It is a difficult task for the profession to accept appropriately the inevitable regulations but actively resist regulations which are unrea-

sonable. (It is sometimes difficult to tell one kind from the other, however.)

II. Professional codes of ethics.

A. Frequency. Most health care associations, especially large ones (5,000 members or more), have codes of ethics. Smaller organizations are less likely to have codes; however, organizations in the health care field are more likely than organizations in other professions to have such codes. The numbers of associations which have adopted codes have been increasing in recent years.[1] Note that if an organization does not have an ethical code, it does not necessarily mean that the members are unethical. Many organizations have decided that such codes are unnecessary or inappropriate for themselves.

B. Purposes and functions. That so many associations have codes implies that they have a function for the organization. The actual function in relation to the group's existence may or may not correspond with the ostensible purposes for the code as the group sees them.

1. Educational. This enables group members (and possibly, the public) to know what are effective and appropriate ways of dealing with commonly encountered goal-conflict situations in their professional activities. It is not always obvious how a given higher-order ethical principle applies in a given situation, and a set of guidelines can help a person in such a situation. Knowing about the guidelines can help the public to know how a professional is likely to act and can facilitate the interchange.

2. To enhance the public image of the profession by emphasizing ethical behavior and discipline of those whose behavior deviates from ethical standards.

    a. To augment the ostensible dignity of the profession.

    b. To improve the image of the profession to its own members.

3. To specify the relationships among members of the association.

   a. To reduce competition (for example, by restricting advertising, competitive bidding, and efforts by one practitioner to attract patients and clients from other practitioners) and to preempt an area of practice for one's own group by defining qualifications regarded as appropriate for such practice,

   b. To encourage harmonious and orderly relationships among practitioners. (In practice, codes tend to favor older and more established practitioners.)

4. To promote competence by demanding that members maintain proficiency and expertise. Continuing education, certification programs, and recertification activities are examples.

5. To establish standards and procedures for discipline of members deemed unethical.

   a. A code often provides a forum to which offended individuals, whether fellow professionals or the public, can take complaints of unethical behavior. The presence of such a forum, especially if it has a reputation for objectivity and for taking complaints seriously, can be reassuring to people who interact with professionals and who feel helpless dealing with professional abuse or incompetence.

   b. Resulting public confidence in a profession is beneficial to the profession, unless the level of practice is so low as to lead to constant conflict. But in that extraordinary situation, the profession must clean house for its own sake.

   c. Maintaining standards of practice for members can help a profession avoid efforts by the state to do so. It is far better for professionals to have policing done by sympathetic and understanding fellow professionals than to have it done by unsophisticated laymen, who may tend not to be as sympathetic.

   d. In the aggregate, there is a mixture of self-interest and public interest in any code. Unquestionably, the association wants the highest and most ethical level of practice from its members. Realistically, however, there is a maximum of good practice and a minimum of bad practice which can be attained. How an association can favorably influence levels of practice is an interesting and important question for each group.

C. Contents of codes.

1. Rights and privileges of members.

2. Obligations to those to whom services are provided. Specific situations in which specific obligations are prescribed are often spelled out.

3. Obligations to fellow professionals.

4. Support procedures for members charged with unethical conduct or for those who are handicapped (especially by alcoholism or drug abuse) and who are vulnerable to such charges,

5. Disciplinary procedures against members.

D. Features of disciplinary and support procedures.

1. Grounds for discipline.
   a. Unprofessional conduct, a vague but useful charge that requires exercise of reasonable judgment. It could include anything from taking sexual or financial advantage of a patient to practicing beyond one's competence; it could even go so far as an allegation that a professional's actions give the appearance of impropriety.
   b. Conviction of a felonious or a moral crime.
   c. Fraudulent credentials on applications.
   d. Physical, mental, or emotional inability to practice.
   e. Bona fide malpractice.
   f. Promising cures for incurable disease.
   g. Financial offenses, e.g. fee splitting or gross overcharging.
   h. Maintaining "secret" or unscientific remedies.

2. Reasonable due process is required, although not necessarily as rigid as in a court.
   a. The defendant is entitled to know specifically what is alleged against him, preferably by written complaint.

    b. He must have the time and opportunity to prepare his defense. Almost invariably, that involves the opportunity to confront the individual who complains about him.

    c. He must be able to present his defense before impartial individuals.

    d. Reasonable sanctions should be imposed in the light of the offense.

3. There is often concern on the part of the disciplinary body of an organization that it exposes itself to a libel suit if it disciplines a member. If a reasonable investigation is carried out, however, there is very little likelihood of losing such a suit.

4. Possible sanctions that can be imposed by a group on a member.

    a. An informal admonition or a warning.

    b. A private letter of censure.

    c. Publicizing the offense and the offender to the membership.

    d. Imposing a monetary fine as a condition of retaining membership in the organization.

    e. Requiring further education or probationary supervision of practice.

    f. Limiting the individual's practice as to kind or geographical area. (That sanction would usually involve a licensing board.)

    g. Suspension from the organization for a definite time, or expulsion from the organization.

    h. Removal of a license (in the case of a licensing board).

    i. Whatever sanctions are available, a practitioner brought before an ethics committee is in a serious situation, and he will incur significant problems merely in defending himself. Any public acknowledgment of censure is, of course, an extremely serious matter in a person's career.

5. Support procedures available (depending on the organization).

    a. Counseling.

    b. Legal advice.

   c. In some cases, loans to help finance a defense.

   d. The organization may give moral support, including public acknowledgment of support of its member.

  6. It is apparent that discipline and support of members could impose significant burdens of many kinds on an organization. It is fortunate that complaints of violations of ethical codes are rare.

   a. One reason for the rarity is that a complainant to an organization can get nothing but satisfaction. If he has a chance of getting any money, he goes to a law court.

   b. Most organizations use only a small amount of their resources for disciplining procedures.

   c. Any disciplinary procedure is divisive in an organization. It is very difficult to discipline an associate: it often involves a struggle between the individual's defenders and his detractors, and the development of hard feelings is common. The subject is an unpleasant one, which many members of an organization may be reluctant to think about or discuss.

E. Like any ethical code, professional ethics codes change over time. Changes in social, professional, or economic organization, changes in technology, and changes in fashion lead to different principles. Most people have a tendency to think in terms of their immediate situations as if they were permanent conditions. People do well to recognize that history has created the present from a past which was different, and the future is bound to be different from the present. There is no immutable, professional ethics.

III. Some common medical situations with ethical implications.

A. General considerations.

1. Health professionals, by the very nature of their work, are exposed to the most intimate aspects of people's lives and bodies. The trust put in health professionals

by patients is unique, except, perhaps, for the trust between children and parents.

It is both interesting and impressive that people in
roles of health professionals are able to develop the
emotional control and objectivity to avoid exploiting
the relationship between themselves and patients. Of
course, the very existence of the professions depends
on that self-control, for if, in fact, patients exposed
themselves to a real risk of exploitation when they encountered health professionals, they would chose not
to be treated. It is probably only an indirect result of
training that leads professionals to act in such a re-
strained manner.

It can be argued that health training, which involves
practical experiences with patients, places young, usually idealistic, people in a continuing series of the most
highly emotion-provoking situations, involving death,
pain, and emotional and physical suffering, along with
the sounds and smells of disease, trauma, and abnor-
mality. Virtually no one can remain unmoved by those
situations. Yet, it is vitally necessary that the health
professional learn to be unmoved, for if he is emotionally affected by such cases, he will not be able to function objectively and effectively. Such emotional
distancing, in effect a shutting off of sympathy, cannot
be taught directly and abstractly in a classroom, but,
rather, must be evolved in the course of experience by
each person who undergoes such experiences. Each
individual must use various coping devices, almost all
of which involve a great deal of group support and a
perceived separation between the professional group
and the group of patients. That separation, however,
helps the practitioner and the profession to preserve
self-discipline and to avoid emotional involvements,
and, thus, to practice more effectively.

It is a sobering thought that a practitioner must give
up some of his humanity in order to practice in a hu-
manitarian and ethical manner.

2. One other general medical ethical issue which may become important is that patients and professionals may

have different values and therefore different and conflicting goals with respect to their interaction. Both patient and professional may know the same facts, but
each will want a different action. For example, both
may know that the patient is in pain and that using a
certain drug gives rise to a risk of developing dependence on the drug. To the patient, the immediate pain
relief is more important, while the doctor is more concerned about the risk of dependence.

The problem is most acute where the patient feels very
strongly that a given intervention should occur and the
professional feels just as strongly that it would be unethical for him to make that intervention. Examples
might be in relation to obtaining and administering a
cancer cure that the doctor regards as quackery, or the
performance of an abortion. The latter might be particularly difficult for some practitioners who would
feel that even to refer a patient who requests an abortion to a source from which she could obtain the procedure would be committing a moral wrong. (There is,
of course, the risk that if the practitioner from whom
an abortion is requested does not mention the existence of facilities where abortions are performed, he
may be liable for negligence.)

It is an unenviable and unfortunate situation when
there are such true irreconcilable conflicts between patient and professional. It is particularly difficult to
make general statements about resolving such differences.

Perhaps the best that can be said is that since the patient initiates contact with the health care system,
there is some point in allowing his values to determine
action, unless he wishes something which is illegal or
which the practitioner, upon reflection, regards as unethical or inappropriate. Patient satisfaction is of great
importance to the health professions.

B. Allowing the patient to die.
1. The problem. Usually, the function of health professionals' intervening in a case is the preservation of life.

In addition, the law places the highest sanctions on illegally taking the life of another. But there are many situations in health care in which preserving the patients' bodily existence seems counter to what is reasonable. A person's heart can be kept going for some time, but the resulting "life" bears no real relationship with ordinary human life. Allowing patients to die when it seems appropriate raises ethical concerns for the health professional involved as well as legal concerns that the professional may be subject to either criminal or tort liability. The fear of such legal liability has deterred many health professionals from acting according to the dictates of reason and their consciences.

This kind of situation is a classic example of the method of defining, qualifying, and delineating general principles so their application leads to what are regarded as "appropriate outcomes."

Because of concern that ordinary ethical decision-making was not comprehensive enough to protect patients and families from legal adversity, no matter how they made decisions in this area, various interested parties have brought such cases to court. As a result, certain approaches have evolved. The considerations in those approaches will be summarized below.

Note, however, only a few cases have been tried in a few jurisdictions. The results cannot be said to apply unequivocally in all jurisdictions. The holdings, however, in one jurisdiction have great weight in another jurisdiction, especially when there are no comparable precedents in the second jurisdiction.

In addition, many hospitals and medical societies have written guidelines for dealing with these cases. A practitioner who conforms with such guidelines can be considered to have conformed with standards of practice. It is also virtually certain that a person conforming to such standards would be immune from both civil and criminal liability.

2. Parties usually involved with and interested in such decisions.

a. Physicians, nurses, and other hospital personnel.
b. The patient.
c. The patient's family or guardian.
d. Society and the court system.
e. Persons with a general ethical or religious interest in other human beings.

3. The basic fact leading to consideration of such decisions is that the patient is in a terminal condition. Examples include:
a. "Brain death."
   1) A flat EEG reading, under certain conditions, enables a person to be declared dead.
b. "Irreversible coma."
c. Other cases of imminent death have not been considered as thoroughly.

4. Patient parameters.
a. Is the patient mentally competent to make a critical, life-death decision?
b. Has he declared his desires on the issue of artificial prolongation of bodily existence? If so, how and when?

5. Family/guardian consideration. Do they approve or disapprove of artificial prolongation of bodily existence?

6. Procedural issues.
a. Who must issue orders.
b. Should concurrence by a consulting physician and the hospital ethics committee be required.
c. What kind of orders must be issued?
d. Must they be in writing?
e. Must they be justified in writing?
f. Can they be rescinded?
g. Should a court be consulted prior to writing an order?

7. Kinds of orders.
a. Do not resuscitate in the event of cardiac arrest or similar emergency. Or similarly, "No heroic measures."
b. Disconnect equipment which is artificially prolonging existence.
c. Health professionals usually find it easier to deal with a "do not resuscitate" situation than with a "disconnect" circumstance.

8. General conclusions (adapted from New York, Massachusetts, and California decisions and statutes).
   a. If a patient is competent, he may state that he does not wish heroic measures to be taken. It is expected that a medical facility would honor that wish, on the basis that a competent individual has a right to refuse medical treatment. It is important, however, that such a wish be discussed thoroughly with every patient who is not imminently a terminal case. Frequently, patients and family members, under the influence of depression, fear, or other passions, too hastily express a wish to die when there is a reasonable expectation that they would have a meaningful future. Health professionals should emphatically insure that patients and families are aware of that likelihood before expressing such a wish.
   b. If a patient is incompetent.
      1) The first issue to be determined is whether the patient is terminal and about to die soon.
      2) Generally, if the patient is terminal, a "do not resuscitate" order is appropriate, if the family or guardian and the physician agree, and if the order is written according to hospital policy. The decision is regarded as a medical one and does not require prior court approval.
      The situation is similar for terminating ongoing procedures which merely prolong bodily existence.
      3) If the patient is not immediately terminal, and if he is not irreversibly comatose, court rulings made so far suggest that treatment cannot be interrupted or withheld without a family's or a guardian's first applying to a court. Thus, in that situation, a decision to withhold treatment is regarded as a judicial decision with medical input.
      Some courts have rationalized such decisions on the basis of a "substituted judgment" doctrine, that is, what the patient can be inferred to have desired in such a situation. Applied to a feeble-minded or incompetent person, the doctrine may force much inference.
9. In general, dealing with the situation of allowing such patients to die has gone relatively smoothly. The lack

of major religious opposition has probably been an important enabling factor. The written Papal Opinion, "The Prolongation of Life,"² has been instrumental in the process.

10. A more difficult situation is that of patients with incurable disease who wish to commit suicide to end their suffering. Successful suicide is not a crime any more, but abetting a suicide is. Physicians are reluctant to get involved.

   There are organizations of patients, their families, and interested people whose goal is the furtherance and the legitimization of such rational suicide. Many health professionals belong to such groups. The Hemlock organization is the major such group in the United States.

11. Another alternative for terminal cases is the hospice movement. Such patients may go to special residential facilties for their terminal care, or may receive home visit care from specially trained nurses.

   (It has been pointed out that physicians have tended to underutilize pain control in such individuals, perhaps partly because there is a certain danger, occasionally even a mortal danger, involved in using pain relieving medication in doses high enough to be effective, and partly because of analogizing them too much with other cases in which the development of addiction might become a serious problem. For a patient who is about to die, of course, the significance of the risk of death from a dose of medication sufficient to relieve pain is fundamentally different from the importance of that risk to someone who is expected to recover. The situation is similar to that of allowing a terminal patient to end his suffering, with the difference that the patient only runs a risk of dying as opposed to a certain death.

   As in any other risky situation in medicine, this one involves the issue of informed consent. If the patient is informed of the alternatives, he can, if competent, make his own decision. If incompetent, his guardian can make the decision.

In any event, in a terminal case, addiction is a trivial problem compared with alleviation of pain.)

C. Truth-telling to patients.
1. This is primarily a patient-raised issue. Throughout the ages, doctors and other professionals have notoriously misrepresented the true seriousness of patients' diagnoses or clinical conditions. The most important reasons for this phenomenon follow.
   a. Patients often do better with an optimistic attitude and more poorly with a pessimistic attitude. Good news cheers up the sick person.
   b. The "messenger effect." Someone hearing bad news, by a psychological process of displacement, often blames or becomes angry at the person who conveys the information. In addition, hearing bad news gives people pain. Most people try to avoid inflicting such pain on others, for the teller of the news feels bad because of sympathy with the feelings of those who receive the information. It is especially depressing to have to give bad news frequently, such as on a children's cancer ward.
   c. Bad news to a person is that he is in a hopeless situation, that is, everything that can reasonably be expected to yield the desired result has been tried and will not work. (The existence of cancer, as such, is not too disturbing if the cancer is easily removed. It is, undoubtedly, not the word, "cancer," which frightens people, but the situation that they may have an incurable cancer.)
   d. Telling a patient that he is hopeless is acknowledgment of failure on the part of the medical system and its personnel, and as such, makes the teller feel bad.

2. The issue is related to informed consent. The difference is that if there are decisions to be made on the basis of the bad news, they are not specifically medical decisions but, rather, general life decisions. For example, if a person is in danger of dying soon, he usually has many arrangements to make regarding family and

property. In such situations, physicians who have avoided informing the patient of the bad news have tended to inform the family and to suggest indirectly to the patient that it is sensible for him, as a generally prudent person, to have an up-to-date will, etc. It is difficult to avoid completely the issue of the inevitability of mortality.

3. From the patient's point of view, he doesn't want to be hoodwinked by anyone, even if it is in his own best interest.

4. What little research has been done on the subject suggests that patients, including child patients, usually fare better if they are told bad news.

   a. It seems reasonable to assume that if the information is conveyed in a gentle, sympathetic, and supportive manner, it will be easier for the patient to cope with than if it is blurted out in an offhand or callous manner.

      1) The latter probably occurs most often when physicians are inexperienced or are anxious about the task. They wish to do their disliked duty and leave the scene as soon as possible.

      2) With experience and training, however, it is possible to accomplish the task in a manner helpful to the patient.

   b. It should also be remembered that seldom is a situation completely hopeless. Even if death is a certainty, pain can be relieved and a patient and his family can be helped to face death with dignity. A realistic and appropriately positive approach, emphasizing what can be salvaged in an admittedly bad situation, tends to be helpful to all participants in the gloomy case where a person is certain to die soon.

5. Research has shown that many physicians have fixed ideas on the subject and that they, themselves, declare they would refuse to change their policy about telling patients the truth about bad news even if it were to be demonstrated that a change were in the interest of rational and conscientious medical practice.[3]

D. Research with human beings

1. The experiments of the Nazi doctors led to the formulation of the Nuremberg Code. Subsequent publicity of medical research, in the United States and elsewhere, in which researchers showed a lack of concern for the welfare of research subjects, has led to increased emphasis in the United States on monitoring research so that the rights and interests of research subjects would be honored and protected. Among abuses discovered in the United States have been the recruitment of research subjects by coercion or fraud, the submitting of persons to dangerous conditions, and the failure to prevent or treat harmful conditions occuring as a result of research.

2. The following principles to protect the rights and interests of subjects have received general endorsement:

   a. Subjects should not be recruited from places like prisons or mental institutions, in which coercion to participate is likely to occur. (It was not uncommon for researchers to pay premiums to guards and other prison staff for obtaining prisoners who participated in research. Such a system is an invitation to abuse, and the invitation tended to be accepted readily.)
   Minors or incompetent persons should not be used as subjects unless the information sought could not be obtained by using competent adults. Parents or guardians must provide fully informed consent.

   b. Fully informed consent of the risks incumbent on participation in the study should be obtained before any procedures are performed on a subject. It is obviously inappropriate to tell anyone that "it's perfectly safe."

   c. The research should be conducted with humans only when the information is important (a vague term, to be sure) and when the information cannot be obtained by other means.

   d. The research should be planned in advance with a written protocol which includes a statement of the objectives and of the methods of study and analysis. (That is a fundamental requirement of research, anyway.)

    e. The research must be conducted so as to expose subjects to the minimum risk compatible with the objectives of the study. It must be conducted only by appropriately qualified persons.

    f. The subject must be free to terminate his participation in the study at any time without prior notice.

    g. If it becomes apparent during the course of the research that a subject may be injured or otherwise affected adversely, that aspect of the research project should be terminated forthwith.

3. A controversial issue is whether research subjects who are injured in the course of research should be indemnified by the researcher.

    a. A researcher who disregards the welfare of his subjects is likely to be found liable for a tort of negligence if the subjects are harmed.

    b. Assumption of risk is the likely defense that an experimenter would use against such a suit.

4. Unquestionably, the flexibility of a researcher is diminished if he has to consider the welfare of his subjects. In addition, when research has to go through institutional review processes, such as a hospital ethics committee, it takes away time and effort that could go to the research proper. Frequently, researchers believe ethical requirements represent an unwarranted imposition on them.

    a. The principle behind imposing such requirements is the same as that behind imposing requirements on any practitioner. There is no reliable way of telling which practitioners or researchers will practice ethically. Controls must be placed on all.

    b. To date, the increased ethical concerns and requirements have not diminished the output of medical research in a fundamental way.

E. Abortion.

1. The topic has become an important political issue. Many people have strong feelings on abortion, and ef-

forts to mobilize support for a given political position, often with many aspects unrelated to abortion, have been remarkably successful. Religion has been involved in the abortion question more than in most medical questions. The Roman Catholic Church has been a traditional opponent of abortion, and many conservative religious groups hold similar positions.

2. Abortion relates to population policy. For that purpose, however, it is a tactic which is considered only when ordinary forms of contraception have failed.
   a. The expenses and risks associated with abortion are far greater than with contraception.
   b. Many countries have, at times, undertaken efforts to allow relatively free access to abortion. Typically, such access goes on for a few years, then policy becomes more restrictive.

3. Impetus for a policy of legal abortion is the frequency of illegal abortion. Many pregnant females decide to terminate their pregnancies by self-initiated methods or by resorting to illicit practitioners. The incidence of disability and death following such clandestine procedures is much greater than when they are undertaken under controlled medical conditions.

4. Ethical considerations in abortion.
   a. It is seen by some as the taking of a potential person's life, without fault on the part of the fetus. In other situations in which life is legally taken, justification is in terms of the danger presented by the individual or in terms of his past criminal behavior. No justification of this kind is seen for abortion.
   b. Others regard the fetus as not being a person in any real sense and, thus, claim abortion is appropriately defined as a medical procedure and not a homicide.
      1) Abortion is seen as a medical decision between the pregnant female and her physician. The Supreme Court viewed the matter as an issue of the right of privacy.[4]
      2) As a uniquely women's problem, abortion has been focused on by feminist political interest groups as an

area in which women's lack of political and economic power has caused them poor treatment by men.

3) The problem of power is compounded by the fact that merely acknowledging that she has a pregnancy she wishes terminated places a woman in a disadvantaged position. Unlike the case for many interest groups, publicity is a handicap rather than an asset.

c. Some believe that the loss associated with aborting a pregnancy is less than would occur if the pregnancy were to go to term and impose hardship (for example, with a defective child, or with a mother who is too young, sick, or otherwise too burdened to care properly for the child and otherwise maintain her own life). It has been pointed out that if parents do not care for a child, the child becomes a burden on society in many ways, including financial. Society has not always wanted to assume such burdens.

d. Distinctions are usually made between early abortions, such as in the first trimester of pregnancy, and later ones, when there is greater risk associated with the procedure and when the fetus begins to look more and more like a baby. There is much more reluctance on people's parts to do a late, as opposed to an early, abortion. The principles may be similar, but the emotional attitudes tend to be different.

e. An unwanted pregnancy, or one which would lead to family hardship, is a situation with no good resolution. Those in such positions, or society generally in dealing with the problem, have to choose from approaches which all have strong, undesirable characteristics. Virtually no pregnant females are happy about undergoing abortion. They usually choose to submit to the procedure, feeling that they have no alternative.

5. Overview

a. Society recognizes the bad aspects of either sanctioning abortion or of forcing females to seek illegal abortions or suffer the consequences of carrying the fetuses to term. Each alternative engenders strong emotions and motivates people to hope for something different and better.

b. It is expected that social policies will oscillate, perhaps outlawing abortion for a time, living unhappily with the consequences, then legalizing abortion for a time, living unhappily with the consequences, then again outlawing it, in a chronic policy circle. There are no completely rational solutions, but even if there were, the very nature of the problem predisposes to recurring motivation to do things differently. The motivations evoked are often strong. A concise summary, in fact, of the feelings of polarization that have been aroused on the issue, is that of Daniel Callahan: "The debate releases the most unfettered emotional appeals and outbursts, as if moral passion on the subject would be compromised by recourse to rational argument."

F. Access to medical care: who receives care and who is excluded.

1. This is an area of the general ethical problem of access to resources. It is a major problem of economics, involving not only who receives what medical care, but also how much of society's resources ought to be invested in medicine. A further implication is how to deal with social conditions which give rise to a demand for medical care which would not be necessary if proper preventive measures were taken. If people in general had different habits with respect to use of substances like alcohol, tobacco, foods, or automobiles, there would be much less need for medical care. If such a state of affairs could occur, however, it would be in a society much different from the one with which we are familiar.

2. Individual economics, supplemented by charity, had been the most important determinant of access to medical care through the early part of the century.

3. Health insurance, disseminated on a mass scale, greatly increased access to care and expanded the health care system. Government policy through tax considerations was an important factor in the expansion of health insurance coverage. The passage of Medicare

legislation, another government policy, in one stroke tremendously increased health insurance coverage in a high medical needs group which was underserved with respect to those needs.

4. Government programs also aided people directly in receiving medical treatment.
    a. Hospitals and clinics were built directly or indirectly financed by tax revenues.
    b. Health agencies were staffed through use of government funds.
    c. Medical services and drugs were furnished directly through government agencies such as city and state hospitals, the Veterans Administration, or armed services programs for servicemen and their dependents. Medicaid, too, could be regarded as a direct provision of medical care, but it is more like insurance than a direct provision.

5. Government contributed to medical care by sponsoring research, both directly and indirectly, through service and research grants.

6. Most of the health care system expansion and utilization of the system have occurred since World War II, when the American economy was correspondingly expanding. Recently, however, the potential costs of widespread assurance of care have been better appreciated. (It has almost appeared that demand for medical care has increased, the more medical care demands have been filled.)

7. The ethical question for social policy is to determine to what extent government should, itself, provide or strive to induce others to provide medical care to those who would not have access, if inability to pay prevented a person from receiving care.

8. Such social policy questions resolve into political and economic interest questions and require much balancing. Because these questions, involving what is the equivalent of some involuntary income redistribution, are heavily emotion-laden, and because a rational approach to such problems is the exception rather than

the rule, people deciding such questions tend quickly to reach a general conclusion as to what should be done. Discussion of issues does not rise above an advocacy level, and does not serve as well as might an integrative forum to improve policy.

But in many ways that is the nature of political discussion, which is different from a negotiation between disciplined parties with relatively well-defined interests and purposes.

Text References

1. Chalk, R., Frankel, M.S., and Chapter, S.B. *Professional Ethics Activities in the Scientific and Engineering Societies.* Am. Assoc. Adv. Sci., Washington, D.C., 1980

2. Pope Pius XII. The Prolongation of Life. *The Pope Speaks* 4; 393–398, 1958, cited in Reiser, *op. cit.* infra

3. Oken, D. What to tell cancer patients: A study of medical attitudes *JAMA* 195; 1120–1128, 1961. Reprinted in Reiser, *op. cit.* infra (See also Novak, D.H., Plumer, R., Smith, R.L., Ochitill, H., Morrow, G.R., and Bennett, J.M. Changes in physicians' atittudes toward telling the cancer patient. *JAMA* 241; 897-900, 1979)

4. *Roe v. Wade,* 410 U.S. 116

General References

Reiser, S.J., Dyck, A.J., and Curran, W.J. *Ethics in Medicine,* M.I.T. Press, Cambridge, 1977

Barber, B. (Ed.). *Medical Ethics & Social Change. Annals Amer. Acad. Polit. & Soc. Sci.,* vol. 437, May, 1978

Curran, W.J. Court involvement in right-to-die cases: Judicial inquiry in New York. *NEJM* 305; 75–79, 1981

Humphrey, D. *Let Me Die Before I Wake.* Hemlock, Los Angeles, 1981

Jackson, D.L. and Youngner, S. Patient autonomy and "death with dignity": Some clinical caveats. *NEJM* 301; 404–408, 1979

President's Commission for the Study of Ethical Problems in Medicine and Biomedical and Behavioral Research. *Deciding to Forego Life Sustaining Treatment.* Government Printing Office, Washington, 1983 (One of a recent series of relevant works published by the Commission)

Shannon, T.A., Ed. *Bioethics.* Paulist Press, New York, 1976

Veatch, R.M. *Case Studies in Medical Ethics.* Harvard Univ. Press, Cambridge, 1977

Cases of Interest

In the Matter of Shirley Dinnerstein, 6 Mass.App. 466, 380 N.E.2d 134

Superintendent of Belchertown State School v. Saikewicz, 373 Mass.Rep. 728

In the Matter of John Storar: Companion case to Eichner v. Dillon, 438 N.Y.2d 363; 420 N.E.2d 64

In the Matter of Karen Quinlan, 70 N.J. 10, 355 A.2d 647

Questions on Chapter 15,
Medical and Professional Ethics

1. Give four important interests of health professionals.
2. Give six important government roles in health care.
3. What is the ethical issue involved in the very process of making ethical decisions?
4. What are the usual elements of due process in a professional disciplinary hearing?
5. a. Give examples of sanctions a professional organization can impose against a member. b. Give examples of support procedures an organization can provide to a member under fire.
6. What seem to be general rules regarding DNR (do not resuscitate) orders: a. For competent patients? b. For incompetent patients?
7. What important aspect of medical care is often insufficiently fulfilled with the terminally ill?
8. What is meant by the "messenger effect?"
9. Define in contract and tort terms how a researcher may not be liable if a research subject suffers harm in the course of participation in a study.
10. What are the four major factors that make abortion an important issue?

CHAPTER 16
Finding the Law: Legal Research and Citation
Thomas E. Shea

Finding the Law: Legal Research and Citation

Thomas E. Shea

I. Introduction.

Researching a particular point amid the expanse of the law is a task which is generally not beyond the ability of a competent layman. The purpose of this chapter is to serve as a guide to researching the law. It is intended as a selected guide, incorporating what seem to be the most useful research aids, rather than an attempt to be an exhaustive list of all available sources.

A. Two important distinctions in law.
  1. The difference between Federal and state law. A particular legal issue may be within the purview of either Federal or state law, or there may be concurrent jurisdiction. Where there is a conflict between such laws, the Federal law will prevail, providing that it is constitutional.
  2. The distinction among statutory law, regulatory law and case law. Statutory law consists of the laws passed by a legislative body, such as Congress or a state legislature, and signed into law. Regulatory laws are promulgated by various governmental agencies pursuant to statutory authority. Case law is composed of judicial decisions, which either may either interpret the Constitution, statutes, or regulations, or may create and apply judge-made law.

B. Research Sources.

1. Law school libraries. Official policies vary from one law school to another with regard to use of the library by non-students, but many will give permission for such research.

2. State, county, and city law libraries. Although intended primarily for judges and lawyers, these law libraries are generally available to the public. Their collections will probably be less extensive than a good law school. One significant disadvantage is an absence of more than a few law reviews and journals. An advantage is ease of access. Most will be quite willing to provide basic assistance in assisting a non-lawyer to locate the right set of references. Call your local bar association for the location of these libraries.

3. Private law libraries. These vary from fairly complete to inadequate. Large law firms and office buildings catering to attorneys often have good libraries, but it may be difficult to obtain permission for their use.

4. College, university, and public libraries. Some of these libraries have surprisingly good legal collections. As the public's interest in the law has increased, so have these collections. Often, these libraries will include all the references necessary for a research effort.

II. Federal law.

A. Federal statutory law.

1. Slip laws. The public laws of the United States which have been enacted by Congress and signed by the president are first printed in unbound pamphlets known as "slip laws." A slip law contains the exact text of the law. A slip law also has marginal notes and references to the legislative history.

2. *Statutes at Large.* This is the official source of Federal statutory law. It includes all public and private laws as well as resolutions, reorganization plans, proposed

and ratified amendments to the Constitution, and proclamations by the President. Part I of the *Statutes at Large* contains public laws and resolutions, and Part II includes all other material. The *Statutes at Large* are "positive law", meaning that they serve as legal evidence of the law. Marginal notes provide information concerning the legislative history of the statute. Each volume of the *Statutes at Large* contains an index, and numerical and chronological lists of the laws therein.

3. *The United States Code (U.S.C.)* (1976 edition). This is a series of ten volumes of statutes arranged by topic into sections called titles. Each title covers a general area of Federal law. Congress has enacted eighteen titles of the *Code* into positive law, and they are therefore legal evidence of the law. The other titles are prima facie evidence of the law, the positive law being contained in the *Statutes at Large*. The *U.S.C.* contains a comprehensive four-volume index which serves as the best method for locating a Federal statute.

The citation form for the *United States Code* is: (33 U.S.C. § 401) (that is, volume 33, section 401).

4. *The United States Code Annotated (U.S.C.A.)*. This series of approximately 200 volumes contains the Federal statutes arranged in the same manner as the *United States Code*. In addition, each section of the *U.S.C.A.* contains comprehensive annotations of Federal and state court cases which have applied that law. These annotations provide an excellent means of researching the manner in which the laws have been interpreted. The citation form for the *United States Code Annotated* is: (31 U.S.C.A. § 401).

B. Federal case law.

1. The Federal District Courts. Each state has at least one Federal District Court. These courts are responsible for trying Federal cases and serve as the courts of general jurisdiction for the United States. Significant decisions from all of the district courts are collectively published in the *Federal Supplement*. Unless the trial

judge's decision is appealed, it is final. The *Federal Supplement* consists of a series of volumes of Federal District Court decisions, some of which are final and some of which have been reversed or modified on appeal. Preceding the text of each decision is a series of headnotes, which summarize the decision. Although these are not an official part of the decision, they are useful for locating particular sections of the case.

The citation form for the *Federal Supplement* is: (116 F.Supp. 870) (that is, Volume 116, page 870).

2. The Circuit Courts of Appeal. There are 11 of these courts, whose function it is to hear appeals from the District Courts, based upon a regional division of jurisdiction. These appellate courts base their decisions on the transcripts of the trials as well as written briefs and oral arguments by counsel. All of their decisions are published in the *Federal Reporter* and the more recent *Federal Reporter 2d*. As in the *Federal Supplement*, each case is preceded by a series of headnotes. Circuit Court cases are of greater precedential value than District Court cases because of the principle of stare decisis, whereby lower courts are obligated to follow the precedents of higher courts. On occasion, the Circuit Courts differ in their interpretation of a legal question since they are not obligated to follow each other's precedents. When such a split in the circuits exists, a District Court is obligated to follow the lead of its particular Circuit Court.

The citation form for the *Federal Reporter 2d* is: (330 F.2d 73).

3. The Court of Claims. This court, located in Washington, D.C., was created by Congress as a court of limited jurisdiction to consider monetary claims filed against the Federal government. It serves as both a trial and appellate court in different situations. In its former capacity, the Court of Claims trial judges hear cases that have been filed against the United States government. The trial judge's opinion is tentative only and must be adopted by the Court before it becomes

official. A party dissatisfied with the decision may appeal this official decision to the Court in its appellate capacity. The decisions of the Court of Claims are reported in the *Court of Claims Reports* and the *Federal Reporter 2d.*

The citation form for the *Court of Claims Reports* is: (207 Ct.Cl. 349) and the parallel citation to the *Federal Reporter 2d* is: (518 F.2d 594).

4. The Supreme Court. The decisions of the Court (capitalized) are officially reported in the *United States Reports.* Unofficially, the cases are published in the *Supreme Court Reporter* and *United States Supreme Court Reports.*

Official citation is to the *United States Reports:* (254 U.S. 611). The parallel citation to the *Supreme Court Reporter* is: (41 S.Ct. 61) and the parallel citation to the *United States Supreme Court Reports* is: (65 L.Ed. 437).

C. Federal administrative and regulatory law. Because Congress and the President cannot attend to the myriad of details involved in running the government, they have delegated authority to various agencies to make regulations and decide cases in specialized areas. The rules promulgated by the agencies are far greater in number than the laws passed by Congress and the cases far more numerous than those decided by the courts.

1. *The Code of Federal Regulations (C.F.R.).* The main source for the rules and regulations of Federal agencies is the *C.F.R.,* which is divided into titles according to topic. There is a separate index, as well as an index for each volume. Contents of the *C.F.R.* are prima facie evidence of the regulations or rules involved.
The citation form is: (22 C.F.R. § 210.8).

2. *The Federal Register.* This daily publication includes newly proposed and promulgated rules and regulations of Federal agencies as well as Presidential proclamations and executive orders. A cumulative guide is published monthly. The primary purpose of the *Federal Register* is to serve as notice concerning proposed

and newly promulgated regulations. It can also be used to check on any changes in the *C.F.R.*
The citation form for the *Federal Register* is: (22 Fed.Reg. 9641 (1957)).

III. State law.

A. State statutory law.

The basic statutory schemes of the individual states are similar to that of the Federal government. Most states have codified their laws into a series of volumes which are updated by pocket parts (revisions which are inserted in a pocket at the back of each volume). Virtually all of these codes include indexes, but the quality of the indexing is not uniform. Persistence and imagination are necessary to insure a thorough search for the state laws on a particular subject.

The correct citation form for a state statute is usually similar to that for the *U.S.C.* An example of the correct citation form is often found on one of the first few pages of each volume.

B. State case law.

The structures of state judicial systems are varied. There are usually at least two types of trial courts with different monetary jurisdictional limitations. Every state also has an appellate system. The appellate systems of some states are generally similar to that of the Federal courts with an intermediate appeals court and a supreme court, handling both civil and criminal appeals, though other states have separate intermediate appellate courts for civil and for criminal cases. The structure of the court system of a state is determined by its constitution and statutes.

Approximately two-thirds of the states publish official reporters of the decisions of their appellate courts. Additionally, state court cases are published in the *National Reporter* system (West Publishing Co.). Each series in the system reports the decisions of the highest court in the state as well as some lower appellate court decisions for a group of geographically related states. The *National Reporter* system includes the following: *Atlantic, North Eastern, North Western, Pacific, South Eastern, South Western,* and *Southern, Reporters.*

C. State administrative and regulatory law.

This is a quagmire. Although some states publish complications of agency regulations similar to the *C.F.R.,* most do not. The best way to locate a rule or administrative case decision is to obtain it from the agency itself. Most agencies will honor requests for such information. The basic structures and responsibilities of the agencies are governed by statute.

IV. Research aids and specialized sources:

A. *Corpus Juris Secundum (C.J.S.):*

This set of 101 volumes plus index is a legal encyclopedia, published by West Publishing Co., which is updated with pocket parts. The various titles which comprise *C.J.S.* are preceded by a comprehensive outline. *C.J.S.* provides a good general summary of the law and is well annotated with references to Federal and state law. It is important to note that the basic text of *C.J.S.,* as is true with other such sources, primarily relates to the most generally accepted viewpoint. In order to research the law of a particular state, it is necessary to refer to the annotations for citations to state decisions.

The citation form for *Corpus Juris Secundum* is: (20 C.J.S. *Corporations* § 1898).

B. *American Jurisprudence 2d (Am.Jur.2d)*

American Jurisprudence 2d is a multi-volume legal encyclopedia published by the Lawyers Cooperative Publishing Co. Like *C.J.S.,* it has a separate index as well as an outline preceding each general topic, and it is kept current with pocket parts. It tends to be less formal than *C.J.S.*, and its writing style is more fluid. It is annotated with references to Federal and state court decisions, as well as references to *American Law Reports.*

The citation form for *American Jurisprudence 2d* is: (16 Am. Jur.2d, *Conflict of Laws* § 35).

C. *American Law Reports (A.L.R.).*

There are three editions of this work, of which the second and third are of current importance. These reports are essentially a collection of legal expositions on a wide range of legal topics. The treatment of a specific topic is more in depth than *C.J.S.* or *Am.Jur.2d.* A one-volume index covers the second and third editions, which are complementary rather than duplicative. *A.L.R.* is intended for detailed legal research on a particular subject rather than for general coverage of broad topics, as is the case with the previously mentioned legal encyclopedias.

The citation form for *American Law Reports 2d* is: (42 A.L.R.2d 148).

D. Law reviews and journals.

Law reviews and journals are unique among professional publications because most of them are edited and published by associations of law students. The reviews contain articles authored by law professors or practicing attorneys, as well as notes and comments written by law students. The articles and the notes and comments tend to focus on narrow topics and recent developments in the law, although some articles are devoted to summarizing the state of the law. Law reviews and journals also provide a forum for the exposition of new ideas and concepts. The most comprehensive coverage of a specific legal issue is likely to be found in a law review article. *The Index to Legal Periodicals* provides subject and author indexes for locating an article. Permanent volumes of the index are published yearly, with quarterly supplements for the current year. Perhaps the main disadvantage of law reviews is their limited availability. Because of the expense involved, law school libraries are usually the only sources which have substantial collections.

E. Treatises.

For research in fundamental areas of the law, treatises can prove invaluable. Legal treatises are published on a wide variety of topics and may contain one or several volumes. Because they are intended primarily as research tools, treatises are well indexed. Most are updated with pocket parts, but the basic texts of some tend to be dated. Treatises are usually more useful for researching basic and well-established principles rather than the developing edge of the law.

F. Dictionaries.

A surprising amount of information about the law can be found in law dictionaries, which are available at almost every library source mentioned above. The two most popular are *Black's* and *Ballentine's*.

G. Loose-leaf services.

This is a broad category of reference materials, most of which are highly specialized multi-volume sets of binders with loose-leaf pages. These are constantly updated. Loose-leaf services attempt to consolidate all the statutes, regulations, and court decisions on a particular topic in one source. Most of the various loose-leaf services also include commentaries or summaries of the law.

There are three main publishers of loose leaf-services. Bureau of National Affairs (BNA), Commerce Clearing House (CCH), and, Prentice-Hall (P-H). Topics covered include such areas as taxation, antitrust regulations, health and safety, government contracts, criminal law, etc.

H. Shepardizing and updating the law.

The stream of cases decided by the courts never ends. Often a lower court is overruled by a higher court, and less frequently an appellate court will overrule one of its own precedents, thus changing the law. Because of these possibilities, once a pertinent decision has been found, it is necessary to check its subsequent history to determine if it has been later reversed, modified, or overruled. The word, "shepardizing", is synonymous with this process. Shepard's, Inc. (thus the verb) publishes a series of citators for this purpose. A citator provides a list of all cases which have cited a given case or statute. Thus, by looking up a particular case or statute in the appropriate citator, one is easily able to find all subsequent cases in which it has been mentioned. Furthermore, by means of abbreviations, the citator tells whether these cases have approved of, disagreed with, reversed, or modified the subject case.

Citators can also prove very useful in locating additional cases on a particular subject. By shepardizing a case, it is possible to find a series of decisions on the same subject. Because the subject case will almost surely discuss more than one legal point, it will be cited by later cases for more than one reason. Therefore, not all of the cases listed will be relevant to the subject being researched.

Separate citators have been published for each series of case reporters and the *U.S.C.* In the library, the citators are located after the last volume of a case reporter. Because the citators are periodically updated, it is necessary to consult the supplements as well as the permanent volumes in order to insure a thorough search.

V. Understanding a court decision.

In their decisions courts interpret and apply statutes, regulations, and the common law to the factual situations presented in the adversarial system. In order to be able to interpret a decision, it is necessary to understand its component parts.

A. Facts. The facts of a case form the basis for the decision. In a jury case, it is the jury who decide what are the facts;

in a nonjury case, it is the trial judge who makes these determinations. The only function of an appellate court in this respect is to determine whether the factual findings of the jury or trial judge, the triers of fact, are beyond reason. The factual determinations of the jury or trial judge will not be upset by an appellate court unless they are clearly erroneous as a matter of law.

B. Issue. An issue of a case is an essential point or decisional focus. In their briefs, the parties attempt to focus the judge's attention on the issues of a case most favorable to their position, but, ultimately, the judge decides what are the issues of a case regarding his decision.

C. Rule. A rule is a statement of the law which is applied to the facts. Often rules are incomplete or ambiguous, requiring the courts to interpret them. Such an interpretation is also a rule as also may be a statement of the common law developed by the courts. The rule of a decision, especially of an appellate court, serves as a precedent. Once a rule is stated in a decision, only that court or a higher court may alter it.

D. Holding. The holding of the decision is its outcome, the result of the rule applied to the facts, and who wins or loses.

E. Dicta. In a decision, a court may discuss rules which are not directly related to the facts of the particular case at hand. When a court states a rule that is not necessary for deciding a case, the rule is referred to as an "obiter dictum." Dicta (plural) serve as guidance, but do not constitute binding precedent for lower courts.

General References

Anderson, W.S. (Ed.). *Ballentine's Law Dictionary with Pronunciations* *(3rd ed.)*. Lawyers Co-operative, Rochester, 1969

Black's Law Dictionary with Pronunciations (5th ed.). West Publishing, Saint Paul, 1979

Cohen, M.L. *How to Find the Law (7th ed.)*. West Publishing, Saint Paul, 1976

Elias, S. *Legal Research: How to Find and Understand the Law.* Nolo Press, Berkeley, 1982

A Uniform System of Citation (12th ed.). Harvard Law Review Assoc., Cambridge, 1976

Questions on Chapter 16, Finding the Law: Legal Research and Citation

1. Name the two major legal encyclopedias in the U.S.
2. Decisions of which courts are reviewed in the *Southern Reporter?*
3. A citation in an article is given as 116 F.Supp. 870. a. What does that mean? b. What court decisions are published in that series?
4. When may a Federal District Court not follow a precedent set by a Circuit Court of Appeals?
5. What Federal publication publishes proposals to change U.S. Forest Service regulations?
6. In a case about tugboats, (*The T. J. Hooper,* 60 F.2d 737) Judge Learned Hand stated, "A whole calling . . . never may set its own tests", a comment that extends to the health professions. What is the legal name for such a comment?
7. How can one ascertain if a decision reached some years ago has been superseded?
8. How can one determine what are the regulations governing hospital licensing in a given state?
9. Besides the U.S. Court of Claims, what major Federal Court system has decisions published in the *Federal Reporter 2d?*
10. In what publications are there parallel citations to those in the *United States Reports* series?

Legal Maxims and Quotations

Compiled by Nathan T. Sidley

I. Introduction.

The lore and statements of the law contain many pithy declarations of policy. Some are enshrined as legal maxims. Broad summarizing comments, generally true but subject to exceptions, they connote an important flavor of legal thinking.

Quotations regarding the law are also presented. They reflect beliefs of commentators about various aspects of the law. Some originate from persons not actively involved in legal practice. Their tone in those comments tends at times to be skeptical, indicating that conflicts between law and ethics may occur, and that those in a position to make and enforce law sometimes pay more attention to their own parochial interests than to general public concerns.

II. Maxims and quotations.

A. Ancient latin maxims.

1. *De minimis non curat lex.* Cro. Eliz. 353.*
   The law does not concern itself with trifles.

---

*Citations are to old English collections. Abbreviations are those used in *Blacks Law Dictionary* (3rd ed.) West Publishing, St. Paul, 1933.

2. *In jure non remota causa sed proxima causa spectatur.* Bac. Max. reg. 1.
In law the immediate, not the remote, cause of an event is looked at.
(It were infinite for the law to judge the causes of causes, and at their impulsions one of another; therefore it contenteth itself with the immediate cause and judgeth of acts by that, without looking to any further degree.—Francis Bacon)

3. *Nemo debet esse judex in propria sua causa.* 12 Coke 114a.
No one can be a judge in his own cause.

4. *Nullus commodum capere potest de injuria sua propria.* Co. Litt. 148b.
No one shall benefit from his own wrongdoing.

5. *Omnis innovatio plus novitate perturbat quam utilitate prodest. 2* Bulst. *338.*
Every innovation causes more harm from novelty than benefit from utility.

6. *Omnis ratihabitio retrotrahitur et mandata priori aequiparatur.* Co. Litt. 207a.
A subsequent ratification is retrospectively equivalent to a prior mandate.

7. *Optimus interpres rerum usus.* 2 Inst. 282.
Usage is the best interpreter of things.

8. *Qui facit per alium facit per se.* Broom, Max. 818 et seq.
He who does something through another does it himself.

9. *Verba chartarum fortius accipiuntur contra proferentem.* Co. Litt. 36.
The words of a document shall be interpreted most strongly against the party offering the document (in evidence).

10. *Vigilantibus, non dormientibus, jura subveniunt.* 2 Inst. 690.
The laws serve those who are vigilant, not those who sleep on their rights.

11. *Volenti non fit injuria.* Wing. Max. 482.
He who consents cannot receive (in law) an injury.

B. Maxims of Equity and of the Common Law.

1. He who comes into equity must come with clean hands.

2. Equity will not suffer a wrong to be without a remedy.

3. Equity delights to do justice and not by halves. (All parties to an issue should appear in court to have their rights adjusted.)

4. The law looks to the substance and not to the form.

5. The law will not require the doing of a useless, unreasonable, or impossible act.

6. Evasions and subterfuges through which violation of the law is accomplished are not to be tolerated.

7. Actions speak louder than words.

8. Public policy demands an end of litigation.

9. Fundamental principles cannot be set aside to meet the demands of convenience or to prevent apparent hardship in a particular case.

C. Quotations.

1. Going to law is losing a cow for the sake of a cat. —Chinese proverb

2. Laws are generally found to be nets of such a texture as the little creep through, the great break through, and the middle size are alone entangled.—William Shenstone

3. The severity of laws often prevents their execution ... When the penalty is excessive, one is often obliged to prefer impunity.—Baron de Montesquieu

4. It would be very hard upon the profession if the law was so certain that everybody knew it.—William Murray, Lord Mansfield

5. When laws, customs, or institutions cease to be beneficial to man, or are contrary to the will of God, they cease to be obligatory on us.—Lyman Beecher

6. Laws are silent in the midst of arms.—Cicero

7. When I hear any man talk of an unalterable law, the only effect it produces on me is to convince me that he is an unalterable fool.—Sydney Smith

8. The best way to get a bad law repealed is to enforce it strictly.—Abraham Lincoln

9. A multitude of laws in a country is like a great number of physicians, a sign of weakness and malady.
—Voltaire.

10. To make an empire durable, the magistrates must obey the laws, and the people the magistrates.
—Solon.

11. Let the public mind once become thoroughly corrupt, and all attempts to secure property, liberty, or life, by mere force of laws written on parchment, will be as vain as to put up printed notices in an orchard to keep off canker-worms.—Horace Mann

12. Possession is eleven points in the law.—Colley Cibber

13. Accuracy and diligence are much more necessary to a lawyer than great comprehension of mind, or brilliancy of talent . . . His business is to refine, define, split hairs, look into authorities and compare cases . . . If he would be a great lawyer, he must first consent to be a great drudge.—Daniel Webster

14. The first thing we do, let's kill all the lawyers.
—William Shakespeare

15. Ignorance of the law excuses no man; not that all men know the law, but because 'tis an excuse every man will plead.—John Selden

16. If the courts do not respect the law, who will?
—Roscoe Pound

17. Laws grind the poor and rich men rule the law.
    —Oliver Goldsmith

18. Good men must not obey the laws too well.—Ralph Waldo Emerson

19. "If the law supposes that," said Mr. Bumble, "the law is a ass—a idiot."—Charles Dickens

20. Howsoever long it hath continued, if it be against reason, it is of no force in law.—Sir Edward Coke

21. . . . th' supreme coort follows th' iliction returns.
    —Finley Peter Dunne

22. In the law, if nothing else turns up, clubs are trumps.—Thomas Hobbes

23. The law is all one in great things and small.—Sir Edward Littleton

24. The criminal law stands to the passion of revenge . . . as marriage to the sexual appetite.—Sir James Stephen

25. There is no country in the world in which everything can be provided for by the laws, or in which political institutions can prove a substitute for common sense and public morality.—Alexis de Tocqueville

26. Everybody is presumed to know the law except His Majesty's judges, who have a Court of Appeal set over them to put them right.—Justice William Maule

Glossary of Legal Terms, with Pronunciation*
Compiled by Gertrude M. Allen

Accessory
A person not present at the criminal act who aided, counseled, or commanded the committing of a crime.

Accessory after the fact
One, knowing a crime has been committed, who helps the offender by concealment or by impeding the apprehension of the offender.

Accessory before the fact
A person who assists or advises the carrying out of a crime.

Accessory during the fact
One who stands by and makes no effort to prevent the commission of a crime.

Accomplice
One who knowingly and without being forced joins with the principal offender in committing a crime.

Accord and satisfaction
The mutual giving and accepting of something in place of what is stated in a contract.

Act of God
An event which could not be anticipated or guarded against by reasonable foresight and prudence; an unpredictable, natural occurrence such as a tornado.

---

*This glossary is a selective one. Most of the important common words in the text are included. In addition, for the reader's interest, various commonly encountered legal terms, especially in relation to health practice, are also here, even though they may not appear in the chapters.

431

Ad damnum
(L. ăd dăm´nŭm;* to the damage)—The statement of the amount of damages claimed by the plaintiff in his writ. (See Writ)

Adjective law
The portion of the law that deals with the rules of procedure governing evidence, pleading, and practice. (Opposed to Substantive law, which see)

Adjudication
The decision of the court.

Admissible
(Of evidence)—Allowed by the court as being of proper and pertinent character for consideration in a decision.

Affidavit
(L. ăf ĭ dā´vĭt; he has made an oath)—A voluntary statement, in writing, made under oath. (See Oath)

Affirmation
A solemn and formal declaration that a statement is true, made by one who has conscientious scruples against taking an oath. (See Oath)

Agent
A person authorized to represent or act for another person in a business transaction.

Alcoholism
The excessive use of intoxicating beverages.

Aleatory contract
A contract, the performance of which is dependent on uncertain or hazardous conditions; a gamble.

Amicus curiae
(L. à mī´kŭs kū´rĭ ē; a friend of the court)—A lawyer, not a party to an action, who files a brief or makes an oral argument in appellate procedure, to protect the interest of concerned persons; friendly intervention.

Annulment
The judicial pronouncement rendering void or invalid a marriage contract because of pre-existing conditions.

Appellate court
A reviewing court with power to affirm, reverse, or modify the decision of a court of original jurisdiction. (See Jurisdiction)

---

*See Pronunciation of Legal Latin at end of Glossary

Arguendo
(L. är gū ĕn´dō; in arguing)—A statement made as an illustration to clarify some point in a case being tried.

Arraignment
The initial bringing of a defendant to criminal court to answer the alleged charges against him.

Assault
The apparent intent to do bodily harm by force or violence.

Assault and battery
The unlawful beating or physical harm to another. Assault is the apparent intent to use force; battery is the actual use of force.

Assignment
The transfer of property rights to another, such as a lease.

Attachment
The act of seizing a person's property for custody for a court, in order to cover alleged indebtedness in an action before the court.

Bail
n. A monetary guarantee to assure the appearance of the released defendant in court.

Bail
v. To release an arrestee.

Bailiff
An officer of the court assigned to protect the jury and to carry out the orders of the court.

Bailment
The temporary transfer of goods from one party to another for a particular purpose.

Barratry
Filing of groundless legal actions to prolong litigation, for the purpose of harassment.

Bill of attainder
A legislative act of punishment for high offenses, such as treason, without judicial procedure.

Bill of exceptions
A formal written objection to judicial decisions made during a trial; if allowed, the bill is acted on by the appellate court.

Bind over
The action by the court to establish bail and release the arrestee for a later appearance in the same court or another court.

Bond
A secured certificate making a promise to pay.

Booking
Registering on the police blotter an arrested person's name, alleged crime, and vital facts; it may include photographs.

Brief
A written document, prepared by counsel, stating the law involved and its application, and presented to support a particular position in a case before the court.

Burden of proof (Two senses)
1. The duty to prove facts. Sometimes the burden is on the plaintiff, sometimes on the defendant. 2. The degree of certainty to which facts must be proven. The three main classes are a) preponderance of evidence; b) clear and convincing proof; and c) beyond a reasonable doubt. (See Evidence)

Capias
(L. kā´pē ăs; thou mayest take)—A writ allowing a sheriff to take custody of a prisoner.

Certiorari
(L. sĕr shĭ ō rā´rī; to be informed)—A writ from an appellate court to review the record of a case to correct errors of law.

Champerty
Proceedings in which a person, not a party to a suit, continues litigation at his own expense, anticipating a share of the proceeds in the suit.

Collateral source
A payment to an injured party for damages, from a source other than the wrong-doer.

Common law
Fundamental law of the United States, derived from the English; its authority stems from usage, not from legislation. (See Statutory law)

Comparative negligence
The relative amount of negligence on the part of each party involved in a tort action; damages are mitigated accordingly. (See Tort)

Competency to stand trial
The ability to comprehend the nature of the criminal charges alleged against one, understand court procedures, and cooperate with counsel in one's defense.

Complaint
A statement made by the plaintiff, filed in court, alleging a wrong, and seeking the court's assistance for relief. (See Plaintiff)

Condition precedent
An action agreed on, which must occur before an agreement becomes enforceable.

Confidential communication
Facts or information revealed in private conversation, such as that between husband and wife, doctor and patient, or lawyer and client; not admissible as evidence.

Conservator
A protector appointed by the court to handle the affairs of an incompetent person.

Consideration
A value received in exchange for another value when making a contract. (See Contract)

Conspiracy
Two or more persons joining together to commit a criminal act.

Constable
An officer with duties similar to a sheriff, but having less power and acting within a smaller jurisdiction. (See Sheriff)

Contempt (of court)
Willful disregard of the authority of a court, or failure to carry out its orders.

Continuance
Postponement of a court action to another date.

Conversion
The wrongful assumption of authority over another's property, denying the rightful owner of its use.

Criminal responsibility
The mental capacity to distinguish right from wrong, or to adhere to the right.

Cross complaint
An action by which a defendant sues the plaintiff in the same case in which he is being sued.

Custody
The care and control of another person, such as a child by a parent or a prisoner by a guard.

Damages
The fair compensation allowed by the court for injury suffered by the unlawful or negligent act of another.

Defendant
A person named in either a civil or criminal action, alleged to have committed a wrong.

Defenses to actions
These may be a denial, justification, confession, avoidance of the facts, or alibi.

Demurrer
A motion, generally obsolete, by which the defendant admits to the facts but alleges that they are not sufficient for the plaintiff to continue the action against the defendant.

Deposition
The testimony of a witness taken or written under oath, outside the courtroom, for use at a trial.

Directed verdict
The action of the court when the evidence presented to establish a prima facie case is insufficient; no further action based on the same facts can follow. (See Prima facie)

Discovery
The process of acquiring knowledge of facts, titles, and documents relating to evidence necessary for the trial of the case.

Dismiss
To discharge or remove a case from further court action, either temporarily or permanently.

Double jeopardy
Under the Constitution of the United States a person cannot be tried for the same offense a second time. (See Jeopardy)

Due process
Paraphrased, "every man's right to his day in court," it involves notice and the opportunity to be heard and to defend, in court, charges alleged against a person.

Embracery
An illegal or corrupt attempt to influence unduly or instruct a jury.

Equal protection clause
Under the Fourteenth Amendment of the Constitution of the United States this clause provides like treatment for all persons in like situations; it bars discrimination.

Equity
Principles of fairness by which justice may be attained where there is no specific relief under ordinary law; a supplement to common and statutory law, the basic principles of which were developed in the English Court of Chancery.

Estoppel
A bar or impediment against pleading, alleging, or denying certain facts or legal points.

Evidence
The information presented at a trial, both testimony of witnesses and exhibits.

Execute
To complete or perform the requirements stated in a deed, will, or contract. To sign a document.

Executor
The person named in a will to carry out the terms of the will.

Ex parte
(L. ĕks pär´tē; from a side)—The proceedings taken by one party, usually without notice or contest; for example, an injunction. (See Injunction)

Expert witness
One qualified by education or training in a specific area to testify in a legal action. (See Witness)

Ex post facto
(L. ĕks pōst f ăk´tō; after the fact)—An act occurring after an action which alters the status of the action; for example, declaring an act to be a crime after it has been accomplished.

Felony
A crime of more serious nature than a misdemeanor, punishable by imprisonment in a state's prison or by capital punishment. (See Misdemeanor)

Fiduciary relation
The special reliance of trust and confidence placed on one person by another. If the trust is abused, a remedy may be sought in court. Examples are guardian to ward, attorney to client, health professional to patient or client, etc.

Fraud
Deliberate corruption of the truth to obtain something of value.

Fungible
Interchangeable; treated as equivalent items; for example, gallons of gasoline.

Future interest
An interest in property or an estate that cannot be taken advantage of by a party until some future time. For example, a trust fund (which see) that a person will own only when he reaches 21.

Garnishment
The process whereby property, money, or credit, belonging to one party but held by a second party, is used to satisfy a judgment obtained by a third party against the original party. (See Judgment)

Good faith
The honest intention of a person not to take advantage of another.

Grand jury
A jury selected to determine whether the evidence presented warrants an indictment. (See Indictment)

Gross negligence
The wilful and wanton lack of care, showing no regard for the consequences of one's acts.

Guardian
A person appointed by the court, given the power and charged with the duty to care for another person's physical body as well as his property.

Guardian ad litem
(L. ăd līt´ĕm; for the suit)—A person appointed by the court to represent the interests of an infant or an incompetent who is a party to litigation.

Guilty
The pronouncement of the court when the defendant is judged to have committed the crime charged.

Habeas corpus
(L. hā´bē ăs kôr´pŭs; you have the body)—The writ available to a confined person allowing his appearance before the court for inquiry into the legality of the confinement. (See Writ)

Hearsay
Evidence offered in court that does not stem from first-hand knowledge.

Holder in due course
A person who receives a negotiable instrument, presuming it to be valid, is immune from recourse against enforcing it even it if proves to be invalid.

Hypothetical question
Certain facts, assumed or proven, are presented to an expert witness for his opinion.

Indefinite sentence
A criminal sentence in which maximum and minimum times are set by statute, but the actual time served is determined by prison or parole authorities, based on the prisoner's behavior. (Also called "Indeterminate sentence")

Indictment
A formal, written accusation by a grand jury charging a person with a crime.

Infant
Any person who has not reached the legal age of majority and who, therefore, cannot act sui juris (which see).

Information
A sworn, written accusation of a crime presented by a prosecuting authority.

Informed consent
A reasonable decision made after knowing the appropriate facts in a situation.

Injunction
A court order either to carry out or refrain from carrying out actions.

Insanity
The legal term for the unsoundness of the mind.

Instrument
A formal, written legal document such as a contract, promissory note, check, will, mortgage, or insurance policy.

Intent
The state of mind a person reaches in performing a certain act.

Interrogatories
Written questions presented before trial, requiring written answers given under oath by one party to the opposing party. (See Discovery)

Intestate
The state of having died without a valid will.

Jeopardy
The danger of conviction and criminal punishment faced by a person when put on trial for an alleged crime.

Joint
A common interest shared by two or more persons.

Judgment
The determination of the court in any action.

Jurisdiction
The authority of the court, defined either by geographical area or by class of cases, to hear and decide criminal or civil actions.

Jury
A group of citizens, chosen by law to determine the facts in a case.

Juvenile delinquent
A child, ordinarily between the ages of 7 and 17, who is found to have violated a law or ordinance. (See Ordinance)

Law merchant
Customs of commerce which have become law by usage and by statutory enactment.

Leading question
A question, the wording of which suggests the answer; such is frequently used in cross-examination.

Least restrictive alternative
A doctrine invoked in the involuntary commitment of mentally ill persons. The least limiting conditions consistent with the safety of the individual and the community should be imposed, including, in some instances, outpatient psychiatric treatment.

Libel
A written or published statement harming another person's character or causing ridicule of a person.

Lien
A charge against a person's property for nonpayment of a debt.

Limitations, Statute of
The legal regulation that governs the maximum time allowed by the court for filing papers in a case.

Locality rule
The rule that in a professional negligence case, the standard of practice should be that of the community in which the professional person practices.

Magistrate
A public official with power to issue a warrant for arrest; sometimes a limited judiciary function in criminal matters is also exercised.

Maintenance
Interference in litigation, through aiding the prosecution or defense, where there is no personal interest.

Malice
Intentional harm with no thought of the consequences, or its legal equivalent.

Malpractice
Professional misconduct on the part of a professional practitioner.

Malum in se
(L. mä´lŭm ĭn sē; offense in itself)—A wrong so evil and immoral that it is illegal, even though it might not be prohibited by statute; an offense at common law.

Malum prohibitum
(L. mä´lŭm prō hĭ´bĭ tŭm; a wrong prohibited)—An act prohibited by statute in the public's interest, although it may not be evil or immoral, for example, a 55 mile per hour speed limit on an expressway.

Mayhem
Intentionally and unlawfully injuring, maiming, or disabling a person.

Mandamus
(L. mǎn dā´mŭs; we command)—A court order commanding the performance of a specific action.

Manic depressive disorder
Mental illness characterized by alternate periods of self-deprecation and hyperactivity.

Mens rea
(L. mĕnz´rē´ä; guilty mind)—A guilty mind showing criminal intent or evil purpose.

Miranda warning
Every person taken into custody by an arresting officer must be read the Miranda warning before being questioned. It includes the following: that what a person says may be held against him, that a person may remain silent, and that a person may contact a lawyer. *Miranda v. Arizona*, 384 U.S. 436 (1966).

Misdemeanor
An offense punishable by a fine or imprisonment for less than five years in a penitentiary.

Misprision
The failure to prevent the commission of a crime or failure to report a crime knowing one has been committed.

Misrepresentation
A statement that is not in accordance with the facts.

Moot
An abstract case based on an undecided issue; moot court is used in law schools for student practice in argument for appellate courts.

Motion
A written request to the court for a ruling.

Murder
An illegal killing of a human being.

Negligence
The failure to act with reasonable care.

Negotiable instruments
Written securities, including checks, drafts, bills, and notes, the rights to sue on which can be transferred from one party to another by indorsement and delivery.

Next friend
An individual who acts for a child in a court action, though he is not the child's guardian.

Nisi prius
(L. nī´ sī prī´ ŭs; unless before)—Usually refers to the forum of a judge and jury where the facts in a case are tried; not an appellate court.

Nolle prosequi
(L. nŏ´lĕ prŏs´ ĕ kwī; to be unwilling to prosecute)—The legal action by which the prosecutor or plaintiff in the suit terminates any further proceedings in court.

Nolo contendere
(L. nō´ lō cŏn tĕn´ dĕ rē; I do not contest it.)—A criminal plea which is an admission of criminal guilt for sentencing purposes, but which acknowledges no liability in case a related civil action should occur.

Non compos mentis
(L. nŏn kŏm´ pōs mĕn´ tĭs; not of sound mind)—A person who is mentally deranged; insane.

Novation
The substitution of a new contract for an old one by agreement; it usually involves the same terms as the former contract but with at least one new party in place of the original contract makers.

Oath

A formal swearing to tell the truth.

Obiter dictum

(L. ŏb´ ĭt ĕr´dĭk´tŭm; something said in passing)—The discussion of side issues, not essential to the decision of a case.

Objection

Counsel for the plaintiff or defendant protests the admission of certain evidence and asks the judge for a ruling on it.

Ordinance

A regulation made by a municipal government.

Ordinary prudence

The conduct followed by an average, careful person considering the consequences of his actions.

Original jurisdiction

The authority invested in a court to hear a case in the first instance (as opposed to an appellate court).

Pardon

An act of the executive, releasing a person from punishment for a crime, usually done because of unusual circumstances.

Parole

A conditional release from prison, but still under supervision until the original sentence has been completed.

Parol evidence

Oral as opposed to written testimony, referred mostly to evidence given in court. Also, oral evidence given about a written contract.

Perjury

The act of wilfully and knowingly lying while under oath. (See Oath)

Petition

An application to a court requesting action on a matter.

Petit jury

A trial jury; it is usually composed of six or twelve people. (Opposed to Grand jury, which see)

Plaintiff

The party who brings an action against another, called the defendant. (See Defendant)

Plea bargain

A negotiation between the prosecution and the defense, whereby the defendant pleads guilty to a lesser charge in order to obtain a more lenient sentence.

Pleadings
The papers filed in a case stating the facts and issues involved.

Power of attorney
A document allowing one person to act for another in specified kinds of transactions.

Presumption
A legal conclusion assumed from a set of facts presented.

Prima facie
(L. prī´ma fā´shĭ ē; at first sight)—Facts assumed to be true unless disproved. In a law case, enough evidence to allow for a judgment if the evidence is not disproved.

Probable cause
The facts presented in a hearing, sufficient to convince a reasonable and prudent man that a person suspected of a crime has committed a crime.

Probation
The release of one convicted of a crime by the court to the supervision of an officer, setting conditions which, if not obeyed, may lead to imposition of punishment.

Probation surrender
If the conditions of probation are violated, the probation officer returns the individual to court for imposition of a sentence.

Professional negligence
The neglect or nonobservance of acts of care prescribed by the standards of professional responsibility.

Pro tanto
(L. prō tăn´tō; for so much)—A payment for a part of a claim which does not bar further action.

Proximate cause
A foreseeable, natural, and continuous sequence of acts, which results in an injury that otherwise would not have occurred.

Public defender
An attorney appointed by the court to defend an indigent person who has been accused of a crime.

Quantum meruit
(L. kwŏn´tŭm mĕr´wĭt; as much as deserves)—When there is no fully executed contract, the defendant pays the plaintiff what he reasonably deserves for services rendered.

Quantum valebant

(L. kwŏn´tŭm vă´lē bănt; as much as they were worth)—In the absence of a contract, this constitutes an implied promise to pay a reasonable price for goods.

Quash

To vacate or void an indictment, a subpoena, or a writ. (See Subpoena and Writ)

Rebuttable presumption

A proposition, drawn from probable reasoning, which can be disproved by evidence.

Recidivism

Repeated criminal acts by an offender.

Recognizance

A formally declared and recorded obligation to the court to appear and answer to a charge. No bail is required. (See Bail)

Reformation

The manner by which a contract is corrected by a court when the overt agreement does not express the true intent of the parties involved.

Remand

To return a lawsuit to a lower court for further action or to send a prisoner back to jail.

Replevin

A legal action seeking the return of property alleged to have been wrongly taken.

Res ipsa loquitur

(L. rēz ĭp´sà lŏk´wĭ tĕr; the thing speaks for itself)—The circumstances are such that lacking negligence on the part of the defendant, the plaintiff could not be injured.

Res judicata

(L. rēz jōō dĭ cā´tà; a matter judged)—The final judgment of a court settling a point in a controversy.

Respondeat superior

(L. rē spŏnd´ē ăt sŭ pē´rĭ ĕr; let the master answer)—The employer is responsible for a wrong committed by his employees or his agents, acting within the scope of their employment.

Right of contribution

The right of a party to recover for damages proportionately from other parties who are liable when there is common liability.

Right to refuse treatment
A general right of all persons, competent or incompetent, to refuse medical treatment.

Right to treatment
The right of a hospitalized person to receive minimum standards of care and treatment.

Scienter
(L. sī ĕn´ tēr; knowingly)—The degree of knowledge a person has about an act, which determines his responsibility for that act.

Seal
To authenticate a document by marking it with a distinctive impression, formerly of great importance in the law of contract.

Sentence
The punishment imposed by the court for a particular crime.

Sheriff
(A.S. shire; a territory under an earl, a county; reeve; an ancient administrative officer)—The chief executive officer of a county, chosen by election, and responsible for executing laws and keeping the peace.

Special guardian
A person appointed by the court, with limited powers, to perform specified duties for a ward. (See Guardian ad litem)

Stare decisis
(L. stā´rē dĕ sī´sĭs; let the decision stand, from *"stare decisis et non quieta movere"*; let stand the decision; do not disturb settled matters.)—Following the rules and principles laid down in previous decisions.

Status quo
(L. stā´ tŭs kwō; existing state)—A condition at a given time and place.

Status offender
An offense not subject to criminal sanctions; examples: truancy, vagrancy, being a stubborn child or runaway.

Statute of frauds
A statute stating that civil actions of certain kinds cannot take place in court unless there has been a written contract or memorandum.

Statute of limitations
(See Limitations, Statute of)

Statutory law
The laws enacted by state or Federal legislative bodies.

Strict liability
A legal responsibility for an injury even when the party is not at fault.

Sua sponte
(L. soo͞′a spŏn′tē; of his own will)—Willingly or voluntarily.

Subornation
The inducing of another to commit perjury.

Subpoena
(L. sŭ pē′na; under penalty)—A command from the court to appear at a certain time and testify or be held in contempt. (See Contempt)

Substantive law
The basic law that creates rights, duties, and obligations, rather than procedures of law.

Sui juris
(L. soo͞′ī joo͞′rĭs; of his own right)—Qualified to act under one's own right.

Summary process
Short and simple court action, without juries, etc.; such process might be used, for example, in the eviction of a tenant.

Summons
An order from the court to appear on a certain day to answer charges.

Supplementary process
The examination of a debtor by the court to determine his assets in order to execute a judgment.

Surety
A person's promise to carry out an agreement if the original person fails to do some act, for example, an insurance company bond.

Tolling
Temporarily stopping the counting of the period of elapsed time for purposes of the Statute of limitations. (Which see)

Tort
A legal wrong or injury to another person.

Trial de novo
(L. dē nō′vō; anew)—The retrial of a case, either following a

bench trial or on appeal to a higher court, where the decision in the first instance has no standing.

Trust
A right of property, which is held by one party for the benefit of another.

Trust fund
Money or property which is held in trust. (Which see)

Undue influence
The taking advantage of another by misuse of his confidence or his special position.

Unjust enrichment
The principle that a person should not profit at the expense of another.

Venire (veniremen)
(L. vĕ nī´rē; to come)—A panel of citizens selected as jurors.

Venue
(Fr. vĕn´ū; the action of coming)—The judicial district in which a court action occurs.

Verdict
The decision of the jury or the judge.

Voir dire
(Fr. vwär´dēr; to speak the truth)—The preliminary examination of a prospective juror or of an expert witness.

Waiver
The act of abandoning a claim, right, or privilege.

Warrant
A court order for arrest, search, or seizure issued in the administration of justice.

Workers' Compensation (Workmen's Compensation)
A means created to protect a worker against injury suffered during his employment. Statutorily required insurance which limits an employer's liability to employees.

Writ
A written order of the court to a person authorized or required to execute the order.

Writ of error
The legal remedy for requesting a review of the judgment of a lower court.

Pronunciation of Legal Latin*

Legal Latin terms, (like scientific Latin) are pronounced by the so-called "English method" (that is, as if they were English words), which is different from both Church Latin pronunciation and that of the ancient Romans.

The accent is on the first syllable in two syllable words (dixit—dĭx ´ĭt)**; in longer words the accent is on the penultimate syllable (the one before the last one) if the vowel in that syllable is long (excusat—ĕks kū´zăt); otherwise, it is ordinarily on the antepenultimate syllable (the one before the penultimate) (detinet—dĕt´ĭ nĕt).

Every vowel is pronounced (rete—rē´tĕ; exeat—ĕks´ē ăt)

Some special pronunciations:

1. i at the end of a word is long (qui—kwī).
2. i in the first syllable of a word is long if the second syllable is accented (iambus—ī ăm´bŭs; fiebam—fī ē´băm).
3. e, o, and u at the end of an unaccented syllable are pronounced almost long (rete—rē´tĕ; volo—vō´lŏ; populi—pŏp´ū lī).
4. es at the end of a word is pronounced like the word, "ease" (milites—mĭl´ĭ tēz); os at the end of a word is pronounced like the "oss" in "gross" (dominos—dŏm´ĭ nōs).
5. ei, oe, and ae are pronounced as long e; c preceding any of those vowels is soft (coelum—sē´lŭm).
6. c, s, or t before i-followed-by-a-vowel are pronounced like sh. (facias—fā´shĭ ăs); x in similar position is pronounced ksh.

---

*Compiled by Nathan T. Sidley
**Diacritical marks are used in the same manner as in the *Webster's Collegiate Dictionary.*

Answers to End-of-Chapter Questions

Answers to Questions on Chapter 1, Origin and Functions of American Law

1. "The usage and customs of immemorial antiquity" common to the people of England.
2. The Court of Common Pleas, the King's Bench, and the Exchequer.
3. The Chancellor's Court. Equity jurisdiction and probate jurisdiction.
4. English law is based on a continuing judicial interpretation of cases; Continental law is based on a code. (Actually, the difference is not that profound. There are codified statutes in common law jurisdictions, and judges and scholars must interpret codes in Continental countries.)
5. In decisions of the neighboring states of Maine, Vermont, and Massachusetts. Massachusetts, most populous, having a greater case volume than the other states, and with a high judicial prestige, would be the source likely to carry greatest weight.
6. The legal responsibility falling on the manufacturer or other handlers of a product, for damage which ensues because the product is defective in some way.
7. It is ubiquitous and unavoidable that judges consider the social consequences of their decisions.
8. a. Yes.
   b. Very doubtful.
9. That ultimately the function of law is to maintain social order; if logic, theory, or previous decisions interfere with that function, they will be overruled in the interests of social adaptation.
10. Records of the decisions and opinions of the English courts. They established the fundamental basis for the continuity of English case law.

Answers to Questions on Chapter 2, Ethics

1. An order.
2. Ethical situations arouse strong emotions, which are related to biased perception and simplistic conclusions.
3. a. What are the facts of the case?
   b. What are the values which relate to the facts?
4. a. Survival of the community.
   b. Individual survival.
   c. Influencing others.
5. a. Law has a formal enforcement staff.
   b. Law is restricted to objective, visible, and definable behavior.
   c. Ethical principles are abstract and general.
   d. The law can only punish deviation.
   e. One can be rewarded for following ethical principles.
6. a. Deontology.
   b. Teleology.
7. Leaving too much freedom to individual decision-making threatens social order. Setting forth principles which eliminate individual decision-making latitude creates a system too complex for the average person and too inflexible to cover field situations.
8. True.
9. True (In the author's opinion).
10. "Immanent justice" is the notion that nature will punish a wrongdoer.

Answers to Questions on Chapter 3, Constitutional Law

1. False.
2. False.
3. False.
4. c.
5. True.
6. True.
7. True.
8. b.
9. False.
10. True.

Answers to Questions on Chapter 4, Criminal Law and Procedure

1. d.
2. b.
3. a.
4. True.
5. b, d, e, f.
6. False.
7. c.
8. False.
9. False.
10. a.

Answers to Questions on Chapter 5, Civil Procedure

1. True.
2. False.
3. True.
4. Long arm statutes.
5. Apply to the court to quash the subpoena, on the grounds that such disclosure would violate the physician-patient privilege. Additional grounds are that the records are those of other patients; they are, therefore, irrelevant to the instant case and would not be admissible in evidence.
6. A class action suit, for injunctive relief in this situation.
7. c.
8. A petition for judgment n.o.v., on the grounds that there was no legal basis in the case for that kind of award.
9. False. Depending on the jurisdiction and the kind of case, the agreement of even seven out of 12 jurors may be enough to decide the issue.
10. a. The degree of certainty required to prove an issue.
    b. The responsibility for proving something.

Answers to Questions on Chapter 6, Evidence

1. False.
2. False.
3. False.
4. True.

5. Yes, if his witness is a hostile witness.
6. Yes. It is an admission by a party to the action.
7. Yes. Under the doctrine of present recollection revived, the notes, if used to refresh memory, must be made available to opposing counsel.
8. Submit an offer of proof, which becomes a part of the record to be considered by the appellate court.
9. No. The privilege is that of the patient, not the doctor. If the patient waives the privilege, the doctor must testify or risk being held in contempt of court.
10. Yes. For the husband-wife privilege to be operative in a civil case, the communication must have been intended to have been confidential. The presence of third parties ordinarily indicates that communication is not intended to be confidential.

Answers to Questions on Chapter 7, Torts

1. a. Duty of care.
   b. An act of omission.
   c. A breach of duty.
   d. Proximate causation of plaintiff's harm by defendant's action.
   e. Damages.
2. a. Protect himself.
   b. Mitigate damages.
3. He has no obligation.
4. A person has knowingly exposed himself to a situation in which damage might occur.
5. The doctrine of comparative negligence. Ernest would be likely to be considered somewhat negligent, but not as much as John.
6. a. The plaintiff's harm is a type that ordinarily occurs from negligence.
   b. The causes of the negligence are within the defendant's control.
   c. The plaintiff's voluntary action is not also a cause of the harm.
7. a. Assault.
   b. Battery.
   c. False imprisonment.
8. a. Trespass to land.
   b. Trespass to chattels.

9. a. Defense of property.
   b. Yes. Once William had the wallet back and George was immobilized with a broken arm, there was no danger that either the wallet would be taken or William might be attacked by George. William was then not acting in self-defense or in defense of property, but was committing his own tort on George.
10. Absolute liability for unusually dangerous activities.

Answers to Questions on Chapter 8, Malpractice

1. The basis can be either, although most cases tend to be based on a tort theory.
2. No. A specialist is held to a higher standard because he holds himself out as a specialist, that is, a professional with more knowledge and capability.
3. Yes, if he has the right to control the actions of the other. He is the "captain of the ship" and is responsible for those he controls.
4. No. In an emergency, if consent cannot be obtained, no consent is necessary. Moreover, in the case of a minor, the consent of the parents is ordinarily obtained.
5. Usually not, in accordance with the local community standard. Some courts allow a broadening of this rule, however, especially for specialists.
6. He should insure that another competent physician is in charge of the case and is provided with all necessary information. He should also inform the patient in advance.
7. It is sufficient, but because of proof problems, written consent should always be obtained where possible.
8. Yes, if there are reasonable alternatives.
9. Not if the physician is an independent contractor and the hospital has not been negligent on its own part.
10. When general standards of medical practice require.

Answers to Questions on Chapter 9, Coping With the Medical Malpractice Problem

1. 10 percent. No perceived liability, insufficient potential reward.
2. Lower class members and blacks.
3. False.

4. False. Insurance companies don't make as much on investments, and more money must come from premiums.
5. False, but almost true. They are in Class 4. Only orthopedic surgeons and neurosurgeons pay higher rates.
6. It provides for independent evaluation of malpractice claims.
7. a. It is less costly than a trial.
   b. It is less time consuming.
   c. The arbitrator can be more flexible in developing evidence.
   d. Emotional appeals might be reduced in effectiveness.
8. When the patient knew or should have known about the fact. It might not be for several years. If the physician tells the patient, the statute begins to run immediately (on an adult, at least).
9. a. The attorney's fee is contingent on the amount recovered in the case.
   b. Approximately one-third of the net recovery.
   c. Approximately $250 per hour.
10. a. Professionals generally have a mutual, self-protective feeling vis-a-vis outsiders.
    b. A professional who has been disciplined may be able to retaliate against fellow professionals who have undertaken the disciplinary action.
    c. It is difficult to discipline a colleague with whom one has friendly relations.

Answers to Questions on Chapter 10, Contracts

1. Acceptance by performance. There is a valid contract.
2. Probably not. The terms of their agreement are so vague that it is unlikely to be considered a contract. If Stan actually had built the house, the court would have to interpret what is an appropriate profit.
3. a. Seek to have his money returned.
   b. Seek to keep the car but at a more equitable price than one would pay for a sound one.
   c. Sue for breach of warranty, for the amount required to repair the defect. (If it cannot be fixed, sue for the amount to replace the car with a sound one.)
4. Yes. He can sue to have the sale contract voided on the basis of fraud.
5. Promissory estoppel. If he notified the school soon enough, that is, before action was taken on the pledge, he might be able to avoid liability.

6. Yes, he may. William made a counter offer, and in so doing, he revoked the original offer. John is free to make a completely new offer.

7. No. the contract could have been fulfilled within a year if Mary had died (even though she didn't). The contract was outside the statute of frauds. If the purpose of her going was illegal (for example, if they weren't married), he could use illegal contract as a defense, however. If they were married, he could claim that the contract was against public policy because, as her husband, he is obliged to support her anyway.

8. Sue in quantum meruit for partial performance. (If Tom has to pay more than the $25 agreed-on price in order to have someone else do the plowing, the difference will have to be deducted from the amount Tom owes to Walter.)

9. Rescission, substitution, novation, accord and satisfaction, and waiver. (Merger and bankruptcy are not quite the same level of discharges.) Appropriate performance of the terms of the contract is, of course, the most common way of discharging a contract.

10. a. He can sue for specific performance and demand that Charles complete the sale of the book.

    b. Specific performance is a case in equity, not a case at law. Formerly, a plaintiff had to seek such remedy in a separate court, not the court that awarded money damages for breach of contract. (The two forms of action had different historical origins.) Usually, the same court can entertain either action today, even though they are still separate actions.

Answers to Questions on Chapter 11, Family and Domestic Law

1. X will not be successful on the basis of the agreement. All of the incidents of the marriage or divorce are controlled by the state. X must prove a statutory ground such as incompatibility or cruel and abusive treatment. X may be entitled to alimony if she is successful, but the amount of it will be subject to court's approval.

2. Probably not. X lived together with Y in a common law jurisdiction as husband and wife. Therefore, the marriage should be upheld.

3. Probably not. The custody decision is a delicate one. The judgment is based on many factors, most of which center on the best interests of the child. Y's occupation requires him to

travel. Morality may be a factor, but *X* has carried out her job well, and chances are she will prevail.

4. Probably not. The answer would depend on several factors. The marriage implies that the husband will supply certain necessities. A coat is probably a necessity. Here, however, the husband is a dishwasher. Their station does not imply an expensive coat. Also important are whether she has independent means or if he has previously provided her with a coat.

5. The answer depends on numerous considerations. The most often mentioned is that the legal separation leaves the marriage intact. The parties, after seeking a separation, must thereafter seek a divorce if they intend to remarry.

6. Yes.

7. Yes.

8. There is no ability to pay if the spouse is jailed.

9. Seek a modification of the support order, which reflects his inability to pay.

10. The ordinary contract can be modified by voluntary agreement between the parties. All of the incidents of a marriage are, however, controlled by the state. It cannot be entered into, modified, or terminated except according to state policy.

Answers to Questions on Chapter 12, Wills

1. A will must be in writing; it must be signed by the testator and witnessed by the statutory number of witnesses; the testator must be of sound mind; he must be free of undue influence or coercion, and the will must indicate a testamentary intent.

2. a. No.
   b. Yes, depending on relevant state or Federal tax laws.
   c. Possibly, if the spouse does not take the required statutory action to waive the provisions of the will.
   d. Yes.

3. Yes, probably.

4. A person may make a transfer to a trust, establish a joint bank account, present as a gift, or convey title in various other methods which give a present interest in property so as to affect the title to the property after death.

5. The testator may draft or execute a new will at any time prior to death, provided he meets the requirements for a valid, enforceable will. Provided that his son fulfills the appropriate

requirements, he may seek a share determined by statute, if the will does not indicate that the son was intentionally disregarded.

6. There is no requirement that the written document always be in existence. It may be proved by notes or testimony. There is a presumption, however, that if it is not found, it has been revoked intentionally by the testator. This may be countered by evidence, such as testimony that prior to his death the testator referred to his will.

7. His estate is handled through the probate court, and an administrator is appointed. The estate is distributed according to the provisions of the intestacy statute of the state. The wife usually would receive the greatest share of property; the children come next.

8. A means of property ownership in which, while they are married, a husband and wife are considered to be one person. On the death of one spouse, title to the property is passed to the other. (See Chapter 11, Family and Domestic Law.)

9. It is taken over by the state by escheat.

10. Apply to the probate court to have John removed as executor and to appoint someone else, either a different sibling or a neutral third party.

Answers to Questions on Chapter 13, Special Legal Problems in Mental Health

1. The individual's *present* functioning.

2. The individual's mental functioning *at the time of the offense.*

3. False. State statutes uniformly distinguish between admission for mental health treatment and a legal adjudication of incompetency. In the past, commitment often resulted automatically in the individual's being deemed incompetent. Today, hospitalization for mental health treatment results in the automatic loss of few civil rights.

4. Yes. The Supreme Court in *Jackson v. Indiana* banned indefinite commitment after an adjudication of incompetency. The Court ruled that within a reasonable period of time there had to be a determination as to whether the individual was likely ever to be competent. If not, the State had to discharge the individual or have him hospitalized through civil processes.

5. The minimum standard that must be met is that of clear and convincing evidence. A state is free to use the more stringent standard of beyond a reasonable doubt, but is not free to use

the least stringent standard of preponderance of the evidence.

6. The two questions evaluated are whether the individual is mentally ill, and whether, as a result of the mental illness, he poses a danger to self or others.

7. Courts have ruled that in order to meet obligations resulting from a right to treatment, a state facility must provide (a) a humane physical and psychological environment; (b) staff adequate in quantity and quality to provide treatment; and (c) individualized treatment plans.

8. The initial issue in deciding whether an individual may refuse treatment is an assessment of competency. Courts have differed in the requirements established for assessing competency. One approach is to require a judicial declaration of incompetency in all cases where a facility wishes to treat despite a patient's refusal. The other is to authorize intra-facility arrangements, where the determination of competency may be made by a nonjudicial decision-maker.

9. False. The facility is not an insurer (that is, absolutely liable), for the conduct of its patients. Rather, the facility has the obligation only to exercise reasonable care in its role as custodian.

10. False. First, a therapist need only alert a potential victim if reasonable means to protect the person might require such a warning. Usually other means (for example, call the police, initiate a hospital commitment, etc.) are sufficient to reduce the danger, and a warning would not be necessary. Second, mere suspicion of danger has not been defined as a sufficient basis requiring violation of confidentiality and action to protect a victim. Although specific criteria have not been articulated, there must be some reasonable foreseeability of danger in order to require that the therapist initiate protective measures.

Answers to Questions on Chapter 14, On Being Involved Personally in a Lawsuit, as a Plaintiff, Expert Witness, or Defendant

1. Unrealistic expectations from the court, with failure to anticipate the costs.

2. They may wish to avoid projecting an image of being too interested in the fee.
   They may feel uncomfortable about the size of the fee.

They may fear that financial worries would motivate a patient to forego an important treatment.

They may be reluctant to increase the patient's suffering, when he is already suffering from his health problems.

3. Think about possible problems that might occur in connection with one's business dealings and discuss them with those with whom one engages in business.

4. Observe the actions of the professional in areas with which the layman is familiar. The layman infers from that how the professional might do in areas where the layman is unfamiliar.

5. a. It saves time as compared with examining the expert on his qualifications.

   b. If the expert has unusually impressive credentials, it may have more impact on the fact-finder to take the time to demonstrate those qualifications.

6. Review both your testimony and the anticipated cross-examination with the attorney who engaged your services, well in advance of the trial. Emphasize to him that he must do all he can to protect you when you are under fire (though he will do that anyway in order to preserve the value of your appearance).

7. The patient has died so that nothing further can be done for his immediate benefit. However, the anesthesiologist would be wise to ensure that his equipment is checked, to see if faulty equipment may have been a contributing factor to whatever caused the death of the patient.

8. Dissatisfaction with the concern shown by health professionals to patients' needs and interests. Of course, sometimes patients are very satisfied at the time with their health care but initiate a suit when they later discover that their care has been defective.

9. The tendency to present oneself and one's actions in the most favorable light. It is important that the attorney be completely conversant with the weak points of his client's case and the strong points of the adversary's so that the attorney can cope most effectively with problems which are likely to arise.

10. True. The attorney's responsibility is to the defendant-insured. In a way, however, the attorney is in a conflict situation. The insurance company is paying him; thus, there is a certain pressure on the attorney to take the insurance company's interest into account. Most attorneys can resist and compensate for the pressure, but some may give in to it a bit. The defendant is probably wise to note that the pressure

may exist and therefore, he will be especially observant of how the attorney handles the case.

Answers to Questions on Chapter 15, Medical and Professional Ethics

1. a. The opportunity to practice properly.
   b. The opportunity to maintain skills.
   c. Adequate remuneration.
   d. Good patients.
2. a. Direct provider of service.
   b. Employer of health professionals.
   c. Payer for services.
   d. Regulator and licensor.
   e. Research supporter.
   f. Public health activities.
3. Weighing alternatives takes time and, thus, requires sacrificing some other potential disposition of time.
4. a. The right to know exactly what is alleged.
   b. The opportunity to prepare a defense.
   c. An impartial tribunal.
   d. Punishment appropriate to the offense.
5. a. A warning or admonition; a letter of censure; public censure; a fine; probationary supervision; restriction of practice; suspension; expulsion.
   b. Counseling; legal advice; loans; public declarations of support.
6. a. The patient has a right to refuse such treatment and request that such treatment not be given, if he should be unable, at the time, to indicate a refusal.
   b. If the patient is terminal and if the family and physician agree, such an order is usually appropriate. If the patient is not terminal, it is probably best to apply to a court for the decision.
7. Pain relief.
8. The tendency for people to become upset at the bearer of bad news, as if he, himself, were the cause of the misfortune.
9. If the subject were competent and fully informed of the potential risks but consented voluntarily to participate anyway, he could be considered to have assumed the risk. If the subject is paid, that could be regarded as consideration for a contract. The subject might be rewarded enough, by having the opportunity to contribute to medical science and humanity, for that also to be regarded as consideration.

10. a. It relates to population policy.
    b. It relates to issues of life and death.
    c. Illicit abortion is an important cause of morbidity and preventable death.
    d. It relates to issues of sex.
    e. It has become an important religious and political issue.

Answers to Questions on Chapter 16, Finding the Law: Legal Research and Citation

1. a. *Corpus Juris Secundum.*
   b. *American Jurisprudence 2d.*
2. Appellate courts of the states in the Gulf of Mexico region. (The specific states covered in that series include Louisiana, Mississippi, Alabama, and Florida.)
3. a. *Federal Supplement,* Volume 116, page 870.
   b. Significant decisions (not all decisions) from the Federal District Courts.
4. When that precedent has been set in a different Circuit, and a different precedent has been set by its own Circuit Court.
5. *The Federal Register.*
6. Obiter dictum.
7. Using a citator to obtain the subsequent usage and fate of the decision.
8. If the state has a generalized code of regulations, the regulations in question may be sought there. One may ultimately have to correspond with, or even personally visit, the hospital licensing agency, however.
9. The U.S. Circuit Courts of Appeal.
10. *Supreme Court Reporter* and *United States Supreme Court Reports.*

List of Cases Referenced

Index

abandonment, 197, 306
abortion, 403
absolutism, 24
abuse, 306
abuse of process, 254
acceptance, 264, 265, 271ff.
acceptance by performance, 271
accessory, 431
  after the fact, 75, 431
  before the fact, 75, 431
accomplice, 431
accord and satisfaction, 279, 431
accreditation, 208
act, 154
  criminal, 72
  freedom not to, 51
  of God, 431
action, class, 114
actus reus, 74, 335
ad damnum, 253, 432
adjective law, 432
adjudication, 432
administrator, 321, 322
admissible, 432
admission (to mental hospital), by
  guardian, 338
  involuntary, 337ff.
  of minors, 339
  voluntary, 337
admissions, prior, 138
adoption, 306, 307
adultery, 299
advertising, false or deceptive, 50
affidavit, 432
affinity, 294, 296
affirmation, 432

affirmative harm, 219
affirmatively appropriating, 58
agent, 432
alcoholism, 432
aleatory, 274
  contract, 432
ALI test, 334
alienage, 60
alimony, 302, 303
almost suspect categories, 60
alteration, 279
alternative, least restrictive, *see*
  least restrictive alternative
alternative, less restrictive, 49
ambulatory, 318
American Jurisprudence (Am.Jur. 2d),
  419
American Law Reports (A.L.R.), 420
American Psychiatric Association,
  336
amicus curiae, 432
analysis, ethical, 30
annul, annulment, 295, 304, 432
answer, 112
apparent agency, 161
appeal, 96
  right to, 96
appellate court, 432
apprehension, 167, 168
arbitration, 240ff.
arguendo, 433
Aronfreed, Jason, 35
arraignment, 91, 433
arrest, 87ff.
  by warrant, 88
  warrantless, 88

counsel, right to, 47, 55, 94, 95
counterclaim, 113
  compulsory, 113
  permissive, 113
counteroffer, 270
Court of Claims, 416, 417
Court of Claims Reports, 417
court(s), probate, 2, 299, 320
credentials, fraudulent, 391
credit, full faith and, 123
creditor, 319ff.
  beneficiaries, 275
  bond, *see* bond, creditor
crime, 71ff.
  capital, 54
  infamous, 54
crimes, preparatory, 75
criminal responsibility, 333ff., 435
cross-claims, 115
cross complaint, 435
cross examination, 141
cruel and unusual punishment, *see* punishment, cruel and unusual
cruelty, mental, 300
  physical, 300
custody, 302, 304ff., 435
  joint, *see* joint custody

damage, 154ff.
damages, 159ff., 167, 168, 265, 279, 436
  amount sought, 109
  exemplary, 280
  general, 159
  liquidated, *see* liquidated damages
  punitive, 159, 249, *see* punitive damages
  specific, 159
  nominal, 167, 280
danger, clear and present, 49
dangerousness, 338, 345
de Montesquieu, Baron, 427
de Toqueville, Alexis, 429
death with dignity, 401

deceased intestate, 316
decedent, 320
deceit, tort of, 268
declarations against interest, 138
  dying, 138
  of physical or mental condition, 138
defamation, 50, 172, 173
  per se, 172
defectives, mental, 268
defendant, 436
defense of others, 85, 170
  of property, 85, 170
defenses, against intentional tort suits, 169
  to actions, 436
delivery, personal, 110
demurrer, 436
dentists, 185
deontology, 28
deposition, 111, 436
  on written questions, 116
  oral, 115
desertion, 299
detention, preventive, 89
development, moral, stages of, 33
Dickens, Charles, 429
dictionaries, 421
dictum, dicta, 423
diminished responsibility, 83, 335
direct examination, 140ff., 368
directed verdict, 436
disaffirm, 268
discharge, 197
  of contract, 278
discipline, standards and procedures, 390ff.
discovered peril, 164
discovery, 91, 115ff., 436
  compelled, 118
  rule, 246
disease or defect, mental, 81
dismiss, 436
  motion to, 112
distress, emotional, 168
diversity, 109